DEAD MEN
TELL NO TALES

Studies in Maritime History
William N. Still, Jr., Series Editor

DEAD MEN TELL NO TALES

THE LIVES AND LEGENDS OF THE PIRATE CHARLES GIBBS

JOSEPH GIBBS

The University of South Carolina Press

Published by the University of South Carolina Press
Columbia, South Carolina 29208

www.sc.edu/uscpress

Manufactured in the United States of America

Endpapers: Map of the West Indies, 1796, courtesy of the Mariners' Museum, Newport News, Virginia

16 15 14 13 12 11 10 09 08 07   10 9 8 7 6 5 4 3 2 1

Library of Congress Cataloging-in-Publication Data

Gibbs, Joseph, 1965–
    Dead men tell no tales : the lives and legends of the pirate Charles Gibbs / Joseph Gibbs.
    p. cm. — (Studies in maritime history)
    Includes bibliographical references and index.
    ISBN-13: 978-1-57003-693-4 (cloth : alk. paper)
    ISBN-10: 1-57003-693-4 (cloth : alk. paper)
    1. Gibbs, Charles, 1794?–1831. 2. Pirates—United States—Biography. I. Title.
    G537.G5G53 2007
    910.4'5—dc22
    [B]

                                                                                    2007007329

This book was printed on New Leaf Ecobook 50, a recycled paper with 50 percent postconsumer waste content.

CONTENTS

ILLUSTRATIONS

PREFACE

This work tells the story of mariner James D. Jeffers, largely by critiquing the "confessions" he made before his 1831 hanging under the alias Charles Gibbs. Elements of them have long been enshrined in Caribbean piracy lore, either without challenge or else with much embellishment, and I have tried to stay close to his original admissions as published, place them in historical context, and distinguish between what other evidence can and cannot support.

Much falls into the latter category. While books should answer the questions they ask, some issues raised herein about the man's admittedly violent life cannot at present be answered beyond a reasonable doubt. This will explain the use of such qualifiers as "apparently," "evidently," "may," "presumably," and "seems"—words that are anathema to most writers but that were necessary to signal where documentation ceased and interpretation began.

Many facts about the real James Jeffers may have been lost to history. This is not a new caveat for maritime writing. A chronicler of Newport, Rhode Island, in citing a key nineteenth-century text on privateering, observed that it "compiled a great variety of sources, some of which may no longer be available." The author of a work on the early U.S. Navy bemoaned the absence of documents "probably long ago discarded as routine records of no historical importance."[1]

Portions of this book synthesize details drawn from multiple sources. In some places several paragraphs occur before a footnote provides the references; this reflects efforts to impart a narrative feel and avoid countless *ibids*. These sources are often newspaper accounts, either in their original form or as they were "borrowed" by other periodicals.

While contemporary articles about Jeffers are invaluable, all treatments of his fascinating 1831 confessions need careful handling. Most permutations of the "Charles Gibbs the Pirate" story can be traced to a few pieces in the New York press, particularly the *Journal of Commerce*. These much-reprinted stories contained elements that were unclear or suspect in their first incarnation. They became more distorted as the man's tale was retold.

For that matter, published accounts of acts of piracy during Jeffers's lifetime were simultaneously sensational and vague. Journalists might relate—and distort—what had reputedly passed between ships that "spoke" briefly at sea, or pass on sketchy accounts of incidents culled from newspapers weeks or months out of date. Writers were also known to invent or exaggerate episodes, which an apologetic *Niles' Weekly Register* editor correctly observed "cast a doubt over those barbarities which really exist."[2]

The most solid material that exists about Jeffers's life concerns its last phase. The original Southern District of New York Circuit Court indictments from his 1831 trial for mutiny and murder have survived in the National Archives. Handwritten onto template forms, they provide background for the proceedings that ended with the double hanging of Jeffers and Thomas Wansley. The same record group contains court minutes from the trial, detailing information such as indictments returned, pleas entered, names of jurors and witnesses, verdicts, and sentences. Despite precise handwriting, the minutes are not infallible. For example, entries for Wednesday, March 9, 1831, erroneously give Wansley's first name as Richard.[3]

The archives do not contain a *Vineyard* trial transcript, but one by a shorthand writer named W. E. Drake was published separately in New York. While its contents are important, they may be incomplete or represent paraphrasing rather than direct quotation, as its versions of some speeches are shorter than those given elsewhere.[4]

Other archival materials provide varying degrees of help. Some customs forms and crew lists from the era's ships embarking for foreign ports still survive in National Archives repositories. The central Washington holdings contain muster lists from U.S. warships, prisoner exchange and service data, reports of engagements with pirates, and so forth. A National Archives venture undertaken with the Works Progress Administration (WPA, later the Work Projects Administration) produced volumes of compiled ship registration information from some major American ports.

These findings are balanced by notable omissions. Ship registration information is often incomplete from certain ports for certain periods. The Second World War evidently interrupted some WPA efforts to collect and publish the data. The first volume of Boston-Charlestown records up to 1795 was issued in 1942, but no later serials appear to have been published, although materials compiled for them still exist. There is also an apparent lack of published coverage for other places crucial to the Jeffers story, such as

Charleston, South Carolina, and the port of New York.[5] In the latter municipality, records from Bridewell and Bellevue prisons for 1830–1831, which
could document the final acts of Jeffers's and Wansley's lives, have not survived, though Common Council minutes shed some light on their jailer,
police officer Henry Merritt.[6]

Attempts have been made to respect maritime terminology while keeping general readers in mind. When the data are available, craft are identified
by specific rigging type (brig, schooner, sloop, etc.) On occasion the term
ship is used as a catchall, although in the age of sail that word was technically
reserved for vessels that had three masts, all of which were square-rigged
(that is, using square-shaped sails, hung perpendicularly to the bow-to-
stern/fore-to-aft axis). That said, any contemporary rigging designation may
have been used loosely, a point historian David Cordingly underscored when
he tried to pin down "that baffling word 'sloop.'"[7]

As in Jeffers's day, the geographic terms *Caribbean* (a sea) and *West Indies*
(a group of islands) are often used interchangeably herein. In transcribing
source material, vessel names were regularly italicized regardless of initial
rendering, while some words were de-italicized when the original emphasis
was deemed unnecessary.

Acknowledgments

My first thanks go to the editors, peer reviewers, and staff of the University of South Carolina Press for their confidence in my manuscript and for including it in their Studies in Maritime History series. Regarding the task of trying to run "Charles Gibbs" to ground more than two centuries after his birth, the help of many people needs to be acknowledged.

Private researchers Barbara Carroll of Exeter, Rhode Island, Vicki Killian of Takoma Park, Maryland, and Alison Rapp of Falls Church, Virginia, went through various archives on my behalf, often looking for elusive references to contemporary people and vessels. Ship-identification efforts were also undertaken in England by London-based researcher Stephen Bennett. Expert constructive criticism on many nautical issues came courtesy of John Frayler, historian of the Salem (Massachusetts) Maritime National Historical Site, and Jeff Remling, curator of collections and director of operations for New York City's South Street Seaport Museum. National Archives personnel who assisted in various capacities include Rebecca A. Livingston in Washington, D.C., Michael Moore in Waltham, Massachusetts, Gregory J. Plunges in New York City, and Barbara Rust in Fort Worth, Texas.

Similar thanks are owed to the personnel of many libraries, organizations, societies, and universities who rendered assistance and/or directed me to further sources. They include Professor Benicio Oscar Ahumada, Departamento de Estudios Historicos Navales, Armada Argentina; Irene Axelrod, head manuscript librarian at the Phillips Library, Peabody Essex Museum in Salem, Massachusetts; Ruth Barriskill of Guildhall Library, London; Prof. David Canter of the Centre for Investigative Psychology, University of Liverpool; Kenneth R. Cobb, director of the New York City Municipal Archives; Lynnette Dillabough, Claudia A. Jew, and Jeanne Willoz-Egnor of the Mariners' Museum, Newport News, Virginia; Joseph Ditta, Kristine Paulus, and Jill Reichenbach of the New-York Historical Society; author John Douglas, former Federal Bureau of Investigation special agent and past head of the FBI's Investigative Support Unit; David G. Engle of California State University (Fresno); Jim Gehrlich, head of archives at Weill Medical College, Cornell University; Peter Goodwin, manager of the Sagadahoc History and Genealogy Room of the Bath (Maine) Historical Society; Dr. Janet Wells Greene, historian and library director, and Ian Murray, past president, of the General Society of Mechanics and Tradesmen, New York, New York; Emma Haxhaj of *Lloyd's Register,* London; Timothy L. Decker and Brenna King of the New Jersey Historical Society; Richard Foster, Margaret Vollmer, and the staff of the New York Public Library; Kimberly Krazer, registrar, and the staff of the Newport (Rhode Island) Historical Society; Barbara List, director of collection development for Columbia University Libraries; Lauren Mandel and Carin O'Connor of the Bostonian Society; Thomas C. McCarthy of the New York City Department of Corrections; Megan Milford of the Massachusetts Historical Society; Carey Lucas Nikonchuk of the South Carolina Historical Society; Sally Reeves of the Louisiana Historical Society; Dr. David J. Starkey of the Maritime Historical Studies Center, University of Hull, United Kingdom; Margaret Tenney of the Harry Ransom Humanities Research Center, University of Texas at Austin; Richard Thompson of Historic Salem (Massachusetts); Mauricio Tovar, head of la División de Servicios al Público, Archivo General de la Nación, República de Colombia; William Vareika of William Vareika Fine Arts, Newport (Rhode Island); Robert Vietrogoski, archivist at the Columbia University Medical Center; Laura Waayers of the Naval Historical Foundation; Irene Wainwright of the New Orleans Public Library; Louisa Watrous of the Photography & Licensing Department and the staff of the G. W. Blunt White Library, at Mystic Seaport, Mystic, Connecticut; Margaret Winslow of the Office of Rights and Reproductions, Delaware Art Museum; and the staffs of the Maryland Historical Society and the Rhode Island Historical Society Library.

Karen Haspil, Hanan Jumean, Matthew Ismail, Karen Peterson, Lorin Ritchie, and Holly Skelton of the library of the American University of Sharjah made available many needed materials either by personal research or by arranging interlibrary loans. The many public and university libraries that gave access to their holdings or helped locate available sources include the British Library Document Supply Center in West Yorkshire, United Kingdom; Boston College (special thanks to Anne H. Kenny and Robert Bruns); Boston University (special thanks to Katherine Kominis); Brandeis University; Brown University; the University of Chicago; Cornell University; the University of Minnesota; Princeton University; Stanford University; and the public libraries of Newton and Wellesley, Massachusetts, and Brooklyn, New York.

This work was written across parts of three continents, and several instances of special generosity should be acknowledged. My first thanks in this context go to Carol and Patrick McNally of Newton, Massachusetts, wife and son respectively of the late Dr. Raymond McNally. As a young reader, I loved his books, and as an adult I was honored by his friendship prior to his death in 2002. In opening their home to me in summer 2004, Carol and Patrick gave me the unique privilege of writing in Raymond's surroundings. Gratitude also goes to Conney and Tina Lofstrand of Mariestad, Sweden, and Roland and Irma Bertilsson of Stöpen, Sweden, for hospitality and friendship during the same summer (and in boat-builder Conney's case for conveying some of his extensive nautical expertise).

As with my last book, Tanya Karpiak of Newton, Massachusetts, and Eva and Niall Heney of Medford, Massachusetts, provided invaluable feedback and professional help. Professional colleagues who assisted in various ways included Dr. Ann Hamilton of the University of Central Oklahoma; and at the American University of Sharjah, United Arab Emirates, Prof. Kim Bigelow, Dr. Judith Caesar, Anna Marie Castillo, Dr. Robert Cook, Dr. Reagan McLaurin, and Dr. Hugo Toledo. Special mention goes to AUS Prof. Ana Gavassa who (with family members Giovanni Gavassa and Edmundo Gavassa of Bucaramanga, Colombia) provided Spanish-language materials on revolutionary Cartagena and Buenos Aires.

My strongest and fondest thanks are reserved for Tatyana and Michael Gibbs, who for many months tolerated a husband and father who spent more time with "Charles Gibbs" than with them.

With those acknowledgements given, please note that any errors herein are the author's responsibility.

DEAD MEN
TELL NO TALES

1

"So mild and gentle a countenance"

A 1978 BOOK ABOUT PIRATES described Charles Gibbs as "an ex-privateer and as vicious a rogue as ever sailed. On one occasion, Gibbs had chopped off a captured captain's arms and legs; on another he had burned an entire merchant crew to death."[1] Such bloodthirsty prose is representative of most accounts of a man often encountered in histories of early nineteenth-century Caribbean-area piracy. Certainly, Gibbs's execution in 1831 for his role in an incident involving mutiny, murder, and ship stealing lends it credibility. However, the above quote contains little which can be conclusively proved. Gibbs's privateering career is hard to confirm or deny. And while he admitted to a violent life, no contemporary tales include him dismembering or burning captives alive.

Even the pirate's name is open to question. The man known to seafaring history as Charles Gibbs was tried and hanged under an alias. Awaiting execution, he told a few people his real name was James D. Jeffers and that he had been born in Newport, Rhode Island, to a prominent family who thought him long dead. Whether that name was itself genuine, or how it should be properly spelled, concerned few contributors to the Gibbs-the-Pirate saga.[2] Accounts continuing into the last century stressed morality-play elements: a good upbringing undone by drink, bad company, and loose women. The stories related how "Charles Gibbs," as he is still routinely referenced, heroically served his country's navy in the War of 1812; failed as a Boston businessman; then became a privateer-turned-pirate, assuming a leadership role in a Caribbean gang taking dozens of vessels and perhaps hundreds of lives.

Even in this terrible guise, he could show—albeit briefly—redeeming qualities. After one sea capture, he saved a young Dutch woman from his rapacious, murderous comrades. Against their wishes, he spirited her off to the pirate band's west Cuban lair. There was a tragic end to the romance. To uphold the brotherhood's vow to eliminate witnesses, he allowed her to be killed.

But these were versions of stories the man himself told while awaiting trial and hanging. And testimony from Jeffers—this work presumes this was his real name—needs special handling.

Under any circumstances, much of James Jeffers's account fits the context of the post–War of 1812 flowering of privateering and piracy off the coasts of Latin America and the southern United States, an enterprise that attracted American and European adventurers. Jeffers claimed to have begun his privateering career, which led directly to piracy, on a craft licensed by Cartagena in modern Colombia. Having revolted against Spain, this former colony gave out commissions authorizing shipowners to take prizes from the estranged mother country. But these documents were easy to get and correspondingly suspect, and crews holding them were known to attack indiscriminately. In some nautical circles, one maritime historian wrote, "the term *Cartagenian privateer* was a euphemism for pirate."[3]

Many crews, such as those Jeffers claimed to have served with or led, dropped the pretense of privateering altogether, hoisting the red flag that served as the era's equivalent of the Jolly Roger. Jeffers's recollections of cruises off the Cuban coast, of collusion with Havana merchants, and the habitual killing of captives all tally with contemporary reports. Therefore, the confessions Jeffers made a few weeks before his hanging appear to provide a firsthand account of Caribbean piracy's last, inglorious epoch.

Yet aside from an 1821 brush with the U.S. Navy, little Jeffers claimed to have participated in as a maritime criminal can be documented to a satisfactory degree. Jeffers as a source is simultaneously fascinating and challenging. His published statements are often confusing and abound with inconsistencies and contradictions. Many problems can be rationalized but not resolved. What is more troubling is that Jeffers invented aspects of his upbringing and maritime background. Into those fabrications he wove facts—real places, events, people, and ships. Some of the tales he later retracted made it into the pirate Canon anyway. That said Jeffers stuck by his claims to villainy, even when the noose was fitted around his neck.

In assessing James Jeffers's case, the challenge is deciding how far to trust him. Separating fact from fiction may be impossible to do with finality, especially when firing at long historical range. But it is worth trying because the saga of Charles Gibbs remains a touchstone of American sea lore. Some chroniclers saw in him a manifestation of the piratical Golden Age, best described in the famous *General History of the Pyrates*, sometimes attributed to Daniel Defoe. One contemporary likened the man's crimes to those of, among others, William Kidd, a high-profile figure in the *General History*. When a 1924 book noted that the pirate known as Charles Gibbs "was hanged at New York as recently as 1831," the time reference highlighted him as an echo of an earlier, romanticized phenomenon.[4]

A second reason is the sheer scale of his alleged career. In its take on the Gibbs-Jeffers story, a New York newspaper related that "he has repeatedly stated that he was concerned in the robbery of more than *forty vessels*, and in the destruction of more *than twenty, with their entire crews*. Many of those destroyed had passengers on board, which makes it probable that he has been an agent in the murder of nearly FOUR HUNDRED HUMAN BEINGS!!"[5]

A Rhode Island print shop put the italics and the bloody details on the cover of its pamphlet on the subject, announcing that in its pages "GIBBS *confesses that within a few years he has participated in the murder of nearly 400 human beings!*" More than a century later, the story's amazing scope prompted nautical chronicler Edward Rowe Snow to place Charles Gibbs among those pirates who "rise above the common level of their profession. In certain ways they have distinguished themselves so that they are classed in a different light from other marauders of the sea lanes." As James Jeffers in 1831 reportedly convinced one navy pirate chaser he was genuine, it seems safe to affirm a recent description of Charles Gibbs as being among "the last pirates to use the Caribbean as a base." Yet enough obscurity remains to support what a visitor to Jeffers's cell wrote: that the condemned man was "one of the most singular and mysterious beings that ever figured on the theatre of human life."[6]

Jeffers's strange story first came tumbling out as the thirtyish man sat in New York City's Bridewell prison in early 1831, awaiting trial for a relatively small crime on an arch pirate's resume: his role in a mutiny on the *Vineyard*, a vessel traveling between New Orleans and Philadelphia with fifty thousand silver Mexican dollar coins on board. That episode had begun at sea off North Carolina's Cape Hatteras shortly after midnight on November 24, 1830. Jeffers—who had signed on as Charles Gibbs—and a few others killed the *Vineyard*'s captain and first mate, their plans having been laid a few days earlier. After dividing the money, they sailed their prize to the New York coast.

Off Long Island the pirates, for such they now were by U.S. law, set fire to the *Vineyard,* then headed for land in two small boats. The rough sea caused one to sink with all hands; Jeffers and three others in the second boat made it ashore, although they had to lighten the craft by throwing most of their loot overboard. They still might have gotten away with what silver remained, but while drinking at a Gravesend inn, *Vineyard* survivor John Brownrigg belligerently referred to his companions as murderers. The outburst from the man, who claimed no role in the *Vineyard* affair and would later testify against the others, was overheard, leading to their arrest.[7]

Up to this point, to his jailers Jeffers was nothing more than a member of a single forecastle conspiracy. No detailed contemporary description of him has survived, though it is documented that he bore a scar on or over his nose. But he was surprisingly well spoken in jail and in court, and when he smiled, an observer wrote, Jeffers "exhibits so mild and gentle a countenance" that he simply did not look like a criminal.[8]

His alias, coupled with the fact that the prisoner told his captors he was a Rhode Islander, led some to suspect he was a son of that state's former governor, William Channing Gibbs. But Jeffers maintained he was not related to that prominent Newport family (to the best of his knowledge, neither is this author), although evidence does exist of land transactions

Bridewell Prison "as it stood about 1834." An 1859 lithograph by George Hayward. Courtesy of the Picture Collection, Branch Libraries, New York Public Library, Astor, Lenox, and Tilden Foundations

between it and the Newport sea captain who was probably Jeffers's father—a point discussed later.[9]

Despite the life of crime to which Jeffers would later admit, he did not necessarily act like a master villain. Being transported from the Flatbush jail to the Bridewell in New York City, he did nothing to stop his *Vineyard* accomplice Thomas J. Wansley from talking of the mutiny in front of their police escort. Instead, the lawmen later testified, Jeffers prompted him and made his own damning admissions.[10]

Secured in the Bridewell and denied lawyers for months until the eve of trial, Jeffers likely brooded on his situation. Besides the anticipated testimony from Brownrigg, he might have sensed that another codefendant, Robert Dawes, would also speak for the prosecution in exchange for his own life.

It is difficult to reconstruct the sequence of events from contemporary sources—a statement that applies to most of Jeffers's entire saga. But in February 1831, Jeffers told deputy keeper Henry W. Merritt, who had been one of the officers escorting him from Flatbush, that he wanted to talk privately with a judge. Merritt extended the invitation to local police magistrate James Hopson, who had no connection with Jeffers's case, which was to be heard by the federal Circuit Court for the Southern District of New York. Bad weather kept Hopson, then about fifty-eight, from arriving at the Bridewell until Sunday, March 6, the day before Wansley's trial was to begin. Hopson later related, in dialogue form, the start of his conversation with the prisoner:

[Question.] Gibbs, are you going to tell me the truth, or is it to amuse me, and to make me write a long story that will not amount to any thing?
[Answer.] I shall tell nothing but the truth; and it is only on condition that you will swear not to divulge any thing I may say, when I am on my trial, and no time after, if I should get clear.

Readers must judge for themselves the mindset of a man on trial for his life making such a request. Equally remarkable is the fact that Hopson agreed. He later explained: "My reply was . . . that I should not take my oath, but I would give him my word that it should be kept a secret according to his request." Presumably Hopson's "oath" was that of a New York judge, his "word" that of an individual.

The prisoner responded by spilling out a tale few fiction writers could equal. Lucid but largely unrepentant, Jeffers spoke of a bloody pirate career beginning in 1816, which included intervals serving on privateers commissioned by two Latin American states, Cartagena and Buenos Aires. Overall, he admitted having a hand in the capture of at least forty ships, several of which he named offhand. Frequently, he said, he and his comrades destroyed the vessels—in many cases their crews and any passengers as well.

An exception involved an otherwise unidentified Dutch ship from Curaçoa, bound to Holland. In this case, he spared one passenger, a young woman about seventeen or eighteen, the rest of whose family his comrades slew. He took her away to the notorious pirate rendezvous at Cape Antonio, on Cuba's west coast. After two months, Jeffers said tersely at this first meeting with the magistrate, she was killed. Hopson noted that this story alone evoked remorse in the man.[11]

———————

Hopson kept his word, and none of this appeared during Jeffers's day-long trial on Tuesday, March 8. Dealing only with the *Vineyard* mutiny, it featured testimony from Brownrigg and Dawes (charges against him being dropped). As had happened at Wansley's trial the day before, the jury found him guilty of murder. Jeffers and Wansley were sentenced to hang together on April 22.[12]

The findings released Hopson from his promise of silence, and he paid at least two more visits to Jeffers, the first on Saturday, March 19. Hopson would relate that on that date Jeffers "conversed with great freedom: repeated to me the vessels he first informed me had been robbed and destroyed." The magistrate occasionally asked about specific ships, wondering if Jeffers knew anything of their fate. In most cases Jeffers denied knowledge.

Jeffers's confessions were ostensibly those of a man trying to clear his conscience. Yet Hopson was wary of the condemned man's story, parts of which—at least as filtered through the 1831 New York press—seem contradictory or incoherent, belying Samuel Johnson's famous remark that "when a man knows he is to be hanged in a fortnight, it concentrates his mind wonderfully." Hopson began their March 23 session by telling the prisoner that "I expected all he had told me could not be true." Jeffers's response is not recorded.[13]

The prisoner also began to provide versions of his life to Merritt and others. The press soon got hold of the story, and articles appeared summarizing, detailing, and then discussing the condemned man's tales. They caused a sensation, but some readers were unconvinced. One New Yorker noted a "great diversity of opinion, in relation to the history of Gibbs, and the extent of his crimes." The debate became so spirited that it led "to the using of gross and intemperate language, by gentlemen, from whose education and standing in society, better things ought reasonably to be expected." Some doubt must have stemmed from questioning why the prisoner would confess to a multitude of atrocities while denying a role in the sole murder for which he had been convicted. Asked about those crimes for which he had confessed but had not been tried, Jeffers showed little overt remorse—except for the story of the young Dutch woman.[14]

—◆◆◆◆◆—

To test Jeffers on his admitted captures is frustrating, the results usually inconclusive. Though he assigned relatively few dates to his crimes, he occasionally identified vessels by name and hailing port. But while candidates for those craft do turn up in surviving ship registration data, the materials rarely record a vessel's ultimate destiny. As Jeffers said his comrades often scuttled prizes and murdered their crews, their fates would go unreported anyway.

When links might be established between vessels on his list of victims (as published) and documented acts of piracy, inconsistencies emerge. What might be classified as minor lapses include his reference to an 1821 capture, the Charleston-based *Lucies*, first as the *Caroline*, then as the *Luciur*. Larger issues arise with his claim to having destroyed the Boston-based *Belvidere*. Pirates in 1821 boarded and robbed a vessel by that name of Beverly, Massachusetts, but then released it; a few months later the same craft fought off a different set of attackers. Additionally, Jeffers admitted to robbing and burning the *Jane* of Liverpool, and a vessel so-named from that port was stopped by privateers in 1817, though on this instance at least it was allowed to proceed on its way.[15]

Besides gaps in records, several innocent and overlapping solutions present themselves: coincidence regarding vessel names, faulty memory made worse by passage of time, sloppy note taking, the era's uncritical editorial standards, and so forth. As Jeffers was an admitted heavy drinker, he might have experienced his piratical career as a rum-sodden blur. Addressing the problems of memoirs and related writings, crime historian Philip Sugden noted that "over time our memories deteriorate more profoundly than many people inexperienced in the use of historical evidence realize, and reminiscences recorded long after the event are characteristically confused on chronology and detail. There is a very human tendency, too, for us to 'improve' upon our memories, to make a better story, to explain away past mistakes, or simply to claim for ourselves a more impressive role in past dramas than we have acted in life."[16]

Or was Jeffers simply a full-throttle liar? Probing the criminal mind is outside the scope of this work, but author and retired FBI profiler John Douglas observed in his book, *The Cases That Haunt Us,* that "one thing that motivates many serial offenders is the desire to create and sustain their own mythology. The press is often a willing collaborator. . . . The reasons they feel a need to do this are obvious to those of us in criminal investigative analysis. These are insignificant nobodies whose only 'accomplishment' in life, the only time when they feel in control and fulfilled, is when they are causing suffering or fear in others."[17]

In correspondence with this author, Douglas cited several cases involving convicted killers who inflated their score. Some did this to punish law enforcement agents by making them follow dead-end leads; others simply craved attention. Discussing modern examples, Douglas observed, "Like many criminals I've interviewed they seek power and control over others. It's very natural for them to boost the number of 'scores' particularly if the punishment is going to be the same."[18]

Many lawmen of 1831 would have agreed. Some contemporaries did, in fact, deem "the terrible pirate Charles Gibbs" to be a fraud. But those who took him seriously pointed to an episode in which the condemned man was given a Jocelyn's chart of the West Indies. This contained, in a journalist's words, "the names of about 90 vessels boarded by pirates from 1817 to 1825." Asked to "mark those of whose robbery he had any recollection," Jeffers made only one, referencing the *Lucies*. "When questioned afterwards in regard to that vessel, he gave such an account of her, and of her subsequent recapture [by the USS *Enterprise*] . . . as left no doubt respecting the truth of his statement." The writer noted that "had he [Jeffers] been desirous of increasing the black catalogue, here was so fine an opportunity, that he would undoubtedly have availed himself of it."[19]

The story of the *Lucies* figured in another 1831 occurrence that may lend substance to Jeffers's claims. Lawrence Kearny, the navy officer who recaptured the *Lucies* while in command of the USS *Enterprise*, was now stationed in New York, read about the confessions of the prisoner known as Charles Gibbs, and visited Jeffers in his cell. During their exchange, Jeffers volunteered particulars of the episode at Cape Antonio, and Kearny was said to have come away accepting that the prisoner had been involved in the incident. Moreover, Kearny's commander-in-chief, President Andrew Jackson, who knew about the pirates of New Orleans from personal experience during the War of 1812, took seriously a summary of Jeffers's claims that reached his desk. So did the author of an 1853 history of the navy, who observed that "the noted pirate Gibbs" had been present at the *Enterprise*'s Cape Antonio raid.[20]

None of these examples should be seen as endorsing all Jeffers said. As Kearny's biographer put it, Jeffers had "confessed so glibly that there was doubt cast upon some of his stories." The *Journal of Commerce* felt the gist of his tales was credible, but cautioned "that [all details] are all true we do not undertake to affirm."[21]

One that was disproved was Jeffers's claim to have served on two American warships, the USS *Hornet* and the USS *Chesapeake,* during famous sea battles in the War of 1812. Despite giving an especially convincing account of the *Chesapeake*'s 1813 defeat by a British ship, this part of Jeffers's story—which he had not related to Hopson—broke down under scrutiny. Shortly before his hanging, at about the time he dropped the Charles Gibbs alias, he "declared that his sole object in making such representations [about service on those warships] was to conceal his true name, and prevent his friends from being visited with the stigma that his crimes would cast upon them." If true, then he had no problem with infamy as long as it was under an alias. But this was not his only falsification. Jeffers also invented a story about running a grocery in Boston that failed due to his mismanagement. This banal fiction—which again, was not part of his original admissions to Hopson—at least filled in the chronological gaps between his alleged War of 1812 heroics and what was probably his actual initiation to maritime life in 1816. Yet a real Charles Gibbs co-owned a short-lived Boston grocery at about that time, either a remarkable coincidence or more likely proof that Jeffers, like many liars, drew on real things when inventing stories. As a result all of his statements must be assessed with caution, even if one agrees with an 1831 observer who applauded Jeffers's continued reliance on the Charles Gibbs alias during his trial. It was a sign, the writer noted, of the pirate having "so great a degree of regard" for his family name.[22]

After Jeffers was hanged alongside Wansley on April 22, 1831, his story continued to stimulate the publishing trade. Monographs on pirates and murderers had been common in the Old World and the colonies, and the eastern United States was a literate marketplace; many capital trials in New York between 1791 and the Civil War resulted in a pamphlet coming off a local press.[23]

The original newspaper stories about the *Vineyard* trial and the subsequent execution were widely reprinted and inspired several separate works. One 1831 example, turned out by a New York print shop at No. 231 Fulton Street, was a 20-page pamphlet including poems and a few crude woodcuts. Materials in this, *The Confession of the Terrible Pirate Charles Gibbs, as made to Justice Hopson and others, at different times,* were largely based on coverage from New York newspapers, though the origins of some contents have proved hard to trace. Overall they give a relatively balanced picture, citing the Jeffers name, questioning the man's motivations in confessing, and reporting challenges to his claim of service on the *Hornet* and *Chesapeake.*[24]

They contrast sharply with another 1831 work, *Mutiny and Murder,* published by Rhode Island printer Israel Smith. Using the Charles Gibbs alias throughout, it stressed a theme of children's duty to parents and added a moralizing "Address to Youth." Assuming whoever assembled it had solid local knowledge of the Newport boy-gone-bad, parts of *Mutiny and Murder* might add something to the saga. But some third-person newspaper contents were rewritten into first-person statements from Jeffers, and it repeated uncritically the *Hornet* and *Chesapeake* story, even changing some elements. For instance, while Jeffers originally claimed to have joined the *Hornet* thanks to his father's influence, *Mutiny and Murder* had the fifteen-year-old protagonist doing so after running away from home. And while Jeffers claimed he had been sent to Halifax after capture during the War of 1812— an authentic detail, Jeffers had good sources—*Mutiny and Murder* transported its subject all the way to Dartmoor.[25]

Mutiny and Murder influenced Bostonian Charles Ellms when he was writing *The Pirates Own Book,* published in 1837. Further improving the story, Ellms imagined Charles Gibbs as a schoolboy who "was very apt to learn, but so refractory and sulky, that neither the birch nor good counsel made any impression on him, and he was expelled . . ." Sent to work on a farm—whose is unstated—he ran away and enlisted on the *Hornet.*[26]

Ellms's book was reprinted many times, and its 1924 edition was likely the source on which Edward Rowe Snow drew when recounting the Charles Gibbs tale in his 1944 *Pirates and Buccaneers of the Atlantic Coast.* Snow also used a writer's license to flesh out his subject's childhood and education. The future pirate's father was "a well-to-do citizen with an efficient, up-to-date farming property, and was respected and admired everywhere in the community." The child—who "was his father's joy"—is now sent "to the best academy in the neighborhood." After being expelled and forced to work on his father's farm: "Charles . . . soon began to commit acts of such outrageous nature in the neighborhood that the despairing father realized his boy was becoming a problem. If he heard of any new outbreak in the vicinity, it usually was the act of his son. Feeling between the two became more and more strained as the career of Charles continued, finally causing the boy to run away from home at the age of fifteen. Evidently his thoughts for some time had been of the sea, and so his footsteps naturally turned to Boston, the sailing metropolis of New England. At that time the great man-of-war *Hornet*, commanded by Captain James Lawrence was in the harbor. Charles obtained a berth aboard her."

Snow summed up Charles Gibbs as "a brave man, who fought aboard the *Chesapeake* for his country in the War of 1812, became a prisoner of war at dreaded Dartmoor, started a grocery store in Boston, became a notorious pirate, again became a marine fighter in South America, and then after many years was attracted to piracy by chance and hanged for his evil deeds." In 1959 Florida novelist Jack Beater repeated essentially the same story in a work on regional pirate legends. His chapter titled, "The Pirate and the Golden-Haired Virgin," centered on the episode with the Dutch woman, adding new fictions to the original story.[27]

Tracing the facts about the man known to pirate history as Charles Gibbs begins with the name he sought baptism under shortly before his 1831 hanging: James D. Jeffers. As he admitted being from Rhode Island, the search begins there.

Formative Years

THE LAST VERSION JAMES D. JEFFERS provided of his introduction to maritime life, given shortly before his 1831 execution, was that he first went to sea in 1816, aged seventeen, aboard a Newport-based vessel. As this is the least dramatic of the tales Jeffers told of his background, it is the likeliest. Newport origins explain his connection to nearby Providence. As a pirate he was said to have let a ship from, and named for, that city go after robbing it of $10,000 because Jeffers "could not consent to destroy his own townsmen." Letting the *Providence* go was in contrast to the admitted penchant of Jeffers and his mates for destroying captured ships and their crews. Such violence belied an upbringing from parents who he recounted as "good and affectionate" and having offered "Godlike advice." Presumably through them Jeffers attained a degree of literacy. At his hanging he remarked that he had squandered a "good education."[1]

Others disagreed. An observer who saw two of his letters from prison felt they revealed "a good deal of native talent, but very little education. The spelling is bad, and no regard is paid to punctuation, capitals, &c." The same writer was surprised by "the apparent readiness with which he makes quotations from scripture." Perhaps his early years included some Bible study, though as his execution date neared he had many clerical visitors. Only a few other bits of background information exist or can be inferred. Jeffers was undoubtedly an experienced sailor. By his account, he served as navigator aboard his first ship of ill-repute, and subsequently as captain of that and other crews. Testimony in the *Vineyard* trial placed Jeffers at that brig's helm after the fatal mutiny. He may have had the sea in his blood, for the Newport family link hints at nautical ties. An 1831 writer who claimed local knowledge was silent on the father's trade but asserted that the pirate's "Parents and connexions (many of whom are now deceased) were of the first respectability." Contradictory data exist on his approximate age at hanging. During the *Vineyard* court hearings a law officer said Jeffers told him he was thirty, but the *Journal of Commerce* gave Jeffers's age at trial in March 1831 as thirty-two, which tallies with his last-minute claim to have been seventeen in 1816.[2]

Reviewing this, an intriguing candidate emerges: a James Jeffers born in late 1798, son of Newport sea captain Samuel Jeffers. Samuel, born in Rhode Island in 1755, commanded two vessels in American privateering service late in the Revolutionary War, making cruises in December 1782 in the *Trimmer* and the following February in the *General Greene*.[3]

If this man indeed sired "Charles Gibbs" then remarks about the pirate coming from genteel stock reflected how far Captain Jeffers later advanced into polite society. In an 1882 lecture before the Rhode Island Historical Society, William P. Sheffield distinguished between "the more cultivated men who commanded privateers" and "the rough men engaged in this rough work," placing Samuel Jeffers in the second category. According to Sheffield, Samuel Jeffers "was once captured, and his captors had the indiscretion to leave him and two of his men, as prisoners, on board his vessel in the charge of a prize crew. Jeffers soon won in a degree the confidence of the prize master, and one morning it so happened that the prize master and his officers were below at breakfast, thinking no harm; they had left Jeffers and his men on deck. As soon as the master was busy at breakfast the companion way was closed and the men below were fastened down; then the men left on deck were soon overboard, and Jeffers was in command, the helm was hard down, and the vessel on her way to her old home, where Jeffers brought her with his prisoners in safety."[4]

Samuel Jeffers's wartime profession as a privateer (some authorities use *corsair* as a synonym) requires explanation. A privateer vessel was a privately owned one operating with a government license—a letter of marque—authorizing capture of enemy-owned property at sea during war. In effect these were temporary commissions, distributed to ship captains—who were often termed "masters" when in civilian service—willing to couple military and mercantile aims.

Many authors have noted the blurred line between privateering and piracy. Like warships and pirate craft, privateers carried little cargo but large crews, which were needed to work cannon and form boarding parties. Also like pirates, privateer crews did not earn wages, outside perhaps an advance given on enlistment, but shared in the division of a cruise's plunder. But privateers were theoretically subject to regulation; captured vessels and cargoes were supposed to be turned over to naval prize courts, which would oversee their sale and subsequent distribution of proceeds. Privateers and pirates' most desired catch was a ship bearing specie—gold or silver coins packed in barrels and sent to complete business deals somewhere in the world.[5]

Privateers and pirates favored swift, light craft: the single-masted sloop—the pirates' vessel of choice in the eighteenth century Caribbean—competed with the two-masted schooner for dominance of coastal shipping lanes. Vessel designations could be used loosely—"sloop of war" meant any warship below frigate class—but the standard sloop and schooner both employed fore-and-aft rigging, in which the sails were hung parallel to the keel. Put *very* briefly, the benefit to this type of rigging was that the vessel sailed more efficiently against the wind, tacking at a shallower angle than a square-rigger. The latter design, featuring sails hung perpendicular to the keel, held an advantage with the wind behind it, and was preferred for longer, ocean-going voyages. The principal square-rigger was the two-masted brig; variants (such as the brigantine) incorporated some type of fore-and-aft rigging on its mainmast.

The best examples of the nimble schooner would come from Baltimore and Bermuda shipyards. Dangerous looking given its long bowsprit and sharply curved sails, a schooner might need only a handful of crew to operate, but when on the prowl it could accommodate dozens more as gun crews and boarders. American privateering examples varied in tonnage, length, and armament. While cannon provided firepower they added weight, making any craft slower and harder to sail. Accordingly, many marauders of both Samuel and James Jeffers's generations mounted relatively few guns, preferring to use speed to overtake, then board, their merchant prey. Some crews carried only a single long-barreled gun on a pivot or transverse mount placed amidships, akin to the designs of some American revenue cutters. Such a weapon might be camouflaged under a tarpaulin until needed. Capable of being aimed independently of the ship's course, it was perfect for the chase. If all went well it would be needed only to fire a warning shot.[6]

—————————

Sheffield's description of Samuel Jeffers's retaking of his captured craft places him in the mold of many eighteenth- and nineteenth-century English and American privateers; colorful, reckless characters known as much for cunning as combat. One captain overawed a better-armed ship by running out fake cannon, sawed from spare masts and painted black, and putting every available man into the rigging. Another passed off his craft as a warship by having some of his men wear grenadier caps, à la marines.[7]

A well-documented modern study concluded that most Anglo-American privateers of this era "were not plaster saints but, in most of them, a decent, civilized greed outweighed vainglory and blood lust." The writer added, "Like sportsmen, privateers played by a code of rules. A wide variety of *ruses de guerre* were acceptable: privateers often sailed with several sets of false papers and the flags of half a dozen nations in their flag lockers. They lied wildly when they spoke to other ships. But they were generally civil to the few women whom they captured at sea, and they never fired a gun under false colors."[8]

But as noted in the *General History*, "Privateers in Time of War are a Nursery for Pyrates against a Peace." It was only a short step between the two professions, something Jeffers's native Newport frequently witnessed. The town's long rapport with privateers and their pirate cousins began with a 1648 visit from a Dutch mariner who brought a prize taken illegally during a lull in hostilities. Authorities made no effort to prosecute him due to both the lack of an available warship and residents' eagerness to buy his goods.[9]

A few decades later, Newport was at least trying to keep out suspicious vessels. In 1687 officials refused entry to Captain William Wollery, his ship fresh from a reputed pirate cruise. But in the same era the port spawned Thomas Tew, who made profitable voyages to the Arabian and Indian coasts until his death in a sea battle. It also produced several other captains who, like Tew, sailed with pirate Henry Every; at least one member of Every's band was said to have settled in Rhode Island. A measure of the town's view of such activities came in 1698, when the authorities tried to prosecute the captain of a suspect vessel that visited Newport to refit and traded openly in the harbor. The grand jury refused to indict him, largely because the pirate crew included their relatives and friends. New York's corruption-fighting governor Lord Bellomont deemed Newport too friendly to pirates, and a 1702 report accused most of the town's male population of involvement in privateering.[10]

Many presumably crossed the line into outright sea robbery as well, but attacks on Newport's own shipping lessened local tolerance. In early June 1723, pirate Edward Low took a Newport-based sloop, its captain earning an arm wound while resisting. He was fortunate to receive nothing more, as Low had a psychopathic reputation. Before sailing away Low's men ransacked and vandalized the sloop, which then limped to Block Island, from where a boat took the news to Newport. The town hitherto known as friendly to pirates sent out its own expedition against Low. While it failed to

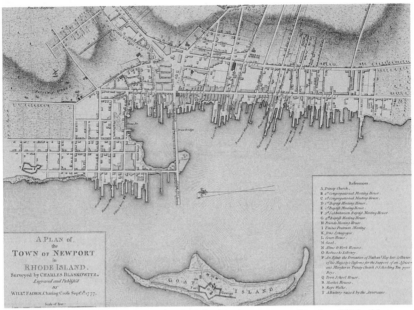

Map of Newport. Surveyed by Charles Blaskowitz; engraved and published by William Faden, Charing Cross, September 1, 1777. Courtesy of the Newport Historical Society, 01.952

find him, a British warship succeeded in capturing his consort—an eight-gun, Bermuda-built sloop called the *Ranger*—and brought its crew to Newport for trial.

This time the local jury condemned twenty-six for piracy. They were executed in a mass hanging at noon on July 17 at Gravelly Point. Many watched the event from small boats. The *New England Courant* reported that a corner of the gallows was draped with the pirates' own "Black Flag, with the Pourtrature of Death, having an Hour-Glass in one Hand, and a Dart in the other, at the end of which was the Form of a Heart with three Drops of Blood, falling from it . . . The Flag they call'd Old Roger, and often us'd to say they would live and die under it."[11]

Newport privateers were active in the mid-eighteenth century wars between England and its European rivals. When the Americans broke with England in 1775, lack of a national navy ushered in the widespread granting of letters of marque; the Continental Congress passed an authorizing act in March 1776. Until 1782, the number of privateers always far outnumbered those of

Continental-commissioned armed ships. Only a handful of the dozens of privateers that went out during the first years of the Revolutionary War hailed from Rhode Island, but they brought back a profitable haul of prizes and captured goods. The thought of easy money apparently lured Samuel Jeffers into action late in the conflict.[12]

The Revolutionary War's end presumably brought his privateering adventures to a close. On March 25, 1792, he married Elizabeth Drew, then about twenty-six, in Newport. James, the fifth of their eight children—and third son—was born November 5, 1798. Given the pirate's later choice of an alias, it is notable that when James was born, his parents were doing business with Newport shipping magnate George Gibbs, a man distinguished enough to sit for artist Gilbert Stuart. Records exist of two land sales by Samuel Jeffers to Gibbs and his partner Walter Channing. In the first transaction on December 7, 1798, the merchants paid $150 for a four-and-three-quarter-acre plot adjacent to Gibbs and Channing's own land. Five years later, Jeffers sold Gibbs and Channing another adjoining plot, part of which was next to "a Road leading to Howlands ferry." About five-and-a-half acres in size, it cost the merchants $250.[13]

A hint of Samuel Jeffers's appearance—possibly that of James as well—may linger in a National Archives document referencing the captain's eldest son, also named Samuel. He had just turned twenty-one when he shipped for Liverpool in mid-1815 aboard the Freetown-registered brig *Starling*. As it was a foreign trip, the *Starling*'s master filed a crew list with the Newport customs office. It describes Samuel Jeffers Junior as 5 feet 7 6/8 inches tall, with a light complexion and brown hair. His experiences could have influenced his brother James to head for sea the next year.[14]

Their parents lived in Newport for the rest of their lives, the elder Jeffers dying on Halloween 1820, aged sixty-five, while returning by ship from Philadelphia. Elizabeth Jeffers died in Newport the following April. Aside from Sheffield's "rough men" remark about Samuel Jeffers and some of his contemporaries, little else is recorded about the captain or his character. But in the autobiographical fictions James Jeffers gave out in 1831 while maintaining the Charles Gibbs alias, his father comes across as a candidate for sainthood, exhibiting remarkable patience with a wayward son. Even after those falsehoods about his early life had been scattered, Jeffers still went to the gallows affirming that he "was born of respectable parents."[15]

The *Hornet,* the *Chesapeake,*
and the "Boston Grocery"

O F JAMES JEFFERS'S INVENTIONS, the one that struck the deepest chord with later writers—despite the condemned man's own retraction—was that as a youth he first went to sea aboard the warship USS *Hornet,* later following its captain, James Lawrence, to the USS *Chesapeake.* Yet even if he was not there, his version of the *Chesapeake*'s June 1, 1813, defeat by HMS *Shannon* (discussed below) is close enough to the standard historical accounts to unsettle any researcher using Jeffers as a source.

It is also interesting that muster and pay records of the *Chesapeake* include references in 1809 to an apparently young ordinary seaman whose name is given as "Ja^s. Jefferies," similar to the "James Jeffreys" and "James Jeffrees" variants cited in some 1831 sources on the pirate otherwise known as Charles Gibbs. His name went through several spelling changes as he was transferred to the USS *Constitution* and later the USS *President,* on which he ended his two-year-plus service.[1]

It would be adventurous indeed to suggest that a shred of fact could lie behind the naval service tale, albeit three years earlier and much less glorious than Jeffers told his 1831 listeners. The James Jeffers born in Newport in 1798 would have been only ten at the time "Ja^s. Jefferies" joined the *Chesapeake,* and no child would have been classed as an ordinary seaman. However, following this otherwise obscure sailor's naval career does illustrate life at sea in the era.

Assigned number 639 on its rolls, "Ja^s. Jefferies" made his first appearance aboard *Chesapeake,* then taking on new enlistees, on March 11, 1809, in Boston. His grade of ordinary seaman was a notch above boy, a designation often referring to experience rather than age, and one below able seaman. Yet he was paid $8 a month, a figure at the high end of what boy designation earned on American warships. These facts hint at his being young but knowing enough of the ways of a ship to qualify for a higher rank, if not better pay.[2]

Again, only a similarity in names and reference to the *Chesapeake* links the recruit to the future pirate James Jeffers. That said, the latter's parents might well have wished at times that they had sent young James off on a warship. An 1831 Rhode Island-published source contended that "in early life, he [James Jeffers] became addicted to vices uncommon in youths of his age," and efforts to discipline him only "seemed to render him still worse." He was "refractory, ungovernable, and disobedient to his parents."[3]

The young James Jeffers sounds a bit like Samuel Comstock, whose role in the 1824 mutiny aboard the whaling vessel *Globe* was detailed in Gregory Gibson's *Demon of the Waters.* Born in Nantucket in 1802 into a pacifist Quaker family that later moved to New York City, Comstock was intelligent and well read, with a fondness for adventure stories; he would at one point in his life try to join a Latin American privateer as an officer. He was also strong-willed, rebellious, and prone to violence from an early age. Educated at strict Quaker schools, he fled home at thirteen hoping to go to sea; sent back to his family, he made life so difficult that his father in desperation put him aboard a vessel with a Quaker captain.[4]

Comstock's reluctant father had actually followed the era's conventional wisdom. According to naval historian Christopher McKee, "Agreement was nearly universal among the pre-1815 navy's leaders: the place to learn professional skills, values, and culture was on shipboard, and preferably in a large warship." Hard-pressed parents held to this view throughout the age of sail. In the merchant trade Richard Henry Dana met a sailor in the 1830s who had been sent to sea by his father, and there were probably many others. Several decades later, Conan Doyle's fictional Sherlock Holmes recommended "a year at sea" for a wayward boy.[5]

Discipline aside, local industry often pointed youths toward maritime careers. Gibson noted that in port towns many "boys were raised with the expectation that they would become seamen." Some went to sea simply because they needed a way to live. Writing of children serving in the British navy, Tom Robson held that "lots of boys of that era were left to fend for themselves as unwanted children, destined for life in institutions and poor houses. They saw the Navy as a way of enhancing their life. The call of the sea was a natural instinct especially for those living on the coast. By finding their way on to a ship they hoped it would lead to a chance of becoming a regular crew member when they reached a mature age."[6]

Youngsters often received relatively undemanding tasks on ships, being allotted to senior personnel as aides, or added to a mess simply to do the cleaning up. Just as easily they could be put into positions of danger, regardless of the vessel's mission. As Gibson wrote, early nineteenth century "New England mothers sent their sons to kill whales in the Pacific Ocean at an age when modern parents would think twice about letting them have the car for a weekend." And if they signed on to a warship, in battle they carried munitions, served the guns, and often received hideous injuries.[7]

So the apparently young sailor "Ja[s]. Jefferies" entered—or reentered—a violent, complex world when he boarded the *Chesapeake* in March 1809. He may have been rowed to the ship at anchor across a chill, even frigid Boston Harbor. An eighteenth-century engraving by William Hogarth shows two boys on such a trip taunting a third, whose mother's presence betrays his newness. One gleefully dangles a bit of frayed rope resembling a cat-o-nine-tails, the multistrand whip with knotted or weighted ends used to administer punishment at sea. The other points out a body hanging from a dockside gallows.[8]

Built in Virginia's Gosport (later Norfolk) Navy Yard and commissioned in 1800, the USS *Chesapeake* was one of several famous early American frigates, that term being used for three-masted, square-rigged warships with a certain length-to-beam ratio and cannon capacity. Its armament varied over the years. In 1807 it carried thirty-eight cannon, most being long-barreled 18-pounders, so-named for the weight of their munitions. Displacing 1,244 tons in the water and measuring 41 feet at its broadest point, the 153-foot-long ship carried a crew of 340. Opinions differed on its performance under sail.

Like most of the rest of the small, underbudgeted American navy, it had served in the turn-of-the-century war against Barbary corsairs. But it was considered ill-starred after an 1807 episode off the Virginia coast. Then, the 50-gun HMS *Leopard* stopped it to search for British deserters, a common occurrence at the time. Events escalated and when the *Leopard* began firing, the *Chesapeake* struck its colors with almost no resistance. The incident provoked a national scandal, several courts-martial, and at least two duels. Normally level-headed sailors began to think of the *Chesapeake* as unlucky, even cursed.

In December 1808, the *Chesapeake* completed a cruise at Hampton Roads, Virginia; two months later, its captain, Stephen Decatur—who had taken over the ship following the *Leopard* incident—was transferred to the USS *United States*, succeeded by Isaac Hull. By early March the controversial ship was in Boston mustering new crewmen, "Jaˢ. Jefferies" among them, for two years.[9]

Some of their experiences likely matched those of English shoemaker's son William Robinson, who joined the British navy in 1805 and immediately regretted it. Lumped together with a levy of criminals, the recruits received a quick medical examination, and, after being bullied and robbed by veterans, were locked below decks for transport. Robinson recalled, "In this place we spent the day and following night huddled together, for there was not room to sit or stand separate: indeed we were in a pitiable plight, for numbers of them were sea-sick, some retching, others were smoking, whilst many were so overcome by the stench, that they fainted for want of air."[10]

On board the *Chesapeake* in early 1809, a change of "slops" (clothes) may have been among the first items doled out to Jefferies, the cost docked from his pay by the officer known as the purser. Given the season, the recruit would have received thicker clothing items with this issue, including a hat and gloves. Having signed on as an ordinary seaman, he may have already known how to wear the outfit as did experienced sailors. Describing a merchant crew, Richard Henry Dana observed that "a sailor has a peculiar cut to his clothes, and a way of wearing them which a green hand can never get. . . . The trousers, tight round the hips, and hanging long and loose round the feet, a superabundance of checked shirt, a low-crowned, well-varnished black hat, worn on the back of the head, with half a fathom of black ribbon hanging over the left eye, and a slip-tie to the black silk neckerchief, are signs, the want of which betrays the beginner at once." The "regular salt" also owned a "sunburnt cheek, wide step, and rolling gait, [and] swings his bronzed and toughened hands half opened, as though just ready to grasp a rope."[11]

Maritime historian John Frayler noted that trousers worn by early-nineteenth-century American sailors were usually made of canvas or "duck," wool, or various homespun materials. If made of duck, they would be a white or natural color; those made from other fabrics were commonly striped. Duck trousers were often worn with "a double-breasted, waist-length blue wool roundabout jacket," and sometimes a waistcoat. Checked patterns often found their way onto shirts. "Wool was highly regarded for providing warmth while wet." Shoes might be secured with buckles or laces, the leather preserved with a grease-and-tar concoction. For bad weather, sailors waterproofed a spare set of clothing with tar: "Not comfortable, but effective."[12]

Having been dressed and docked, the *Chesapeake*'s new Ordinary Seaman Jefferies would have been assigned to a watch, one of two four-hour shifts on duty on the starboard (right) or port (left) side of the ship. European navies assigned each hand a number from 1 to 999; odd numbers were on the starboard watch, even numbers on the port side. (The figures next to the name of "Ja[s]. Jefferies" and its variant spellings in surviving navy muster rolls probably correspond to an American adaptation of such a method, not surprising given the British influence on the early U.S. Navy.) All hands had to be smart enough to execute a bewildering number of commands with speed and precision. Working aloft was especially dangerous. The most compactly built sailors, usually the youngest, tended the highest sails. Dana left a firsthand account of himself as a newcomer "reefing" or shortening a topsail in a heavy sea on a merchant vessel: "I 'laid out' on the yards, and held on with all my strength. I could not have been of much service, for I remember having been sick several times before I left the topsail yard, making wild vomits into the black night. Soon all was snug aloft, and we were again allowed to go below. This I did not consider much of a favor, for the confusion of everything below, and that inexpressibly sickening smell, caused by the shaking up of bilge water in the hold, made the steerage but an indifferent refuge from the cold wet decks."[13]

Those who worked aloft developed extraordinary strength and coordination. Scientists examining the recovered skeleton of one 17th century sailor likened his upper body to that of a trapeze artist, although one also suffering from rickets and teeth ground down from chewing coarse bread. The remains of another sailor from the same century gave evidence of similarly bad teeth, as well as arthritis and a nose broken by a right-handed uppercut.[14]

Sailors took a grimly humorous look at death, which came in many forms. Dana remarked that sailors "must make a joke of everything at sea; and if you were to fall from aloft, and be caught in the belly of a sail, and thus saved from instant death, it would not do to look at all disturbed, or to treat it as a serious matter." Loss of a comrade was viewed pragmatically: one less man to help. Shipboard procedure killed sentimentality. Dana perceived a feeling of general shock when a shipmate died, but once buried at sea his clothes and personal effects were quickly auctioned off. "His chest was taken aft, and used as a store-chest, so that there was nothing left which could be called *his*." Another source described how, after one battle, a sailor was seen to pick up from the quarterdeck a hat with the owner's head still inside. "Matey, you don't now require a hat," he said to the head, which he tossed overboard.[15]

Many duties aboard ship did not actually involve sailing. Crews were drilled at fighting fires caused by accident or lightning strike, or rescuing a man overboard. Much time was spent cleaning equipment or the deck. "While scrubbing we had a bucket of rain-water and a bucket half-full of beach sand, for two sailors," nineteenth-century crewman Frederick Pease Harlow recalled. "We also had a piece of old canvas to use as a cloth to wash the paint work about the bulwarks and this was not very soft so the rust stains and blotches of tar on the stanchions couldn't be removed as quickly as they would have been had the cloth been pliable. Dipping the canvas into the bucket of beach sand helped the work, but even this sometimes failed and then the mate in his generosity would throw a handful of lye into the water and this usually removed the stains, and the skin from your fingers as well." Such tasks were as much about eliminating idle minutes as anything else, the goal being to keep the sailors too busy to get into trouble or plot against their officers.[16]

To keep them so employed was the captain's responsibility, his authority distributed through lesser officers (on merchant vessels, the chain below the captain began with the first mate). Many captains believed sailors needed constant supervision and regulation. William Bligh of HMS *Bounty*, whose crew famously mutinied, held that sailors "must be watched like Children." Whether in private or government employ, the captain and those under him were theoretically bound by maritime laws. In practice it was different. Naval captains overlooked regulations meant to control, for example, how many lashes they could award a transgressor without a court-martial. To Dana, a captain was "accountable to no one, and must be obeyed in everything." Such concentration of authority was meant in part to overcome sailors' natural reluctance to perform makework chores.[17]

Shipboard life required men to conform to authority, something they did not always do cheerfully, and historical studies often highlight the harsh disciplinary methods of the era's navies. Some infamous punishments, such as dragging a man underwater across the barnacle-encrusted keel (keelhauling), appear to have been rare and were outlawed under American regulations. What sailors regularly faced was being beaten with the cat-o-nine tails.

U.S. naval officer Lawrence Kearny wryly termed the cat-o-nine-tails "something of a persuader," although at least late in his career he seems to have rarely used it. But other commanders frequently did, and American and British sailors came to take flogging in stride. Author James E. Valle wrote that "seamen themselves would have understood its rationale. A ship's safety depended upon their prompt and efficient compliance with orders. Slackness and incompetence endangered the welfare of all. When proven shirkers were flogged, overworked messmates might well have applauded. Flogging was traditional punishment, to be stoically borne so long as justly deserved."[18]

While it was a mark of pride to take a flogging without crying out, many could not. One man recounted an incident near the end of the War of 1812, in which "two young . . . mechanics' apprentices" were given six and seven dozen lashes, respectively. "The shrieks of the [first] youngster were dreadful, calling upon God and all the holy angels to save him. After the first dozen another boatswain's mate took the cat; and, when he [the prisoner] had received two dozen, he fainted and hung by his wrists. The punishment was suspended for a few moments until he had revived sufficiently to stand on his feet. He then took four dozen more, making six in all; and, when taken down, he could not stand. The other received seven dozen. He fainted, however, before he had received the first [dozen] and received the greater portion of his punishment in that state. The flesh was fairly hanging in strips upon both backs; it was really a sickening sight."[19]

A man who survived a flogging remembered that after the first three lashes he felt pain in "every nerve from the scalp of my head to my toenails. . . . I put my tongue between my teeth, held it there and bit it in almost two pieces. What with the blood from my tongue, and my lips which I had also bitten, and the blood from my lungs or some other internal part ruptured by the writhing agony, I was almost choked and became black in the face."[20]

Well-disciplined ships were quiet. Only tasks such as working the capstan to raise the anchor might permit a song. At such times, merchant sailor Dana maintained, "A song is as necessary to sailors as the drum and fife to a soldier. They must pull together as soldiers must step in time, and they can't pull in time, or pull with a will, without it." But usually silence on deck was the rule, especially on warships. Captain's orders on HMS *Indefatigable* in 1812 read in part: "The strictest silence to be observed and no singing out on any occasion to be suffered."[21]

On all vessels, sanitation was primitive. Sailors relieved themselves at latrines consisting of holes extending over the bowsprit. The era's equivalent of toilet paper was a rope kept dangling in the water. When stormy weather prevented using the head, sailors were known to urinate and defecate into the hold. They rinsed their clothes by towing them in the sea, and on rare occasions bathed using a bucket of fresh water (soap was useless in salt water) shared among many men. Nothing eradicated the rats that historically plagued all ships, targeting canvas, planks, and cargo containers, and spreading disease. Sailors clubbed them individually, or left out balls of poisoned oatmeal. Under drastic circumstances crews fumigated the hold by lighting pans of charcoal and other combustibles, then closing the hatches and caulking them shut. But this dangerous practice risked fire at sea. Another delicate procedure was that of "careening"—also known as "graving" or "breaming"—by which barnacles and other debris would be removed from below the waterline to help streamline the hull and improve sailing speed. When done away from port, this involved beaching the vessel, rendering it helpless while the growth was burned and scraped off.[22]

Shipboard food was poor and badly prepared, the drinking water collecting rust from the iron tanks in which it was stowed. Meals were built around heavily salted beef or pork—occasionally fish—usually soaked in a "harness cask" of fresh water prior to eating to reduce the brine-and-saltpeter preservative. The other mainstay ration was ship's biscuit, or hard tack, which was often full of insect life. One historian noted that sailors gnawing on the hard, flavorless, infested crackers learned "to distinguish the flavors of the different species: weevils tasted bitter, cockroaches of sausage; maggots were unpleasantly spongy and cold to bite into." Not all sailors considered shipboard rations vile. Breakfast on one nineteenth-century vessel was "lobscouse" or "cracker hash," which sailor Frederick Pease Harlow described as "a mixture of broken pieces of hard-tack soaked in water until it became soft and then mixed with pieces of salt beef, pork and sliced onions to give it a flavor. This was usually more than [other sailors] could stand, but I was very fond of it when it was baked with a crisp top."[23]

Disease killed more sailors than storm or battle. Perhaps the chief problem was scurvy, caused by a lack of vitamins. Dana recalled how one victim's "legs swelled and pained him so that he could not walk. His flesh lost its elasticity, so that if pressed in it would not return to its shape. His gums swelled until he could not open his mouth. His breath, too, became very offensive. He lost all strength and spirit, could eat nothing, grew worse every day." In his case, a cure was at hand in the form of juice from raw potatoes. The sick man was given this concoction "by the teaspoonful at a time, and rinsed it about his gums and throat. The strong, earthy taste and smell of this extract . . . at first produced a shuddering through his whole frame and an acute pain, which ran through all parts of his body. But he persevered . . . and in ten days so rapid was his recovery that he was at the masthead furling a royal."[24]

Besides scurvy, typhus and tuberculosis (and in the tropics, malaria) were a sailor's likeliest killers, and the first three were sometimes termed "sea" diseases. The presence of diseases such as smallpox on a vessel visiting a port might force it to be quarantined. Medicine chests aboard U.S. warships were stocked with the instruments and medicines expected of the era. Their effectiveness depended on the surgeon's competence, but as John Frayler wrote, "Some compounds seem quite sinister by today's standards." He added, "Calomel, once widely prescribed as a purgative, and for the treatment of syphilis, was in fact a form of mercury, mercurous chloride. Sugar of Lead (lead acetate) was used to treat eye problems and gonorrhea. Elixir of Vitriol (a mixture of sulfuric acid and brandy, flavored with cinnamon and ginger) was used as a tonic for stomach ailments. And then there was opium, commonly included in pain medicines such as Laudanum, and as addictive then as it is now." The same author found grounds for calling shipboard surgery "not far removed from butchery," observing that "shipboard response to accident in the Age of Sail was about at the same level of effectiveness as today's first aid. If the bleeding was stopped, broken bones set or removed, the injury bandaged and the patient was still alive, the effort was a success. Then the general health and constitution of the patient became the critical factor in the recovery process."[25]

The watch system went overboard in time of battle when all hands were organized into divisions. The number of divisions on warships depended on how large the captain wanted each gun crew to be. These teams had to be big enough to move guns weighing several tons in their carriages. Larger gun crews meant faster shots, plus more replacements at hand if needed, which was crucial as working a naval cannon was a complex job. The nine-to-fourteen men of a gun crew first undid the ropes securing the weapon when not in action, then dragged it far enough inboard to enable loading. This process began by forcing into the muzzle a bag holding several pounds of gunpowder, followed successively by a wad, the iron cannonball (or at close range, a musket-ball filled shell), and another wad, each rammed deep into the bore. The gun captain then stuck a powder-filled quill into the touch hole at the rear of the gun, piercing the bag with it. Thus primed for firing, the crew pushed the behemoth's muzzle through the gunport, its two-part lid having already been stowed.

Properly aiming such a weapon on a rolling ship required intense training and lots of luck. Crews used handspikes to force the barrel to point toward the target, and used wedges called "quoins" to adjust elevation. When ready to fire, the gun captain applied a slow match to the touch hole, the resulting discharge enveloping all in a cloud of smoke. All hands had to be clear at firing or risk death or mutilation as the massive unit recoiled against its breeching tackle. After swabbing out to remove powder blockage and/or stray sparks, good crews repeated the exercise in two to three minutes.[26]

Only rigid training kept new sailors at their post during the shock of their first combat. A young Englishman whose first battle was Trafalgar wrote home that "when the game began, I wished myself at Warnborough with my plough again." But he soon "set to in good earnest, and thought no more about being killed than if I were at Murrell Green Fair, and I was presently as busy and as black as a collier." Having survived his baptism of fire, the same sailor mocked comrades affected by Admiral Sir Horatio Nelson's death: "They have done nothing but blast their eyes, and cry, ever since he was killed. . . . Chaps that fought like the devil, sit down and cry like a wench."[27]

The exposure of young sailor "Ja[s]. Jefferies" to such life aboard USS *Chesapeake* lasted only about a month. *Chesapeake* needed to replace its sails, and in mid-April 1809 when Hull received authorization for this most of its crew, including Jefferies, were transferred to the USS *Constitution*. A different variant of the sailor's name, "James Jeffries," now appears on the *Constitution*'s muster rolls, number 276 on its ledger, among men "transf[d] from Chesapeake." Earning only $8 monthly, he is listed as having been advanced $13.26 by the purser while receiving $14.97 worth of slops—the advances presumably offset the high clothing costs. By the time of his next (and last) entry on the *Constitution*'s books, his advances totaled $27.55, his slops purchases $25.60. The high figures assigned slops purchases affirms Frayler's observation that "while the typical seaman bought what he could not make, the cost of clothing encouraged him to make everything that he could and patch everything that could be saved a little longer."[28]

His new ship had been launched in 1797, served in the Quasi-War at sea with France and was especially active in action against the Barbary pirates. It had already undergone a major refit in the New York Navy Yard between February 1808 and March 1809, by which time its captain was John Rodgers, who being appointed commander of a new squadron also bore the title of commodore. With *Constitution* as his flagship, Rodgers's squadron began its cruise in mid-August. This trek along the northeast American coast was marked by the September 10 collapse of several upper masts and yards, an

Commodore John Rodgers.
Courtesy of Louisa
Alger Watrous

episode that killed one sailor and was blamed on bad timber. Unhappy with the *Constitution*'s sailing, Rodgers eventually moved his flag to the USS *President,* bringing the crew with him. The two 44-gun frigates accordingly switched most of their personnel on June 17, 1810, in Hampton Roads, Virginia. Jefferies served out the rest of his enlistment on the *President,* its cruise ultimately lasting several months longer than the two years for which he originally signed. National Archives documents list him as being discharged and paid off, still at $8 per month, at New York on August 19, 1811. At this point, he vanishes from navy records.[29]

<hr />

"Ja⁵. Jefferies" had only a brief, peacetime glimpse of the *Chesapeake*'s history. The James Jeffers hanged on Ellis Island in 1831 initially claimed more dramatic knowledge of the ship, gaining it while compiling an impressive but fictional War of 1812 record. The *Journal of Commerce* reported:

> The first account which he gives of himself is, that his father obtained
> a situation for him in the United States sloop of war *Hornet,* Capt.
> Lawrence, during the last war with England, in which vessel he made
> two cruises; in the last of which she captured and sunk the enemy's

sloop of war *Peacock* off the coast of Pernambuco, after an engagement of 20 min.—On the arrival of the *Hornet* in the U.S., Capt. Lawrence was assigned by the government to the command of the frigate *Chesapeake,* then lying in Boston harbor, and Gibbs accompanied him to that ill-fated vessel in the month of April, 1813. "Early in the month of May," says he, "we received a challenge from Capt. Broke, of the frigate *Shannon,* and we instantly made preparations to go to sea, and risk a battle. We stood down the harbor about 11 o'clock, and commenced the action about 3 P.M. off Cape Ann. It lasted about 30 minutes, with great slaughter, especially on board the *Chesapeake.* I escaped miraculously, with only a sabre wound upon my nose, the only wound I ever received in my life. The loss of the *Chesapeake* was 65 killed dead, and 100 wounded—one half mortally. We were taken into Halifax, where I remained about four months."[30]

How his claim was disproved is lost to history. A "layman" who visited the condemned man in his cell in 1831 noted that "some of the particulars related by Gibbs, such as his having been during the late war on board of the *Hornet* and the *Chesapeak[e],* have been proved not to be true, and he has admitted that part of his statement to be a falsehood." While having no bearing on Jeffers's sentencing, it understandably "cast a cloud of suspicion around the whole of his story."[31]

Yet Jeffers had much of the history right. The USS *Hornet* began the war as part of an Atlantic squadron under Rodgers. By the end of 1812, it formed part of a new light squadron under Commodore William Bainbridge, consisting also of the *Constitution* and the light frigate USS *Essex,* meant to operate in the Indian Ocean. In late December, the *Hornet* was left on its own, under James Lawrence, to blockade Bahia. Chased away by a 74-gun British man-of-war, Lawrence, then holding the rank of master commandant, stayed along the Brazilian coast and met the brig HMS *Peacock.* Much as Jeffers told his interviewers, the subsequent battle lasted only about a quarter of an hour before the *Peacock* sank.

For accomplishing this, Lawrence hoped to be rewarded with command of the first-class *Constitution.* Instead he was given the star-crossed *Chesapeake,* which when the War of 1812 began was in Boston Harbor on receiving ship duties. Hurried back into service at the start of 1813, *Chesapeake* went on a four-month cruise under Captain Samuel Evans. *Chesapeake* took at least two prizes, one carrying cargo worth $700,000. With Evans's eyesight failing, in early May 1813 his superiors transferred command of the *Chesapeake* to the hero of the *Hornet.*

Captain James Lawrence, by J. Herring. Courtesy of the U.S. Naval Academy Museum Collection / Naval Historical Foundation, 80-G-K-17587

Though his new vessel was formidable, mounting fifty guns, the reluctant Lawrence was saddled with a poorly trained, surly, partly foreign-born crew. Worse, he was under pressure to confront the HMS *Shannon*, visible outside Boston Harbor, carrying fifty-two guns and a veteran crew captained since 1806 by Philip Broke. Weighing anchor early in the afternoon on June 1, Lawrence was off Cape Ann by 4 P.M. Within seven miles of the *Shannon*, he ordered a gun fired to signal a challenge. Broke let the American ship approach. At about 5:45 P.M., Broke ordered his first broadside, from which the Americans never recovered. With Lawrence mortally wounded and many officers killed, the *Chesapeake* drifted out of control into the British ship. The subsequent boarding ended in a British victory after fifteen brutal minutes. Tallies of the day's losses vary among sources. Spencer Tucker, in his *Handbook of Nineteenth Century Naval Warfare,* states that the Americans lost sixty-two killed and eighty-five wounded; the *Shannon,* which by Tucker's account suffered about half those numbers, towed its prize into Halifax harbor.[32]

Describing something that took place almost eighteen years earlier and at which he surely was not present, James Jeffers erred by just a month in dating the *Chesapeake-Shannon* battle, and there are minor differences with what historians have accepted as the time of the engagement. Even allowing for exaggeration of losses, particularly the number of mortally wounded, his pretended first-person account is reasonably close to the accepted historical one. He also included a reference to morale aboard the *Chesapeake.* It was said that Jeffers stated "that previous to the engagement, the crew of the *Chesapeake* were almost in a state of mutiny, growing out of the non payment of their prize money, and that the [pre-battle] address of Captain Lawrence was received by them with coldness and murmurs."[33]

Consider the following twentieth-century account of the same episode: "In bright sunshine Lawrence ran up a flag bearing the motto 'Free Trade and Sailors' Rights' which no more inspired the *Chesapeake*'s men than the short address he delivered, which they several times interrupted. Some of them chose this moment to demand prize money owed them from previous cruises."[34]

It is worth asking how Jeffers obtained his basic story. If he gleaned it from talking to actual *Chesapeake-Shannon* participants, he showed a good memory for details. Yet the fact Jeffers lied about this rightly troubled the aforementioned layman who in 1831 pondered the same question a modern observer must: how much of the man's overall story was true? "If the narrative which this unhappy man has given . . . be not true," he asked "[why should he] volunteer to tell, of the commission of crimes, which he had not perpetrated. For his piracy and murder on board the *Vineyard* he was about to be tried, and knew full well he would be found guilty. Upon what principle, then . . . could he act, by seeking to increase the public horror of his crimes, and their indignation against him, by adding to the list of dreadful deeds he had actually perpetrated, others, which had no existence but in his own murderous imagination. . . ."[35]

————

Serving on the *Hornet* and *Chesapeake* was just the beginning of Jeffers's claims to maritime posts before embarking on his privateering career in

1816. He said he followed his exchange with inconsequential trips as a sailor passing through ports such as New Orleans, Stockholm, Bristol, and Liverpool. All may of course reflect real visits at one point or another during his career. But as he was still using the Charles Gibbs alias and lying about his early years when he told these stories, they can probably be dismissed from the genuine chronology.

Another tale provokes more interest—that he followed these journeys by starting a grocery in Boston. Contemporary critics did not challenge this story, and later writers embroidered it. As with the *Hornet-Chesapeake* account, looking closely at it yields some interesting finds.

By Jeffers's account—relayed through a reporter's words—"Shortly after his return home [from the reputed War of 1812 exploits] the death of an uncle put him in possession of about $2,000, with which he established himself in the grocery business in Boston." The year was presumably 1814 or 1815. All he said additionally about this episode was that his business lost money, and despite his father's help, which was "accompanied with good advice and his blessing," the venture collapsed. "The stock was finally sold at auction, for about $900, which he soon squandered in alehouses and among profligates."[36]

The crew of the Shannon *boarding the* Chesapeake, *by M. Dubourg after a drawing by Heath. Courtesy of the Naval Historical Foundation, NH 65811-KN*

Six years after Jeffers's 1831 execution, the account began to mutate. The setting was *The Pirates' Own Book,* published anonymously in Boston in 1837 by former Boston stationer Charles Ellms, and which would go through eight more editions over the next quarter-century. Ellms took material from a number of sources, generally without acknowledging them. Moreover, the preface to a 1924 reprint noted, "he not infrequently embellishes his text with the fruits of his own fertile imagination." An example occurs in discussion of Charles Gibbs and his Boston business. In Ellms's version, "He [Charles Gibbs] opened a grocery in Ann Street, near what was then called the *Tin Pot,* a place full of abandoned women and dissolute fellows. As he dealt chiefly in liquor, and had a 'License to retail Spirits,' his drunkery was thronged with customers. But he sold his groceries chiefly to loose girls who paid him in their coin, which although it answered his purpose, would neither buy him goods or pay his rent, and he found his stock rapidly dwindling away without his receiving any cash to replenish it. By dissipation and inattention his new business proved unsuccessful to him."[37]

Editions of the *Boston Directory* from this period contain no references that fit James Jeffers. But fascinatingly, editions for 1816 and 1818 list a provision store co-owned by one Charles Gibbs and Abel Barnes. It was located at 65 India Wharf, built in 1803–1807 on the site of the present Harbor Towers development. To judge from old Boston maps it was a long walk from the Ann Street location that Ellms cited. The business disappears by 1820.[38]

When stories about a pirate named Charles Gibbs circulated in 1831, and word spread of his claim to having run a Boston grocery, memories were jogged. Locals described the business, said one newspaper, as having been "near Liberty Square," which contemporary maps place several blocks from India Wharf. They also recalled it being in operation at "about the time that one Hart, a confectioner, was found murdered in his house close by, and that Gibbs decamped from the city soon after. The fate of Hart is very generally remembered, but his murderer has thus far eluded detection."[39]

As with so many creaky parts of Jeffers's confessions, probing this issue invites problems and questions. If he was in Boston at the same time the India Wharf store was in existence, it would push back the date at which he began his drift toward the Caribbean. Yet why would this young Newporter go into business under an assumed name? If he drew on the actual shop owner's life when choosing an alias, Jeffers probably learned of it during trips back to the United States.

4

Going to Sea in a Lawless Age

SSUMING JAMES JEFFERS WAS indeed ship captain Samuel Jeffers's son, it was natural that he would turn to the sea. His oldest brother had already been on at least one foreign voyage. The War of 1812 probably brought their father's privateering background into focus as a career possibility. Some citizens in that era's oceanfront towns even deemed a slip across the line into piracy acceptable. A late nineteenth-century observer cautioned that "the condition of piracy can not be measured by present lights." He added, "In those times of almost incessant war, when one Government commissioned individuals to rove the seas and rob its enemies' ships of commerce, the step from the privateer to the pirate was natural, and the moral difference not very marked. Men of very good family became pirates because they loved adventure; it was profitable if they were not hanged, and they had nothing to do at home except fight."[1]

So it is possible that this seventeen-year-old of respectable background already had some kind of maritime marauding in mind when Jeffers—so he said before his 1831 hanging—first went to sea in 1816 aboard the Newport-based brig *Brutus*. Such a vessel existed. Built at Freetown, Massachusetts, in 1815, the *Brutus* was 77 feet long and 24 feet across at its widest point. Its designation of 197 tons referred to cargo space, a "ton" in this case referring to about 100 cubic feet. (Since warships lacked cargo holds, naval tonnage figures referenced estimated water displacement.) Registration documents noted that it had "two decks, two masts, no figurehead." Many co-owners are listed between its first registration in March 1816 and its 1825 loss on a Florida reef. Its first master was Charles Gorton of Newport, born circa 1778 and described on surviving crew lists of the era as almost six feet tall, with a dark complexion and brown hair. He had captained merchant ships since at least 1812, when he took the Newport brig *German Peggy* to Havana. He returned there during 1815 in three different craft, bringing back a cargo of molasses to Newport in January 1816 while captaining the schooner *Eliza*. Two months later Gorton, then thirty-eight, took the recently launched *Brutus* to Charleston, taking ten days to get there.

If James Jeffers accompanied him on this trip, he likely got off in Charleston. His name does not appear on the crew list Gorton filed with Charleston's customs collector on April 26, when the *Brutus* sailed for Copenhagen to pick up hemp and iron to transport back to Newport. Nor does Jeffers appear on documents Gorton filed for the *Brutus*'s November 23 trip to Bonavista. Could Jeffers have taken the *Brutus* to Charleston early in 1816 and never looked back?[2]

Had James Jeffers gone to sea with adventure and money in mind, he was not alone. The U.S. southern coasts, particularly those near Spanish colonial holdings, were potentially profitable for the right individuals. The Gulf of Mexico and Caribbean had already attracted American adventurers, some of whom made little distinction between privateering and piracy. Many had operated since the early 1800s out of New Orleans. Like Newport of an earlier era, it had a deserved piratical reputation. Gardner W. Allen's 1929 book *Our Navy and the West Indian Pirates*—a rarity among works on piracy given its citation of sources—described wide-open New Orleans at the Mississippi's mouth as an ideal base for a new generation of marauders: "Being unfrequented by foreign ships of war, it was comparatively safe. Here the privateersmen spent their money freely, mingled with the dregs of the population, and kept the town in a state of turmoil. The more reckless and dissolute among them easily passed the shadowy border line between privateering and piracy. They seized and plundered not only their enemies' vessels, but American shipping as well. Within a few years the bays and inlets of Louisiana had become a favorite rendezvous of pirates."[3]

The United States Navy began policing the area in 1810 and scored some successes against the New Orleans pirates. But the loss of the revenue cutter *Louisiana* in a hurricane and the War of 1812's drain on naval resources allowed the area's brigands to stay in business. The story that Louisiana pirates were American allies during the war arose from aid French expatriate and smuggler Jean Laffite—he seems to have spelled his name this way— gave to the defense of New Orleans against the British. Having been in New Orleans since at least 1807, Laffite justified his presence to American authorities by arguing that he targeted only Spanish ships. Yet Spain was at peace

Then-lieutenant Daniel T. Patterson, from a miniature circa 1810. Courtesy of the Naval Historical Foundation, NH 59496

with the United States. Moreover the 1795 treaty between the two countries forbade Americans from holding privateering commissions against Spain; violators were to be treated as pirates. In early 1813, Louisiana's governor condemned Laffite's activities. Within two years, he and Laffite would offer bounties for each other's head.[4]

Laffite was described as handsome, with polished manners and a businesslike approach to piracy. He operated from Grand Terre Island, which he renamed Barataria after its location in Barataria Bay, west of where the Mississippi opens into the Gulf of Mexico. The early Baratarians were mostly French Creole, reflecting the area's pre–Louisiana Purchase days. After the War of 1812 began, Laffite drew in a host of deserters from U.S. service. Partly with this in mind, an American naval expedition there in mid-September 1814 captured several vessels and scattered Laffite's operation for a while. Navy captain Daniel T. Patterson, who led the attack, reported that Laffite's colony of thatched-roof huts housed between eight hundred and one thousand pirates of mixed nations and races. Many of their vessels flew the flag of Cartagena in New Grenada, modern Colombia, then being one of several recently revolted Spanish colonial provinces. It consisted of an eight-pointed white star on a green bar, bordered in yellow and red.

Its appearance at Barataria testified to how the violent dismantling of Spain's colonial holdings in Latin America after 1808 helped spawn the sea marauders of James Jeffers's generation. Short of established navies and with Spanish ships their nominal prey, the rebel provinces began issuing letters of marque. Cartagena was perhaps the most prolific commissioner of privateers, closely rivaled by Buenos Aires. The latter was the political and commercial center of the United Provinces of the Plate River, modern Argentina. Buenos Aires's vessels flew the United Provinces flag, incorporating a sunburst on a blue-and-white field.[5]

Observers in the United States at first looked approvingly at Latin American privateering, some drawing parallels to their own country's revolution against Britain. An editorial in *Niles' Weekly Register* supported Cartagena's privateers, noting that the republic was "at war with Spain, just exactly as we were with Great Britain during our revolution. There is not one shade of difference." Defending a client in a piracy trial, in which his vessel sailed under a Buenos Aires commission, a lawyer argued that "there was an exact and perfect analogy between" the issuing state's revolt against Spain "and the revolutionary contest of our country." Even federal officials in Baltimore dabbled in privateering, causing diplomat and later president John Quincy Adams to label them "fanatics of the South-American cause." A Henry Clay speech in support of Latin American liberation drew cheers when translated and read out to revolutionary troops.[6]

Some privateer commanders attained a kind of celebrity in American newspapers. One example was Joseph Almeida, who apparently served under commissions from both Cartagena and Buenos Aires at various times. On one occasion in 1818, when his well-armed vessel *Louisa,* its decks crammed with about one hundred men ready to make mischief on Spanish shipping, spoke with another ship at sea, Almeida dryly asked to be reported as "bound round Cape Horn, on a sealing voyage." An editor clarified that in actuality Almeida "will, no doubt, do great execution on the coasts of Peru, &c. Capt. Almeida is under high obligations to the Spaniards . . . and will relieve himself of them as soon as possible."[7]

The names of some "patriot" privateering ships must have struck chords with American readers. A Buenos Aires-commissioned vessel was called *Constitution.* The Cartagena-flagged *Retaliation* docked in Charleston. One of Patterson's captures at Barataria was named for Latin American liberator Simon Bolivar. Other then-current heroes gave their names to vessels cruising in the Gulf and Caribbean in 1817; their number also included the *Mexican Congress* and a brig and a schooner both named *Invincible.* U.S. Navy lieutenant-turned-privateer Henry B. Rapp's Cartagena-commissioned *Hotspur* carried three 9-pound cannon and a brass 18-pounder, and it took heavy casualties trying to take an armed Spanish brig, which had been built in Baltimore as the *Chasseur*. The latter returned crippled to Havana, and when it later captured a privateer all aboard it were reportedly executed.[8]

As that alleged act showed, Spain viewed the privateers as pirates, refusing to recognize its rebellious colonies as sovereign states entitled to grant letters of marque. (Washington would take a similar view during the American Civil War regarding Confederate raiders.) In truth, privateer commissions from the new republics were available with few of the traditional regulatory strings, such as bond posting, attached. Privateer captains did not even have to visit the issuing country to get a letter of marque. Evidence at one 1816 trial included blank commissions made up and dated in Buenos Aires, to be completed and sealed by that government's agents in the United States.[9]

Buenos Aires presumably tightened its commissioning process in 1817 when it adopted regulations based on Spanish ones, but its privateers remained as active as those from Cartagena, the major Caribbean port in New Granada (Colombia by 1820). Cartagena offered an excellent harbor in what an observer called "a delightful region, with about 2,500,000 white inhabitants, and very few slaves—rich in the product of all the necessaries of life, and yielding more gold than all the rest of South America. All things considered, it [New Granada] is probably the most desirable country of any of the new republics. . . ."[10]

Cartagenian/Colombian service attracted adventurers from many nations and backgrounds and brought in plenty of Americans. Fifty-six of the roughly sixty-man crew of one Colombian privateer captured in 1822 were said to have hailed from the United States, and an 1823 estimate placed eight hundred Americans on vessels commissioned by the insurgent republic. A similar number likely served Buenos Aires.[11]

In all cases, their captains' letters of marque would have sanctioned interference only with Spanish merchant craft, still operating out of Cuba and Puerto Rico. In reality, some holders attacked whatever ship was at hand. This was no innovation. What was new was the brutality that began to routinely accompany marauding in the area's waters. Contemporary descriptions of capture at sea, especially in the 1820s, emphasize random violence and cruelty.

A historian looking through the records of the English Admiralty Court in the sixteenth and seventeenth centuries noted that most maritime robbery then involved straight piracy—cargo theft without violence. But the colonization of the gold-rich Americas, amid the clash of European and indigenous cultures, gradually saw the emergence of a more violent breed of criminal. Writing of the buccaneer era, Alexander Exquemelin documented vicious characters like Henry Morgan and Jean-David Nau. better known as François L'Olonnais. Somewhat later, the *General History*'s lineup of Anglo-American pirates included Edward Low, who killed crews and burned ships for reasons ranging from hatred for New Englanders to patriotism—the Londoner becoming enraged at finding captured English sailors and goods aboard a Spanish ship.[12]

While pirates sank on the morality scale, privateers were still distinguishable by better conduct, in part a reflection of government oversight. Indeed, some eighteenth- and early nineteenth-century privateers earned bounties for captives brought into port. Such offers protected prisoners, who were a burden to feed and guard at sea. They were also a threat, as Captain Samuel Jeffers knew from his own Revolutionary War experience, because captives were known to turn on prize crews. Privateers of that era also sometimes released captives in return for a bill of exchange drawn upon their shipowners, a form of ransom that allowed the prize to go free and its crew to feed itself. Some governments operated cartel ships taking prisoners off privateers' hands and transporting them for later exchange.[13]

Yet during the Latin American wars of revolution Cartagenian and Venezuelan privateers were sometimes instructed to kill Spanish captives. The orders reflected the "War to the Death" ongoing ashore. An historian of Gulf-area privateering wrote, "Rival commanders on the mainland, royalist and republican, had been waging for years a war without quarter that General Bolivar in 1813 saw it necessary to establish as a policy of state. So was continued the War to the Death, which worked incalculable injury to Venezuela and to the provinces of the future Colombia."[14]

To their credit, many Cartagenian and Venezuelan privateers ignored such commands, and there is evidence of humane treatment by vessels commissioned from other states. Captain Pierre Brugman, who commanded the schooner *Popa* in Cartagenian service, took Spanish prizes off Haiti in 1816 and dropped his prisoners alive on Cuba in spite of orders to execute them. Late that year the Venezuelan-flagged *Jupiter* and the Buenos Aires–commissioned *Potosi* were both reported to have spared Spanish captives. The aforementioned Captain Joseph Almeida once shifted two Spanish captives onto a vessel bound for New York. An otherwise unidentified insurgent privateer placed thirty prisoners from the Spanish ship *Carlotta* aboard a Portuguese brig, which landed them at Madeira. Privateers from Mexico also seem to have had a good reputation.[15]

Those acting strictly as pirates did not, irrespective of whether they called themselves privateers. Patterson in 1815 charged that New Orleans's pirates routinely eliminated witnesses and destroyed captured vessels as well. Several years later, when a British warship broke up a Cuban pirate colony, its crew reportedly found a dozen otherwise valuable craft "burnt to the water's edge." As historian David Cordingly explained: "Operating outside the law, the pirates could not, of course, go along to the prize courts to get their captured vessels valued and sold, which was the usual practice of privateer captains." They would occasionally keep a craft as a consort or replacement, but most were burned or scuttled.[16]

A trip to some prize courts might discourage even legitimate privateering. Those of Buenos Aires kept two-thirds of whatever a captured vessel and its cargo brought. Many privateer captains considered the percentage extortionate, particularly if they did not own their vessels and therefore had to split any remaining profit with the *armadores* who did.[17] These economic factors probably spurred some captains and crews into a less complicated, more lucrative, albeit more violent line of work.

Such was the maritime atmosphere off America's southern coasts at the time James Jeffers admittedly went to sea. If he stopped off in Charleston in early 1816 courtesy of the *Brutus,* where did he go from there? By his 1831 confessions, at some point that year he signed onto a ship called the *John,* its master named Brown, bound for the mountainous island of Margarita off Venezuela's north coast. During the conquistador years Margarita, not far from two other islands famous in pirate lore, La Tortuga and La Blanquilla, was known for pearls. It later became a regular target of English and Dutch raiders. An early English account noted that "Margarita is very small, and lyeth foure leagues from the maine land: it hath heretofore bene very rich of golde and pearles, and so would haue continued till this present day, had it not beene spoyled by men of warre, because it standeth so farre from the maine land, notwithstanding they yet gather good store of pearles. Vpon this Island are bred better horses and mules then in any of part of the Indies, therefore they carry them from hence to Peru, albeit they haue great store of horses in Peru, but not so good."[18]

By 1816, as will be seen, it was in chaos, and was a way station for anyone considering a career in Caribbean privateering and its close cousin, piracy.

Hopson's notes of his 1831 conversations with Jeffers reveal nothing about how Jeffers got to Margarita, though the *Journal of Commerce* writer's own narrative does. Unfortunately, the journey there begins after the collapse of the fictitious Boston grocery: "His father hearing of his dissipation, wrote affectionately and earnestly to him to come home, but he stubbornly refused, and went to sea again, in the ship *John,* Captain Brown, bound for the Island of Margarita." The port at which he boarded the *John* is unspecified—though presumably not far from Boston—and the common and nondescript names for ship and captain invite suspicion.[19]

Assuming he had actually strayed to Charleston at this time, this research found no strong candidates for Captain Brown's *John* based there or the other principal southern port, New Orleans. However, a certain Rhode Island vessel does fit the bill, and it plied Caribbean waters in the era. Elisha Brown was master of this *John,* which he co-owned with merchant John Cook and the latter's son, also named John. When built in 1800 as a 124-ton schooner at Hallowell, Massachusetts, it was a single-deck craft 71 feet long, its breadth (widest point) about 22 feet. The *John's* original hailing port was Tiverton, Rhode Island, but it eventually worked out of Newport, and a customs form from a mid-1811 cruise to Havana lists eight crewmen besides Brown, who ran a racially integrated ship. Four of his seamen were black, and another, forty-five-year-old David James of Barnstable, Massachusetts, was listed as "yellow."[20]

Elisha Brown's *John* is an interesting example because the owners changed its rigging from schooner-type to brig in 1804. Six years later they added a second deck, upping its tonnage rating to 156. By June 1815 Brown still co-owned the *John,* though the aforementioned Charles Gorton, later to command the *Brutus,* served as master on its trip to Havana. Perhaps this genuine vessel and man echo somewhere in James Jeffers's confessional mix.[21]

⚑ 5 ⚑

The Privateer *Maria*

ARGARITA, WHERE JEFFERS SAID HE began privateering in 1816, was at that time about as turbulent a place as existed in the hemisphere. Buffeted by Latin American turmoil, Margarita was controlled by revolutionary Juan Bautista Arismendi, who in 1815 the Spanish had captured but made the mistake of pardoning. Once his captors sailed off to take part in the siege of Cartagena, which fell that December, Arismendi led a new revolt and massacred Margarita's garrison. Simon Bolivar shifted his base of operations to Margarita early in 1816, bringing a fleet that soon commenced anti-Spanish operations.[1]

Trade continued despite the war, so Captain Brown's *John,* by which Jeffers claimed to have reached Margarita, could have arrived on business. In the highly charged atmosphere, Brown would have obeyed some formalities upon arrival. The dockside ritual had probably changed little since the days of the *General History,* which used a visit to Pernambuco as an example: "The Dread of Pyrates keeps every one off, till you have first sent an Officer, with the proper Compliments to the Governor. . . ." The reception, including whether the crew received permission to stop and trade, often depended on who was sent. Sailors on this diplomatic task used a well-rehearsed set of answers if their craft was on less-than-legitimate purposes.[2]

The circumstances under which Jeffers left the *John* and entered privateering are uncertain, though one early—and evidently garbled—article about his confessions said that he had found himself stranded without funds in a foreign port. Had he been actively looking for privateering opportunities, though, plenty would have presented themselves on Margarita, which even granted its own letters of marque. From the little Jeffers said of this major step in his life, he joined a privateer schooner called the *Maria*. It was captained by a New Yorker named Bell, who Jeffers recalled "was from somewhere up North River, at or near Hudson." Like those routed at Barataria in 1814, Bell held a commission from Cartagena, several days' sailing southwest of Margarita.

A query to the Colombian archives revealed no obvious candidates for Bell's *Maria*. But in an era of fill-in-the-blank forms that could be issued anywhere—and with Cartagena itself in Spanish hands for a time—this omission does not entirely discredit Jeffers's version of events. Bell himself could have used an alias. A captain named White allegedly operated as a pirate during the era as "Captain Bob." An Italian named Giovanni, commanding the Cartagenian schooner *Republicano*, was known as both "Captain Johnny" and "Barba-fuma." *Noms de guerre* might reflect someone's inability to get the real name right. A French captain in Bolivar's service, Devesge, was also known by a host of derivatives including Duverg, Davit, Deveze, and Davis. Variants of the name of privateer Joseph (or Marcellin) Battigne included Bellegarde, Vergara, Rartigne, Rastique, Rustique, and Roustique.[3]

Bell could have been one of many American privateer captains affected by the peacetime reopening of transatlantic commerce to European vessels. The latter now picked up a hefty percentage of the ocean-going trade. The year 1816, according to one source, was one in which the lack of legitimate jobs for American mariners, due to the foreign competition, stimulated a rush on privateer commissions from Buenos Aires, and other Latin American states surely harvested recruits as well.[4]

Not only privateer captains operated under aliases. The names of American-owned privateers routinely changed when switching flags. In April 1816 the schooner *Romp*, captained by William Hutchings, left Baltimore bound for Buenos Aires ostensibly on business. But it carried six 18-pounder carronades, and after about two weeks at sea, Hutchings mustered the crew: "They were informed of the destination of the vessel against the commerce of Spain. A salute was fired, the colors of Buenos Ayres hoisted, the name of the vessel changed from the *Romp*, to the *Santafecino*, and articles under the government of Buenos Ayres signed by the crew."[5]

The *Romp/Santafecino*'s actual owner appears to have been Bermuda-born Thomas Taylor, a former British seaman whose "Buenos Ayres squadron" spent part of 1817 blockading the south Cuban coast. Taylor frequently stopped American craft but conducted himself well, paid for appropriated supplies, and was said to have disciplined one of his captains for an unspecified transgression.[6]

Prodded by Spanish officials, American authorities eventually arrested Taylor in New York and charged him with piracy. The episode the prosecutors used involved the *Fourth of July*, a brig "built, armed, equipped and owned in Baltimore by sundry merchants of that place and com[modore] Taylor." Taylor enlisted a crew in Baltimore and Norfolk in December 1816 and set sail for the Caribbean, where he ran up the Buenos Aires flag and changed the *Fourth of July*'s name to *Patriota* before embarking on a cruise against Spanish shipping. The jury acquitted Taylor after finding his Buenos Aires commission valid.[7]

A similar finding figured in the case of another contemporary "pirateer" named William Mitchell who, like Bell, held Cartagenian papers. Early in 1816 the English-born Mitchell successfully attacked the Spanish island of San Andrés, executing its governor and garrison of six soldiers. Like many of his profession, he dabbled in running slaves, fourteen being aboard Mitchell's schooner, *Cometa*, when the USS *Boxer* captured it in 1816. But a New Orleans court acquitted Mitchell that June, and he made trouble near New Orleans and British Honduras for the next few years, at one time operating a fleet of open boats. In 1819 Mitchell was reportedly back in Barataria with 150 followers, vowing not to be taken. By then, however, the legal tide was turning against New Orleans's quasi-privateers. Mitchell's fate is not recorded.[8]

Jeffers was a willing recruit for the *Maria;* he would have told his 1831 interviewers had he been otherwise. Men captured on suspect ships occasionally claimed to have been tricked or forced aboard. One hanged at Charleston in 1820 said "he had, with others, been deluded into a service which eventuated in piracy, for which he was about to pay the forfeit of his life, while thousands who projected the scheme, were now walking at large in the country with impunity."[9]

A similar story appeared in a letter signed by fourteen Americans imprisoned on Cuba early in 1817. It read in part: "Our vessel [circa summer 1816] being sold for the purposes of privateering, we were obliged to take passage in the schooner *Margaretta*, Peter Anchor, commander, bound to Jamaica. To our sorrow, after being on our passage two days, the captain brought up his Carthagenian commission and said he was bound on a cruize. Finding ourselves taken in in this shameful manner, we concerned each other to leave her the first opportunity." But no such opportunity for desertion presented itself. Rather, the vessel took the Spanish schooner *Sophia*, headed for Jamaica with a cargo of cattle. Afterwards, their privateer captured a Spanish brig packed with 180 slaves. Its captain and owner offered to ransom the craft and its human cargo and were allowed to take a boat ashore. What returned was a Spanish warship that captured most of the privateer crew. The letter writer continued: "Honored Sir, now began the inhuman usage of the cruel Spaniards—cut and mangled to pieces with cutlasses, bound back to back till the blood run from under our finger-nails; we are at present in Cuba jail on the [daily] allowance of this savage nation on half a pint of rice and beans, half cooked . . . ; without clothing, or any thing to hide our nakedness, in iron strong, &c.—No friends allowed to see us." The writer closed by pleading "for the mercies of a free country, for which we have fought and valiantly conquered our enemies."[10]

———◦•⊱⊰•◦———

What information Jeffers gave out in 1831 about Bell seems to have come reluctantly. In his earliest discussions with Hopson, Jeffers refused to identify any still-living associates, although he volunteered that "when I was cruising, the Governor of the Isle of Pinos [or "Isle of Pines," the comma-shaped island south of Cuba's western coast] was concerned with pirates." But this remark came before Jeffers had gone to trial for the *Vineyard* crimes. His identification of Bell came later, when Jeffers knew he was going to the gallows, and was becoming progressively more cooperative and—apparently— truthful.[11]

Little also emerged of the crew of the *Maria*. Jeffers claimed that at a later point—after turning pirate—it carried "about 50 men, principally Spaniards and Americans," the term "Spaniards" being a catch-all for Spanish-speakers. Members of the crew might have resembled those encountered aboard a Norfolk-based American privateer during the War of 1812. An observer recalled, "The lieutenants and prize-masters . . . were a set of clever fellows, but the captain was a rough, uncouth sort of a chap, and appeared to me to be fit for little else than fighting and plunder. The crew were a motley set indeed, composed of all nations: they appeared to have been scraped together from the lowest dens of wretchedness and vice, and only wanted a leader to induce them to any act of daring and desperation."[12]

Bell's commission made the *Maria* a vessel of war, but it is questionable what standards were enforced. Privateer crews had no special uniform; like merchant sailors—and pirates—they would have dressed for comfort, saving special apparel for shore visits or, in some cases, battle. As they were sailing in the tropics, Bell's men presumably adopted lightweight attire, with linen and cotton preferred over wool. Cleanliness may not have mattered. Pirates the schooner *Union* encountered off Virginia's Cape Henry in 1821 were described as "a number of dirty, desperate wretches."[13]

Perhaps some of Bell's crew followed the pattern of British sailors in the West Indies who wore white clothing and fashioned hats from palmetto leaves. Or they may have resembled those aboard one West Indian pirate ship, the crew of which were described as "mostly brown-jacketted, garlic-eating, cheroot-smoking Spanish desperadoes." They had "fiercely-scowling black eyes, and ferocious moustachios" and "when they fell to quarrelling [their] fierce Cuban oaths were seconded by the long dagger-like knives of Andalusia."[14]

The era's Caribbean marauders preferred such edged weapons, as did those fighting ashore in the vicious wars of liberation. This was in spite of the wide variety of firearms in circulation, the technology of which had changed little since the time of the *General History*. As the percussion-cap ignition system was in its infancy in Jeffers's day, the era's heavy pistols were still largely what one pirate historian called "the usual flintlock, brass or iron-barreled affairs of about .50 to .60 caliber. At twenty paces a one-ounce pistol ball could spell death as truthfully as any more recently contrived instrument of war. In reality these heavy weapons were as formidable as a shotgun loaded with a single ball, inaccurate over a long range but carrying a killing shock that would knock down an ox."[15]

With their longer barrels, muskets were more accurate—a shooter might hit a man seventy-five yards away. Fitted with bayonets the smoothbore weapons became spears when close action prevented reloading. The blunderbuss, a seventeenth-century shotgun with a flaring barrel, was still being issued to navy personnel in the nineteenth century, some models having brass barrels to resist salt corrosion. But all firearms were unreliable under wet conditions. Gunpowder itself was so scarce, an Irish native who fought in Venezuela recorded, that locals used swords to execute prisoners.[16]

The most popular edged weapon at sea was the cutlass. Inexpensive and inelegant, most naval cutlasses had curved, relatively short blades—about 29 inches—making them suited to fighting in narrow spaces below decks. On the cutlass "a rounded brass guard like that of a Scottish claymore protected the hand and wrist. It was a lethal weapon, for the swordplay it afforded was both cut and thrust, brute strength as well as skill."[17]

Caribbean pirates in Jeffers's era developed a double-fisted tactic. Those who in 1822 unsuccessfully attacked a sloop hired to serve as a tender to the

Though Howard Pyle's 1895 illustration "Blackbeard's Last Fight" depicts an eighteenth-century action, the weapons employed when ships collided at sea had changed little by Jeffers's era. Courtesy of the Delaware Art Museum

HMS *Tyne* at anchor in LaGuajaba carried cutlasses in their right hand and long knives in their left. Impressed, British crews copied this method, adding a bayonet and scabbard to their cutlass belts.[18]

The region's original European freebooters were called *boucaniers* (or buccaneers) from their reliance on *boucaned* (cured) meat. Writing in the late seventeenth century, Alexander Exquemelin observed that "they cook two meals a day of this meat, without rationing. When it is boiled, the fat is skimmed off the cauldron and put into little calabashes, for dipping the meat in. The meal consists of only one course, and often it tastes better than the food to be found on a gentleman's table."[19]

But among their early nineteenth-century Caribbean counterparts there are few references to meat aboard ship. One suspicious craft had fresh fruit onboard when stopped by the U.S. Navy, which may show consciousness of the causes and cures of scurvy, or simply have been what was for sale ashore. A different crew regularly ate "boiled rice, garnished with rancid oil and garlic," which was "served up in one huge mess-kid" to diners who simultaneously partook of strong tobacco. Dinner on another pirate ship in the 1820s consisted of "garlic and onions chopped fine and mixed up with bread in a bowl, for which there was a general scramble, every one helping himself as he pleased, either with his fingers or any instrument with which he happened to be supplied." Besides liquor, the same pirate crew enjoyed coffee, although they sold most of what they captured "for ten dollars per hundred weight, its supposed half-value at Havannah."[20]

While it is unclear what success, if any, the *Maria* had on Jeffers's first Caribbean cruise, Jeffers maintained that only two months after he joined the privateer its crew mutinied off Florida's Gulf coast. The uprising must have been dramatic but no violence was mentioned, simply that "a mutiny arose, the crew took possession of the schooner, and landed the officers near Pensacola." As that port, which by one account offered "a very fine harbor," was then in Spanish hands, Bell and associates were placed among enemies.[21]

Mutiny was an accepted risk of the sailing profession. English gunsmiths seem to have had ship captains in mind when they designed a pistol that could simultaneously discharge four barrels angled in a "duck's foot" spread —good against a hostile crowd in closed confines. Privateer crews revolted so frequently that merchant captains would not knowingly employ anyone who had been in that business. Predictably, when privateers mutinied money was often the issue. In 1818 dissatisfied crew members took over the privateer *General St. Martin,* dropping the captain and officers ashore near Port au Prince. After sailing to Savannah, five of the crew marched to the office of the merchant who owned the brig, which they threatened to scuttle unless he gave them $30,000. They compromised for $18,000, but when local officials got involved the crew "would not permit the civil authority to board them, and appeared determined to resist." Cannon were trained on the *General St. Martin* and the militia called out. Order was eventually restored and the crew jailed.[22]

Privateer crews were also sensitive to how officers handled them, as was the case aboard the Buenos Aires-commissioned *General Rondeau.* This was a 202-ton Spanish brig—Argentine sources call it a *bergantin*—that had been captured and recast as an 18-gun privateer, with a crew of 160, mostly British but with about 30 Americans. Captained by David M. Miles of Baltimore, the *General Rondeau* was commissioned late in 1819, enjoyed a successful Mediterranean cruise, and then repaired to Margarita. There, Miles, said to have ill used the crew, deliberately left a man ashore drunk, stoking more anger. About twenty miles off the New Grenada coast the mutineers struck, in the process killing Miles's lieutenant, an Irishman named Sweeney, and setting the surviving officers and a few others adrift in a boat. After dividing the loot on board, the crew made for the American coast. There they began breaking into smaller groups, shifting to other ships, several landing in Virginia and the Carolinas. The last dozen or so scuttled the *General Rondeau* before themselves going ashore. Most were arrested, some in cities as far apart as Boston and Charleston.[23]

Even prize crews mutinied. Those sailing a vessel captured by a Buenos Aires privateer "threw the prize-master and his mate overboard" then made for Scituate, Massachusetts, where they were found out and arrested.[24]

The reason Jeffers gave for revolt in the *Maria's* case was indeed "nonpayment of their prize-money." This sounds like captures were made and, assuming Bell went through prize-courts functioning on Cartagena's behalf, the proceeds divided improperly or not at all. Or he may have been a victim of rumors, such as those "that the captain had secreted large sums for himself," which fueled discord among one set of Caribbean pirates in the 1820s.[25]

In fact, Caribbean pickings were slim at this time. The American consul at St. Thomas complained in 1817 of an "increasing number of seamen, whose ill success in the privateers and pirates . . . induces them to relinquish those unprofitable pursuits whenever an opportunity offers and who almost universally swarm to this island to claim my protection and support, so that they daily almost surround my door." The details of Bell's case seem lost to history, but privateer captains also risked problems by obeying their commission's strictures. During an 1816 cruise in which it captured five legitimate Spanish prizes, a Buenos Aires privateer stopped and released about a hundred others, those actions apparently causing some crew members to be "dissatisfied with the colors under which they sailed."[26]

Jeffers did not name the man who replaced Captain Bell, but as on pirate ships, he was evidently elected or at least affirmed by the crew. (A pirate captain's authority and qualities will be discussed later.) Possibly Bell's replacement shared authority with others. The chain of command on both privateer and pirate craft was practical—niceties such as midshipmen were unnecessary. One Caribbean pirate captain in the 1820s had "six or seven" officers, their ranks probably including a quartermaster, navigator (or "sailing master" as the navy phrased it), boatswain, and gunner. Documented cases of officer elections from an earlier age featured heavy drinking and sometimes the ceremonial presentation of a sword to an incoming captain.[27]

Whoever the new leader was, it was not Jeffers, who by his account was named navigator. If true, this did credit to him as a sailor, especially given his recent taking to the sea. Navigators and other "sea artists" were so in demand that pirates often forced captured specialists to join their crew. The mate of an English merchantman claimed to have found himself in such circumstances when captured off Cuba. He survived being forced, or "impressed," aboard—and a later trial for piracy—to leave an account of how the pirate chief "turned to me and said, that, as he was in a bad state of health and none of his ship's company understood navigation, he should detain me for the purpose of navigating the schooner. I tried as much as possible to conceal my emotions at this intimation, and endeavoured to work upon his feelings . . . But I appealed to a monster, devoid of all feeling, inured to crime, and hardened in iniquity."[28]

Despite Jeffers's tangled story he can be accepted in this key position. Later contemporaries certainly considered him an accomplished sailor. In 1831, during the *Vineyard* trial that ended with his conviction and hanging, both the prosecution and defense identified Jeffers as the only surviving member of the doomed brig's crew able to navigate.[29]

6

"Against all nations"

RIVATEER SHIPS IN THE HANDS of mutineers tended to settle quickly into piracy. By Jeffers's account, the removal of Captain Bell and other former officers left the *Maria*'s crew asking whether to continue to obey their Cartagenian commission, or abandoning that questionable legal status for outright robbery, where flags didn't matter, prize courts weren't needed, and profits were potentially higher.[1]

For a short time—the year is presumably still 1816—they continued to sail as privateers. Probably due to a lack of legitimate Spanish targets, the faction promoting piracy grew so strong that in an 1831 journalist's words, "it was then unanimously determined to hoist the black flag, and declare war against all nations." (As Caribbean pirates in this era preferred red flags, a point discussed later, the reference to a black one was probably a literary device.)

Having crossed the line into piracy, they began to board vessels indiscriminately. They let them all go, in each case finding (to quote the same 1831 newspaper account) "no specie on board, and their cargoes not being convertible into any thing valuable to themselves." Their first tentative steps into piracy had left them no better off than under Bell. But veterans among them knew those cargoes could be profitable with the right connections ashore. Jeffers recalled that a crewman named Antonio came forward, volunteering knowledge of a Havana merchant who "would receive all their goods, sell them, and divide the proceeds." This arrangement would turn stolen merchandise into cash, bypassing any need for prize courts.

With Jeffers navigating, the *Maria* landed Antonio a few miles from *El Morro*, the fort guarding Havana harbor's narrow entrance. He contacted the merchant, unnamed in the 1831 accounts, who proved agreeable. According to their arrangement, the crew would bring whatever merchandise they acquired to Cape Antonio—Cabo de San Antonio, off the Peninsula de Guanahacabibes on Cuba's extreme western edge. At the shoreline the crew would meet "drogers," a type of West Indian boat, that would convey the stolen goods to Havana. There the merchant's "Spanish House" would sell them for a split of the profits.[2]

The corrupt merchant was well placed. Havana was one of the continent's busiest ports. Its level of activity rivaled Charleston—though New York dwarfed both—and Havana in 1816 handled more commercial maritime traffic than Boston, Baltimore, New Orleans, Philadelphia, or Savannah. Havana's principal exports in this era were sugar, coffee, molasses, and wax. Its principal import was slaves, many to be resold in American ports such as New Orleans, where it was said that up to ten thousand were being brought in annually. Almost one thousand slaves reportedly arrived in Havana during an eleven-day period in March 1817. On just one day during that same month, ten ships allegedly set out "on the same business." By the end of the

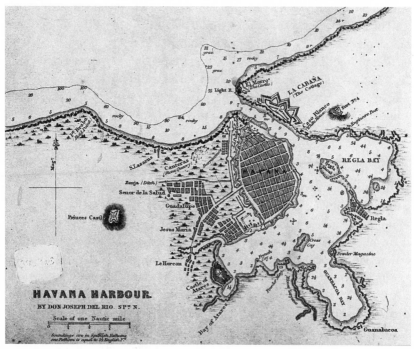

Map of Havana Harbor, Island of Cuba. Courtesy of Mystic Seaport, G. W. Blunt Library Collection, #95-9-5

Map of Cuba, detail from a 1796 chart of the West Indies. Courtesy of the Mariners' Museum, Newport News, Virginia

year, Havana had received an estimated fifteen thousand slaves. Almost as many more were believed to have died during passage.[3]

Havana's reputation for lawlessness was on a par with that of New Orleans. After a night in 1817 in which nine people were killed, the authorities began a campaign against concealed weapons. "The guards are ordered to search all persons, without distinction, for knives," an American newspaper reported, "but they may carry swords, if exposed to view by being hung at the side." But more episodes of multiple murders were reported, and by 1822 an observer wrote that in Havana "not a family, it is said, can go to rest with a tranquil mind—even the police officers are alarmed."[4]

Cuba as a whole had long been a center of pirate activity. Exquemelin wrote in the late seventeenth century that "Cuba is surrounded by innumerable small islands, known as Cays, frequently used by the buccaneers as bases." In Jeffers's era Cubans like Antonio's merchant contact eagerly did business with privateers and pirates who, an 1824 Congressional report observed, "cautiously avoided molesting Spanish vessels, but attacked without discrimination the defenceless vessels of all other nations." It is worth noting that Jeffers's partial list of captures over his admitted career, much of which was spent based in Cuba, includes no Spanish prizes.[5]

Privateers and pirates operating near Cuban coasts picked up provisions by night, furnishing in return stolen goods, which were sold cheaply on the island. Their allies ashore were said to include some of Cuba's best citizens, including mayors and provincial governors. Cuban authorities did mount occasional antipirate expeditions, but once, when Washington pressed for more action, the Havana newspaper *Noticioso* shot back that most so-called privateers fitted out in American ports.[6]

Raiders found Cuban and other Caribbean bases as inviting as Louisiana's bayous had been. Shallow-draft sloops or schooners could attack victims near the coastline. Some gangs simply attacked from shore in open boats, occasionally equipped with swivel guns. Many had been at this game since Barataria's glory days and eluded capture in part because they knew their turf, venturing where warships dared not go because of the shallow water, staying there when pursued.[7]

Cuba's Cape Antonio, which would be the point of contact between Jeffers's crew and the corrupt Havana merchant apparently for years to come, was becoming a place to be avoided. In 1821 a Charleston newspaper printed the following notice as a public service: "Merchant vessels passing Cape Antonio, should not approach the land nearer than to be seen from aloft, as the coast is infested with a number of piratical vessels and boats, who screen themselves from view under cover of the land, and wait the approach of vessels until they come with the usual distance, when passing the Cape."[8]

◆•◆••◆•◆

Having changed captain and profession, the crew of the *Maria* may have also changed their vessel's name. That this happened can be inferred from a discrepancy in magistrate James Hopson's notes of his 1831 interviews with Jeffers. At one point, Jeffers told the judge: "That he [Jeffers] commenced piracy in the year 1816, in the schooner *Sans Sousee* [that is, *sans soucis*, French for "without worries"], belonging to the Island of Margarita." But in a later session Jeffers said that he "commenced in the year 1816, in the Privateer *Maria*." No effort was made to clarify this new name in relation to the *Sans Soucis*, although the accompanying newspaper narrative based on Jeffers's confessions mentions only the *Maria*.

Was Jeffers "remembering better" as execution approached? The slip might signal that he could not keep his story straight, a fact a critical reader must keep in mind. But as a distinction was made between the privateer (the *Maria*) and the pirate (the *Sans Soucis*) it is conceivable that only one vessel was involved, its name changing as it shifted careers. If so, the French alias hints at a Creole, possibly Baratarian, presence among its personnel. Certainly, with its hint of swagger, *Sans Soucis* would fit a schooner going "on the account," a euphemism for piracy, which is where Jeffers and company were headed.[9]

The crew also likely crafted a suitable pirate ensign. Such flags were part of the intimidation process at sea. One gang, cited in the *General History*, deemed their black flag "as good as fifty Men more, *i.e.* [it] would carry as much Terror." The classic black Jolly Roger, bearing a white skull and crossbones—a symbol of mortality found on many old English and colonial American gravestones—was only one of many designs. "Jolly Roger" itself may be a corruption of *joli rouge* (pretty red), referring to the scarlet flags some early raiders preferred. Historian David Cordingly noted that in accounts of piracy, "red or 'bloody' flags are mentioned as often as black flags until the middle of the eighteenth century," and that the red banners were used to signal that if the prey failed to surrender no mercy would be shown.[10]

At Barataria, Jean Laffite was said to have sailed under a "Red Flag of the River," and many contemporaries preferred the same color scheme. In 1822 the USS *Shark* captured a pirate craft named *Bandera de Sangre* (Banner of Blood) and confronted another flying a red shirt for a flag. Some predators began pursuits flying American or English colors, replacing them with red ones if their prey failed to slow down. Yet submission was no guarantee of safety. The era's newspapers were full of horror stories, and the only documented instances of captives being made to "walk the plank" concern Caribbean piracies in the 1820s.[11]

Jeffers is not on record as discussing a particular flag, but he claimed that the crew of the former privateer *Maria*—who swore on a Bible to never divulge each others' names—also voted unanimously, in a journalist's words, "to spare no lives and to burn and plunder without mercy. They knew that the principle inculcated by the old maxim that 'dead men tell no tales,' was the only safe one for them, and they scrupulously followed it."

There is confusion on this point. Jeffers "repeatedly stated that he was concerned in the robbery of more than forty vessels, and in the destruction of more than twenty, with their entire crews." Thus the odds of surviving an encounter with Jeffers appear to have been about even. His figures, however, likely include captures made during "legitimate" privateering stints in service to Cartagena and Buenos Aires.

Still, his admissions of violence prompted Judge Hopson in 1831 to ask, "Why were you so cruel as to kill so many persons, when you have got all their money, which was all you wanted?" Jeffers replied, "The laws are the cause of so many murders." Asked for clarification, he said, "Because a man has to suffer death for piracy; and the punishment for murder is no more. Then you know, all witnesses are sent out of the way, and I am sure if the punishment was different, there would not be so many murders."[12]

Jeffers's confessions were widely reprinted in 1831 and the above quote would provide fodder for contemporary death penalty opponents. It also echoed a point made centuries earlier in Thomas More's *Utopia,* in a passage decrying how thieves and murderers "should suffer equal and like punishment." This naturally induced a thief—or a pirate—: "to kill him whom else he would have but robbed. For the murder being once done, he is in less fear and in more hope that the deed shall not be betrayed or known, seeing the party is now dead and rid out of the way, which only might have uttered and disclosed it. But if he chance to be taken and descried, yet he is in no more danger and jeopardy than if he had committed but single felony. Therefore while we go about with such cruelty to make thieves afraid, we provoke them to kill good men."[13]

Many nations used the death penalty in various incarnations to deter seamen from piracy. Decapitation and hanging were common punishments, sometimes accompanied by other horrors. Brigands captured by the Danish in one medieval antipiracy campaign were forced inside herring barrels, which were nailed shut and sent by ship to the gallows. The English routinely left executed pirates hanging by the shore as a warning, sometimes encased in chains that kept the corpses intact as they rotted.[14]

With Spanish authorities treating them as pirates, privateers fought desperately when pursued. A newspaper reported that the Spanish navy brig *Almirante* captured the Galveston-based one-gun schooner *Eugenia* after a two-hour battle, during which the privateer captain and first lieutenant were killed. The forty *Eugenia* crewmen who survived were taken to Pensacola. Their destination might have been the Florida mines, which were said to be "full of Americans" being punished for service with the anti-Spanish cause.[15]

Other hard fights are on record. Only seventeen of the forty-four-member crew of the privateer *Galveston* survived its taking by a Spanish warship off Havana in 1817. Two years later the Spanish navy brig *Fernando* captured an "insurgent" ship called the *Pagaro* after a four-hour engagement in which the *Fernando* suffered twenty-five killed and twice as many wounded. After the Spanish prevailed, it was alleged "all the prisoners were put to the knife."[16]

But pirates who killed captives were not fighting the "War to the Death." Although done theoretically to eliminate witnesses, the decision to commit mass murder was often an arbitrary one. A pirate recalled before his execution at Cadiz circa 1830 that the decision to butcher captives was usually made quickly. "As soon as we got a ship's crew in our power," he said, "a short consultation was held, and if it was the opinion of a majority that it would be better to take life than to spare it, a single nod or wink from our captain was sufficient." The man—an 1831 writer thought he "must have been a companion" of Jeffers—added that sometimes captives were simply set adrift without provisions. But when the blades came out, the pirates competed to see "who, with his own hands, should dispatch the greatest number, and in the shortest period of time."[17]

As the same man indicated alcohol fueled this carnage, it is notable that Jeffers described himself as a heavy drinker, especially when he had something to forget. The marriage of drink and piracy surely predated that of two pirates hanged in Boston in 1724 who blamed their troubles on Demon Rum. The American navy of Jeffers's era was an alcoholic's playground. Although the amount of grog (rum mixed with water) doled out to sailors was technically not enough to get them drunk, it was enough to set alcoholics in search of more; how they got it was only one of several potential problems. Moral arguments against the spirit ration ran up against wide belief in alcoholism as a character issue rather than a health problem. Intentionally or not, liquor was also a recruitment aid. In his study of U.S. naval discipline, *Rocks and Shoals* author James E. Valle suggested that until the navy stopped issuing it in 1862, "a significant portion of the enlisted men were confirmed alcoholics who had entered the service for the sake of the grog ration." And many former U.S. Navy personnel had joined the Baratarians who, before being scattered about the Caribbean and Gulf of Mexico, already had a reputation for violence.[18]

The pirate career of the former privateer *Maria* started in earnest with the finalizing of the deal with the Havana merchant. Back at sea, it is unclear how long Jeffers and company had to wait for their initial victim. But according to Jeffers, the first in their schooner's sights was an English ship called *Indispensable*. A ship by that name indeed existed circa 1816, but it seems to have plied the south Pacific rather than the Caribbean. Whatever the truth, by Jeffers's account the vessel was headed for Havana, and its fate established a pattern for future cases: "The crew were immediately destroyed; those who resisted were hewn to pieces; those who offered no resistance, were reserved to be shot and thrown overboard." The vessel was destroyed, and sometime later the same treatment was given to a French brig, the name of which Jeffers did not recollect in his 1831 confessions, after its wine and silk cargo had been removed and its crew killed.

Years later, when his vessel raided Cape Antonio, U.S. naval officer Lawrence Kearny's men found clothing the pirates had kept despite it being, in

Kearny's words, "covered with the stains of blood about the collar and breast." The euphemism for cutting a victim's throat was to "slip [one's] wind," and the era's pirates did a lot of it. What did young James Jeffers think of being accessory to all this? When in jail in 1831 and awaiting execution for the *Vineyard* mutiny, an observer wrote that he "gives no evidence of a 'contrite heart' for the horrible crimes of which he confesses himself guilty, yet he evidently dwells upon their recollection with great unwillingness. If a question is asked him, 'how were the crews generally destroyed'? he answers quickly and briefly, and instantly changes the topic. . . ."[19]

He presumably became desensitized to cruelty, perhaps helped along that road by drink. A witness to 1820s Caribbean piracy noted, after seeing a captive tortured to death, how the killers took their own brutality in stride. On this occasion, "the guitar tinkled and the song went round, as if nothing had happened; and the torments which their victim had just undergone, and the cries that he had uttered, seemed to form the subject of their jests, and to be echoed in their barbarous mirth."[20]

Discussing the alleged fate of the *Indispensable,* an 1831 observer wrote that Jeffers and comrades showed no pity to their victims and established a pattern they would reenact many times. "The unhappy being that cried for mercy in the hope that something like humanity was to be found in the breast even of the worst of men, shared the same fate with him who resolved to sell his life at the highest price." It was such behavior, often displayed when cargoes of only minimal value were at stake, which caused a later writer to describe this era's Caribbean marauders as "a far cry from the great seafaring figures of the preceding century. . . . They acted like nothing so much as scavenging sharks—mindlessly brutal, and as willing to steal a sack of coal as a bag of gold."[21]

They were so dreaded that when Richard Henry Dana described a brush with suspected pirates, he avoiding using the term: "Looking astern, we saw a small clipper-built brig with a black hull heading directly after us. We went to work immediately, and put all the canvas upon the brig which we could get upon her. . . . The vessel continued in pursuit, changing her course as we changed ours, to keep before the wind. The captain, who watched her with his glass, said that she was armed, and full of men, and showed no colors. . . . All hands remained on deck throughout the day, and we got our firearms in order; but we were too few to have done anything with her, if she proved to be what we feared."[22]

He was fortunate to be on a ship that outsailed its pursuer. One that did not was the New York–based brig *Laura Ann,* taken off Havana in October

1824. Jeffers claimed to have been active as a pirate that year. While he made no mention of the *Laura Ann,* the description of its capture and burning could give a picture of his mates and himself at work.

The *Laura Ann* had set out from Buenos Aires with a cargo of jerked beef and late on October 20 saw the Cuban shore. The next morning, about twelve miles from Matanzas, an open boat approached, carrying a dozen well-armed men, and met no recorded resistance. Once onboard the pirates sent the captain, named Shaw, to his cabin, and ordered the mate and most of the men into the forecastle, punctuating their commands with pistol shots. They kept a few captured crewmen on deck to help sail the vessel, which they brought to anchor in rough water, about sixty yards from shore. A schooner carrying one cannon and about thirty men now came alongside, and after forcing the second mate aboard, members of its crew ordered him to make masts for their open boat. Trying to find out if money was hidden onboard, they beat up the mate and Shaw, hanging the latter at dusk.

Laura Ann crew member George Brown witnessed Shaw's execution as he climbed down from work he had been ordered to do aloft. He ran into the forecastle even as the mate was called back on deck, and heard the man cry, "Oh God," but did not investigate. While the pirates summoned the rest of the crew—their fates went unreported—he avoided detection by hiding in the coal hole. When they stopped search for him, the pirates set the *Laura Ann* on fire, at which point Brown slipped overboard and swam ashore. He eventually made it to Matanzas, then Havana, where he told his story to a U.S. government official.[23]

Such tales prompted some captains to arm their vessels or at least make other preparations. When pirates boarded the Marblehead, Massachusetts, based *Candace* in 1829, the master and mate agreed "that in case a massacre was begun, one of them should fire into a barrel of gunpowder in the hold and explode the ship. It was thought to be a better fate to kill all in one general ruin."[24]

———◆•••◆———

Jeffers said he and his privateer-turned-pirate mates made only two captures —the *Indispensable* and the unnamed French brigantine—before a change of command occurred. Following the most complete—but still chronologically and sometimes logically shaky—newspaper account of Jeffers's confession, at some point in 1817 *he* was named captain. The *Journal of Commerce* explained the promotion by citing his seamanship, which had already earned him the navigator's post: "The sanguinary scenes through which Gibbs [that is, Jeffers] had passed now effectually wrought up his desperation to the highest pitch, and being as remarkable for his coolness and intrepidity as he was for his skill in navigation, he was unanimously chosen to be their leader in all their future enterprises."[25]

Who the desperate-but-cool Jeffers succeeded is unrecorded—nor was a reason given *why* a new captain would be needed. But mutiny was as common among pirates as it was among privateers. Leaders handled dissidents with violence, the successful display of which was meant to deter others from stirring up plots. One 1820s Caribbean pirate leader and his followers used knives and a hatchet on a reputed conspirator before throwing him overboard. Another fought a duel with his first mate when the latter opposed his captain's plan to kill prisoners aboard a prize. The captain lost.[26]

A change of chieftains could be done democratically as well as violently. When a leader had to be replaced, crews "on the account" commonly did so by a show of hands. Although Jeffers's entire story must be evaluated critically—he may have been a third-rate thug embellishing his resume—his being chosen captain is within possibility. But there are reasons to suspect either exaggeration or at least chronological error on someone's part. Presuming Jeffers to have been Samuel Jeffers's son, born in Newport in 1798, he would have been only eighteen or nineteen when he earned this promotion. Piracy was indeed a young man's business, but pirate captains were usually not *this* young.

Though little has come to light on the demographics of Caribbean brigands in Jeffers's era, going back a century an identical average age of twenty-eight can be computed for the fifty-two members of Bartholomew Roberts's crew hanged in 1722, and the twenty-five members of Edward Low's company hanged a year later. James Skyrm of Somersetshire, who captained Roberts's consort ship *Ranger*, was a patriarchal forty-four. Roberts himself was "near forty Years of Age" when he died in battle. That said, at twenty-five, Londoner Charles Harris, who captained Low's consort ship, also called *Ranger*, commanded men on average three years older than himself.[27]

But Jeffers had yet to see his twentieth birthday when the captain's title was allegedly conferred on him. Even author Edward Rowe Snow, in his creative 1944 take on the Charles Gibbs tale, balked at assigning him command at such a young age. Rather, Snow had his antihero share authority with others: "Gibbs was not chosen the sole commander, but the pirates took turns in running the ship."[28]

Snow's version is plausible. The Caribbean pirates of Jeffers's era probably retained enough of the previous century's tradition to ensure that a title itself meant little. In those touchy pirate democracies, a captain's privileges were few and his share of plunder might be only marginally larger than others. Among the original Caribbean boucaniers, "the captain is allowed no better fare than the meanest on board," Alexander Exquemelin wrote. "If they notice he has better food, the men bring the dish from their own mess and exchange it for the captain's." The *General History* related how a pirate crew only allowed a member "to be Captain, on Condition, that they may be Captain over him." His crew might obey him during a fight but call him to account afterward. On day-to-day terms he was customarily subordinate to the quartermaster. This similarly elected officer "acts as a Sort of civil Magistrate on board a Pyrate Ship," controlling punishments, rations, and the sharing of loot. Unlike legitimate service, in such cases the captain was just another sailor until the time of chase and combat.[29]

Organization and chain of command was doubtlessly as varied among nineteenth-century pirate crews as was the character of their leaders. One 1820s captain was said by one of his crew to have "killed more than twenty people with his own hand, in cool blood." Another was described as a "lean, white-haired, mild little man of some age, who evidently had gained the command through shrewdness and cunning, rather than for any gift of commanding men. He was an Italian; a good seaman and experienced pilot for those seas, but seemed . . . to be entirely worn out and lacking in virility." A survivor's account of the 1821 capture of the schooner *Emily* refers to a Cuban-based pirate crew of twenty-five to thirty as having "four commanders" conspicuous by their brutality.[30]

Assuming he did receive a senior role aboard the *Maria*—or *Sans Soucis* —Jeffers probably fit the mold of pirates earning rank by viciousness, as shown by the 1831 *Vineyard* trial that convicted him of murdering that vessel's mate. The crews Jeffers admitted to sailing with, and leading, included some prolific mass murderers. In a newspaper's words, Jeffers "never had occasion to give orders to begin the work of death. The Spaniards were eager to accomplish that object without delay, and generally every unhappy victim disappeared in a very few minutes after they gained the deck of a vessel."[31]

The reference to Spaniards belies the fact that Jeffers's crew was a mixed one, like many of those seen in the Caribbean in this era. A launch stopping and robbing ships outside one Cuban harbor consisted of "nine villains, viz. one Portuguese, six Spaniards, and two Englishmen." An 1818 report mentioned black and white men raiding together in the West Indies using small boats. The prize crew placed aboard the schooner *Evergreen*, captured off Havana in 1821 but retaken by its original company, was comprised of "an Englishman, another a Dutchman, and the rest blacks, natives of Hayti." The thirty-five-man crew of a pirate schooner taken by HMS *Carnation* in 1822 was largely Spanish Creole but included at least one Englishman who had not been forced. Another pirate schooner that captured a Jamaican sloop returning from Santiago, Cuba, was "commanded by a white man, with a mixed crew of color and countries," Englishmen and Americans among them.[32]

Late in 1816, about the time Jeffers claimed to have been making the switch from privateer to pirate, *Niles' Weekly Register* took note of the emergence "of acts of piracy in the West Indian seas. The depredators appear to be gathered of many nations, and attack equally American and British vessels." Referring to the privateers, still viewed favorably, the same paper acknowledged "some irregularities . . . which we hope for their sake as well as our own, may be restrained in future. In general however, they have behaved quite as well, if not better, than could have been expected. It is not to be supposed that every one who commands a privateer must needs be a prudent and judicious man."[33]

Stronger words flowed from Spain's minister in Washington, Don Luis de Onis, incensed about U.S. ports supplying privateers. Early in 1817 he formally complained to Secretary of State James Monroe that Baltimore and New Orleans were the worst offenders, with "whole squadrons of pirates having been fitted out from thence, in violation of the solemn treaty existing between the two nations." At the same time, the broader American view of privateering against Spain was beginning to change. Lawlessness in or near U.S. waters alarmed some editors. Commenting on a late 1816 incident in which the Venezuelan privateer *Jupiter* captured two Spanish prizes in Louisiana waters just off New Orleans, that city's *Gazette* remarked that "anxious as we are for the success of the patriots, we are not less anxious that they should be taught to respect the laws and dignity of the United States." Another editor observed that "we wish the patriots entire success—if they respect the laws of nations, which in this case has [sic] been frequently violated, and, we hope, may be punished."[34]

With Spanish complaints in mind, Congress early in 1817 discussed a bill meant to discourage Americans from involvement in Latin American privateering. A proposed amendment allowing seizure of any U.S. craft sailing under a foreign commission was defeated. But the final version affirmed that American-owned ships were not to be used against countries "with whom the United States are at peace." For their part, the British reinforced Jamaica with ten additional warships. Later in the year, a royal proclamation ordered British subjects not to take part in the conflicts in "Spanish America."[35]

Spanish officials might apply legal means rather than naval ones against the privateers. To cite two apparently different cases involving one captain, late in 1816 Captain James Barnes's Baltimore-based privateer *Mangore* (or *Mahgoree*), in the service of Buenos Aires, captured a Spanish merchant brig which, when it arrived at New Bedford, the Spanish consul had seized. It is unclear how this was resolved, but in June 1817, Barnes sent a prize named *Providencia* to Baltimore via Norfolk, where revenue officers stopped it. The Spanish consul successfully sued to have the *Providencia* and its cargo of cordage and cutlery sold, the proceeds going to the legitimate owners.[36]

———•••———

Sometime in early 1817 Jeffers and mates steered toward the Bahamas, where their schooner overtook a brig bound for Mexico. Jeffers later said he believed this prize to have been the *William,* carrying a load of furniture in its hold. His memory varied as to its hailing port, either Salem or New York: the vessel's name was a common one. He recalled that the crew were killed, the vessel transported to Cape Antonio where it was presumably scuttled after its cargo was removed and sent to Havana for fencing. At some point during the same cruise, the pirates were chased for a day by an American warship they held to be the USS *John Adams*—a vessel indeed active in anti-piracy operations—and that veered off after the pirates hoisted an unspecified "patriot" flag.[37]

The pirates returned to Cuba early in the summer 1817 with cargo from a ship coming from London that Jeffers identified as the *Earl of Moria* (*Lloyd's List* notes several contemporary British craft called the *Earl Moira*). By Jeffers's account, his shipmates again killed their prisoners and burned the vessel before heading for Cape Antonio. Jeffers would claim to have meted out similar treatment to a Liverpool brig called the *Jane,* a popular name for British ships. While he did not give an approximate date for the episode, a documented incident occurred at about this time involving just such a brig. A Cartagenian privateer attacked this Liverpool-based *Jane* off Havana in early 1817. But it was not destroyed—not on this occasion anyway. Rather, the *Jane* was sent on its way after its captain, named Johns, paid $200 for what *Lloyd's List* called compensation "for the shots fired at his Vessel," notwithstanding that "the Mate and one Seaman on board the Brig were severely wounded." The privateer captain was said to have been Joseph Almeida.[38]

———•••———

After reaching a settlement at Cape Antonio regarding disposition of the cargo from the *Earl of Moria,* Jeffers said in 1831, he himself went to Havana.

There for the first time he met the merchant who was his business partner and made some unspecified arrangements. These may have been financial ones, as he would later claim to have taken about $30,000 with him to America in 1819. He also socialized in waterfront taverns with naval officers patrolling the coast, learning how their ships sailed and their future areas of operation. This was a long-established means of gathering intelligence. Early in the nineteenth century, a French privateer fluent in English frequented Jamaican dives, pretending to be an Englishman and collecting British navy officers' gossip. Some of Jeffers's pirate contemporaries in the 1820s maintained that their pursuers preferred Havana nightlife to chasing suspect vessels.[39]

Jeffers had left his crew at Cape Antonio, where they at some point would build "a small fort that mounted four guns." But upon his return from Havana, he found them in turmoil, several dead and the rest "in a state of complete mutiny and rebellion." The cause is unstated, but Jeffers claimed to have restored order. If true he would have met the standards set down by sea writer Basil Lubbock: "The man who can run a piratical federation with success must possess an unusual gift for commanding men, besides an entirely ruthless nature and fearless disposition. He had to take instant decision and act without hesitation. He had to be able to suppress a drunken riot, or even a serious mutiny by the sheer nervous force of his own personality."[40]

Such unrest was common among the Cuban pirates, whom an 1822 article reported had "boasted of the murder of four hundred people near Cape Romaine. In this, perhaps, they include the persons killed by quarrels among themselves—which are stated to be numerous."[41] As for Jeffers, another test of his authority lay ahead.

In Washington's eyes at this time, Cuban-based marauders were still a distant problem compared to former Baratarians still active in the Gulf of Mexico. The chief suspect was Louis Aury, who commanded a Galveston-based fleet of schooners operating against Spain under Venezuelan and, later, Mexican commissions. Aury's captains, their crews from many nations, reputedly preyed on commerce of any country. Born in 1788 in Paris, and a veteran of the French navy, Aury earned American notice in June 1816 when his privateer schooner *Bellona* captured a Spanish brig off Havana called the *Infatigable*. Aury landed his prisoners at Campeachy and sailed off with the 270-ton prize, originally built at Baltimore as the *Elizabeth*. American newspapers ran ads, probably placed on behalf of the ship's Spanish owners, describing cargo items and trying to find out where Aury's crew had taken the craft.[42]

A year later, Aury's fleet successfully assaulted Spanish-held Amelia Island on Florida's Atlantic coast, just south of the Georgia line. The attacking force overcame the island's roughly seventy-soldier garrison, and then repelled a counterattack. With the island secure, among the first things the victors did was to establish a prize court and issue privateering commissions. About 150 men now settled down on Amelia Island and captured ships began to arrive, some with slaves aboard. By the end of 1817 "Commodore" Aury was issuing writs against one William P. Moore, charged with making off with a 5-gun, 70-ton prize vessel "with an intention to commit depredations on the high seas." Moore, who learned of these allegations while visiting Charleston, told a newspaper that he resented the insinuation.

The American authorities did not welcome a colony of Baratarian and Galveston veterans at Amelia Island. In late summer 1817, a U.S. revenue cutter turned back a vessel bound from New York for Amelia Island with "patriot" recruits aboard. American pressure eventually forced Aury to evacuate to the west Caribbean island of Old Providence, where he took in allies from Galveston. From there, Daniel Patterson predicted, they would "infest the West Indies."[43]

* * *

James Jeffers was already there. One of the few other captures of this period that he would later detail was that of a Dutch ship out of Curaçao bound for Holland, containing silver and West Indian goods. It also had thirty passengers on board, several women among them. One, about seventeen or eighteen, had accompanied her parents and other relatives to sea aboard the vessel.[44]

She was in peril indeed. Accounts of Caribbean piracy in the era contain frequent references to rape. To cite one instance, Caribbean pirate John [Jean?] Louis Dupuis, nominally operating under Venezuelan colors, boarded an English vessel and found a husband and wife. Said an American newspaper account: "The woman was violated by the savages in the presence of her husband, after which both of them were taken on board the privateer. The man was then beaten and abused in a dreadful manner—but finally the rascals becoming merciful shot him and threw him overboard. After which, Dupuis seized upon the woman as his property, and had compulsory intercourse with her!" Dupuis was eventually hanged for piracy at Jamaica. The woman's fate was not reported.[45]

Now, on the deck of the Dutch ship, with Jeffers and the rest of his mates swarming around her, the young woman understandably "fell upon her

"Gibbs carrying the Dutch Girl on board his Vessel," from The Pirates Own Book, *1859 edition. Courtesy of the Mariners' Museum, Newport News, Virginia*

knees and implored [Jeffers] to save her life. The appeal was successful, and he promised to save her, though he knew it would lead to dangerous consequences among his crew." Such was the brief version given by a New York newspaper in 1831. Another account from that year emphasized the drama: the young woman's "unfortunate parents were inhumanly butchered before her eyes and she was doomed to witness the agonies, and to hear the expiring heart-piercing groans of those whom she held most dear, and on whom she depended for protection!"[46]

Almost 130 years later, adventure writer Jack Beater—who, like Jeffers, spun absorbing mixtures of fact and fiction—went further in telling this episode in the life of Charles Gibbs. Beater envisaged the captive as "a buxom, blue-eyed beauty with golden curls and blushing cheeks," and imagined the drama on deck:

> When it came her time to meet the murderer's thrust, she ran to
> Gibbs, fell on her knees, and implored the young man to spare her life.
> Moved more by sudden lust than by any compassion, Gibbs
> hauled the quaking girl to her feet and held her in a tight embrace.

She hid her face against his shoulder while the pirate crew went on with the murder of the Dutch sailors, and as the butchery continued Gibbs made so bold as to bargain with the hysterical girl for her very life. Even though she understood few of the coarse English words he uttered, she was old enough to grasp his meaning and intent. After casting an agonized glance at the bestial faces of the blood smeared pirates, any one of whom would gladly have raped and then murdered her, the helpless fear-choked lass could do little else but nod her head in submission.[47]

She had two months to live.

———◆•✸•◆———

The story seemingly affirms Jeffers's senior status in the pirate crew. Only a true tough guy could violate an oath to kill witnesses. But in sparing this captive's life, he created a disciplinary problem by bringing a woman into a man's world.

History has recorded relatively few female pirates, usually casting such figures as lethal exceptions. Navies traditionally barred women aboard ship, where some sailors were superstitious about even discussing them. *General History*–era pirate captain Bartholomew Roberts formally prohibited his men from bringing women—and boys—to sea as companions. Even keeping a female prisoner aboard ship caused troubles, for she required a special guard who might simply keep her to himself.[48]

Such would seem to be the case then with Jeffers and his Dutch captive. Against his crew's wishes, perhaps against his own better judgment, Jeffers brought her back to Cape Antonio. His 1831 chroniclers quoted him saying that there the woman "received such treatment the bare recollection of which, causes me to shudder!" But his comrades began murmuring not at his treatment of her, nor at any accusation of Jeffers refusing to share her. Rather, the problem cited was her presence as a potential witness.

This life-and-death concern again sparked violence at Cape Antonio. Jeffers one day shot a pirate attacking his mistress, not trying to rape her but rather to club her to death. The shooting failed to calm the situation, and he was forced to put his paramour's fate to a vote. Jeffers would claim that "he made a vigorous effort to rescue her, but that he was overawed by the rest of his comrades, who would listen to no mercy." They told him that "the preservation of their own lives made her sacrifice indispensable," and voted for her execution. Whether out of loyalty to the pirate code, or in acknowledgment of his own tenuous position, Jeffers agreed to abide by their decision. Nothing suggests that he delayed acting on it for long.

How did the Dutch captive die? Jeffers himself maintained that he passively allowed her to be poisoned at Cape Antonio. Other versions of the story had her die at sea, sometimes under more violent circumstances. In one example, from *Niles' Weekly Register*, Jeffers "forced [the woman] for several weeks to be his wife, and then cut her throat and threw her overboard, lest she might expose his atrocities." Whatever her fate, it haunted Jeffers. He declared "that of all the murders in which he has participated, no one has harrowed his soul with so much remorse as the recollection of the cold blooded destruction of this interesting and accomplished female." He confided to magistrate James Hopson in 1831 that "this circumstance hurt his feelings more than any act of his life; and which is the only act he can say he was sorry for."[49]

⚓ 7 ⚓

The Pirate Hunters and Their Prey

THE CREW JEFFERS CLAIMED TO have commanded was only one of many haunting Caribbean-area waters in 1817–1818. Some made out well. The *Tupacamoro,* with a Buenos Aires commission and a largely American crew, captured "a rich Spanish Indiaman" called the *Triton* in 1817. Late in the year the *Tupacamoro* took the Cadiz-bound brig *Santa Christa* on its way out of Lima, carrying a load of copper, cocoa, cotton, Peruvian bark (used to make quinine), and best of all, $50,000. Others had less luck. The privateer *Columbia* abandoned a larger squadron due to lack of pay. It was cruising on its own late in 1818, "with five guns mounted and fourteen in her hold, and sixteen men," when stopped by the revenue cutter *Monroe,* which sent it to Norfolk "for want of papers."[1]

Perhaps the *Columbia* had already veered into piracy. One privateer that certainly did was the *Young Spartan.* Flying an unspecified patriot flag and with a prize ship trailing, it boarded the Baltimore-based schooner *George Armistead* off Havana in mid-1818. Besides stealing some silver spoons, its crew beat the *George Armistead*'s captain and several men on board, threatening one passenger with a knife until he handed over his money. On leaving, they transferred about twenty Spanish prisoners aboard the *George Armistead,* one of whom died after crew aboard the *Young Spartan,* for whatever reason, "fired a volley of musketry among them."[2]

The subsequent jailing of the *Young Spartan*'s captain and some of its crew when it stopped at Savannah showed that the American authorities were gradually realizing how far out of hand the privateering situation had become. *Niles' Weekly Register* complained "that the West India seas appear to be filled with pirates under the independent flag, who rob ships of all nations." With all privateers becoming suspect, the practice of outfitting them in American ports came under scrutiny. It was reported that "eleven vessels, carrying 153 guns, and 1535 men," the craft owned or otherwise fitted out by Baltimore merchants, were cruising against Spain under Buenos Aires commissions. One might have been the *Constitution,* which docked in Baltimore late in 1818, reportedly loaded with $400,000 in specie. The money was said to have been but half of the original load aboard the 800-ton Spanish ship *Castillian,* which the *Constitution* had captured out of Lima and sent on to a Buenos Aires prize court.[3]

On top of these losses, Spain by now recognized that it would have to part with Florida. The United States had long coveted the peninsula, making claims on western Florida as Spain grew weaker after 1810. The mother country's low point came in 1817, when its inability to hold Amelia Island or prevent cross-border Indian raids prompted American interventions. Accepting the inevitable, Spain began to negotiate an agreement with Washington to rid itself of the territory. It would be concluded in early 1819, though ratification by both countries would take two years. At the same time Washington began to move with a firmer hand to police southern waters. A new act of Congress approved in March 1819 ordered the navy to protect American shipping and seize pirates, who faced the death penalty.[4]

A few months after the bill passed, off the mouth of the Mississippi, the U.S. revenue cutters *Alabama* and *Louisiana* stopped and then engaged a suspicious schooner carrying two cannon and about two dozen men. This was the *Bravo,* owned by Jean Laffite, outfitted at New Orleans, and captained by one Jean Desfarges. Abandoning a pair of prizes, the *Bravo* put up a spirited resistance, and when finally captured Desfarges was found in possession of a blank commission issued from Texas. Word of the capture was passed to Laffite, who sought release of the patriot crew, members of which held that they had fired only defensively.

It was the first of several American antipirate successes. In late October and early November, as Desfarges and his men sat in jail, the 6-gun schooner USS *Lynx* captured several pirate craft in the Gulf of Mexico and Galveston Bay. But these victories did not ease the situation enough for the presidents of six insurance firms—their payments soaring—who on December 1 addressed a letter to President James Monroe. In it they listed forty-four recently robbed vessels and asked him to remedy the situation. In its Christmas Day issue, *Niles' Weekly Register* suggested the naval forces responsible for the mouth of the Mississippi area be reinforced. The commander at New Orleans, Daniel Patterson, probably agreed with such sentiments, his handful of craft facing possibly hundreds of raiders operating in the Gulf and Caribbean.

Patterson's efforts must have been buoyed by the conviction of Desfarges and fifteen of his men, the verdict coming in a heavily guarded New Orleans courthouse. By one account of the December 30 proceedings: "After the judge had finished pronouncing sentence upon the hardened wretches, several of them cried out, in open court, 'murder, by G-d;' and in no respect did they appear to be in the least affected." Laffite's organization responded with threats and arson, and Louisiana's governor called out the militia and brought in regular army detachments as well. Laffite then spent time politicking in Washington, but while Monroe pardoned one of the condemned men, Desfarges and the rest eventually hanged. For his part, Patterson stayed at work on the pirate colonies in the bayous and at Laffite's base at Galveston. Many of the survivors migrated to Cuba's northern coast.[5]

James Jeffers was admittedly doing more carousing than cruising during this period. At some point in 1819, the *Journal of Commerce* would relate in 1831, "He left Havana and came to the United States, bringing with him about $30,000." Writer Edward Rowe Snow portrayed Charles Gibbs retrieving the cash from a Havana bank, and his vision of a Newport pirate starting a savings account remains a remarkable image of Yankee thrift. The cash figure— an enormous sum for the time—is credible if one accepts the story that a Cape Antonio–based pirate named Raphaelina by mid-1822 had collected $180,000.[6]

Jeffers gave no reason in his 1831 interviews for leaving Cuba and abandoning privateering *cum* piracy, albeit temporarily. If guilt over the fate of the Dutch woman at Cape Antonio affected him, he did not specify it. Perhaps the lull involved the fact that shortly after the young woman's murder, the *Maria/Sans Soucis* ran aground and was damaged beyond repair.[7]

A replacement vessel would be found for his gang, but the increasing naval pressure might have helped convince Jeffers it was time to enjoy his earnings. He could always return. Every port had ships on the Havana route, and his privateering credentials would be especially welcomed in Baltimore or New Orleans. So by his account, the young Rhode Islander—Captain Samuel Jeffers's son James would have turned twenty-one late in 1819— shipped from Havana to New York lugging what must have been a huge bag of money. In New York he spent several weeks before moving on to Boston.

It is not reported if he stopped at Newport, but he may have visited Providence, for in 1831 a local newspaper reported that the pirate then notorious as Charles Gibbs had at one point mixed with that city's upper classes. It is unrecorded how he attributed the source of his funds.[8]

Passing the time drinking and gambling, Jeffers was unable to settle down in America. He may have preferred roaming, or new troubles may have found him. Edward Rowe Snow imagined Charles Gibbs becoming "disgusted with city sharpers and their clever manipulations," and deciding "to visit the old world." Whatever the reason, Jeffers recounted that he booked passage on the *Emerald*, bound for Liverpool.

Jeffers's only recorded act there was the losing of his heart to a beautiful female, who conquered, then discarded, this veteran of sea fights and romantic tragedy. In Jeffers's words, "I fell in with a woman, who I thought was all virtue, but she deceived me, and I am sorry to say, that a heart that never felt abashed at scenes of carnage and blood, was made a child of for a time, by her." In 1831 the *Journal of Commerce* confirmed the story by locating the very woman, by remarkable coincidence then in jail in New York. How she got there is unrecorded. In Liverpool she was "said, at that time to have borne a decent character," while Jeffers "lived like a gentleman, with apparently abundant means of support."[9]

Writer Jack Beater invented a first name for Jeffers's Liverpool love and envisioned her as "an Irish lass with flaming hair, a honeyed tongue, and freckles across the bridge of her saucy tipped up nose. The rest was an old story, repeated many, many times before and since. The girl, Bridget, made free use of her wiles and charms, and one morning Charles Gibbs awoke to find himself alone in his tumbled bed. . . ."[10]

For the record, no contemporary published account named or described the young woman, who would reappear in Jeffers's story at the time of his hanging. Sailors were supposed to have a girl in every port, and Jeffers had been brutal with the Dutch captive, but according to Jeffers this act of abandonment hit him hard.

Having spent a few months in Liverpool, Jeffers sailed for Boston. He was presumably drunk for much of the voyage. "I gave way to dissipation to drown the torment," he recalled in 1831, referring to the loss of the woman from Liverpool. At about this time, another sensation—guilt—began to require alcoholic treatment. As he put it: "How often when the fumes of liquor have subsided, have I thought of my good and affectionate parents, and of their Godlike advice! But when the little monitor began to move within me, I immediately seized the cup to hide myself from myself, and drank until the sense of intoxication was renewed." Jeffers was likely in the above condition soon after he stepped onto the pier in Boston. He could have been thinking of this period when recalling how "my friends advised me to behave myself like a man, and promised me their assistance, but the demon still haunted me, and I spurned their advice." Instead, he decided to head back to Havana. He probably went via New Orleans. It was from there at about this time that he arranged for word to be sent to Newport that he had died. The James Jeffers known to friends and relatives there would reemerge only in time to meet the noose.[11]

<hr />

If we take the published version of Jeffers's account at face value, upon his return to Cuba circa 1820 he picked up where he left off with the crew of the former *Maria,* apparently again in a commander's role. It seems unlikely that a pirate captain could take such a leave of absence; there is presumably a factual or chronological gap here that cannot at present be resolved.

When their original craft had run aground some time earlier, the Havana fence procured for them a recently built schooner called, for some obscure reason, the *Picciana.* (Was this a feminine derivative of Picciano, a town in the Italian province of Pescara, on the Adriatic?) Phase two of Jeffers's pirate career would involve a new string of cruises, about which relatively little was detailed in the confessions. The *Picciana,* like his former vessel, would remain based at Cape Antonio, and prizes taken during its cruises might have included what he described as the Bremen-based *Dido* and the London-based barque (or bark) *Larkin.* By late 1821 Jeffers and his comrades would operate in consort with a sloop and two other schooners, one of which Jeffers named as the *Margaretta* (or *Margarita*).[12]

Whatever post he did or did not resume among the Cape Antonio pirates, his return roughly coincided with a time when Patterson and the New Orleans Station were getting more weapons in their arsenal. A newspaper on New Year's Day 1820 announced that "the U.S. brig *Enterprize* is about to cruise in the Gulf of Mexico, to look after the pirates which infest it. Built in 1799 as a schooner (later modified into a brig), the 12-gun USS *Enterprise* was commanded by Lieutenant Lawrence Kearny, an officer figuring very much in James Jeffers's story and in the history of antipiracy efforts in the 1820s. Born in Perth Amboy, New Jersey, on November 30, 1789, Kearny became a midshipman in July 1807. The next year he served under

Commodore Rodgers on the USS *Constitution* and followed him to the USS *President* in 1809—which means Kearny and young sailor "Ja⁵. Jefferies" crossed paths. In 1810, Kearny was named acting lieutenant on the *Enterprise*, the ship on which, eleven years later, he would encounter pirate James Jeffers. His first stint on the *Enterprise*—its service till now including action against French privateers and Barbary corsairs—lasted into 1813, when Kearny was promoted to lieutenant commandant and sent to South Carolina, where he spent the rest of the War of 1812, serving with the Charleston-based flotilla. In February 1815 he returned to the *Enterprise,* famous for capturing the brig HMS *Boxer* and several other prizes during the war. Kearny would command it for seven years.[13]

On the New Orleans Station in early 1820, Kearny's missions included a February visit to Galveston to again oust Jean Laffite from his lair. According to a likely embellished version of events, when Kearny anchored offshore: "Lafitte [*sic*] in his splendid barge at once rowed off, and carried the embarrassed officer ashore, where the latter remained for several days as the pirate's guest, being entertained and feasted in the most sumptuous fashion. But all Lafitte's diplomacy was useless. Kearny had orders to see that Lafitte evacuated Galveston with all possible dispatch."[14] Laffite had a worthy opponent in Kearny, who a twentieth-century historian deemed "able and tactful" during negotiations with China in the 1840s.[15]

Patterson kept his New Orleans–based force at work during the year cruising in the Gulf of Mexico, off Florida and in the Caribbean. To increase American visibility, all U.S. warships were routed through the West Indies. Patterson's vessels scored some successes, and reports also exist of captures by British and occasionally French warships. But there was a huge amount of ocean to cover, and away from New Orleans' waters—which all the naval attention made relatively peaceful—American ships continued to fall victim to pirates.[16]

Writing about a century later, historian Gardner Allen noted that little was documented about American antipiracy efforts at the start of 1821. Perhaps they were halfhearted, U.S. Navy officers at the time being told to bring pirates captured in Latin American waters to Cuba, to be turned over to local authorities. Such deference probably became unnecessary after the Senate approved the Florida treaty in February. Surviving reports from Kearny do show the *Enterprise* policing the slave trade in early March, and later that month stopping several patriot privateers, which Kearny released after finding no evidence that they had harassed American ships. The next few months

Engagement between the *Enterprise & Boxer,* Off Monhegan, Sept. 4th 1813 *(above), by Walter F. Lansil. Courtesy of the Collection of William Vareika Fine Arts, Newport, Rhode Island*

Commodore Lawrence Kearny (right), by John Wesley Jarvis, circa 1840. Courtesy of the Collections of the New Jersey Historical Society, Newark, New Jersey

seem to have seen a lull in piratical activity, though Patterson suffered a setback when the USS *Lynx* apparently fell victim to a spring hurricane.[17]

But in late summer Caribbean pirates came back with a vengeance, with at least twenty-one incidents reported from September through year's end. *Niles' Weekly Register* complained in October that "to recapitulate all the cases of piracy that have occurred in our neighborhood, and give a list of all the vessels plundered within the last two months, would, perhaps, fill a whole page!" The same issue reported that a pirate vessel mounting fourteen guns had halted the Philadelphia-based *Orleans* off Cape Antonio. After taking off $40,000 worth of goods, the "Spaniard" pirate captain wrote a note in French, and asked an *Orleans* passenger to share it with a belligerent American officer who happened to be on board. The translated missive is worth quoting in full as an authentic pirate voice:

At sea, and in good luck.

Sir—Between buccaneers, no ceremony; I take your dry goods, and, in return, I send you pimento; therefore we are now even: I entertain no resentment.

Bid good day to the officer of the United States, and tell him that I appreciate the energy with which he has spoken of me and my companions in arms. Nothing can intimidate us; we run the same fortune, and our maxim is, "that the goods of this world belong to the brave and valiant."

The occupation of the Floridas is a pledge [that is, ensures?] that the course I follow, is conformable to the policy pursued by the United States

Richard Coeur de Lion[18]

The cryptic final line shows consciousness that Florida's annexation ended an era. Before the Americans stepped in the territory was rife with pirates, many based on the peninsula's south coast keys.

Opinions vary on the identity of the letter writer. He may have been one Dubois, who cruised in the Venezuelan-commissioned brig *General Arisimendi*. After the "Coeur de Lion" episode, Dubois and his crew reportedly stopped another American craft and "told the story of the *Orleans*, but not that they themselves had written it. They said that the humorous Richard Coeur de Lion had been none other than Jean Laffite."[19]

Another candidate is Jose Gaspar, a mythical figure who reputedly operated from Florida's Charlotte Harbor between 1819 and 1822. He was said to have been a disgruntled Spanish naval officer who stole a warship and turned against his country, waging war on its shipping in the Americas. Legends said "Gasparilla" killed most prisoners but kept the attractive females in a private harem. They also held that he met his end off Boca Grande Pass, attacked by an American warship disguised as an English merchantman. His vessel going down, Gaspar "wrapped a piece of anchor chain about his waist and jumped into the sea."[20]

Such an episode is not mentioned in contemporary records. But in response to the many documented cases of piracy then occurring off the Florida and Cuban coasts, *Niles' Weekly Register* applauded the mid-September news that navy ships were about to set after the raiders, who represented the "fag-end of what was recently called privateering."[21]

One of the most effective pirate techniques was simply to launch fast, small craft from strategic points along the Cuban coast. One observer wrote that these pirate ships "are mere boats, manned with 10 or 15 desperadoes. They are generally found near a cape or the entrance to some port where many merchant vessels are obliged to pass. They are so small and keep so close in shore as not to be discovered by cruizers at the distance they are obliged to keep from the land, while they see every vessel that passes, and are prepared to board and rob merchantmen, or at the sight of a man of war to run among the rocks where they cannot be followed."[22]

A well-armed pirate gang that operated outside the north Cuban harbor of Matanzas in the autumn of 1821 used a launch to board several American vessels in September. They killed the captain and two crewmen of a schooner called the *Milo,* and disemboweled the crew of a brig called *John* before hanging them "by the ribs to the masts" and setting fire to the vessel. The crew of the Bristol, Rhode Island, sloop *Collector,* heading from Matanzas with a cargo of sugar, was more fortunate, though they were beaten and their captain French wounded with a cutlass. The marauders set the craft on fire and took off in its long boat, but the *Collector* had another boat in which the injured captain and crew escaped. What may have been the same gang also boarded the Rhode Island schooner *Louisa.* After beating the mate and threatening the captain—from whom they took $150—they loaded two thousand pounds of cheese and every piece of clothing aboard into the *Louisa*'s longboat. Before departing, "The commander of the boat dressed himself in the captain of the schooner's best clothes, hat and boots, and walking the quarter deck, looked at himself with exultation." The men used an open boat to rob the Boston brig *George* and demanded a specific amount of gold they somehow knew was aboard. The captain refused to divulge its whereabouts, though he handed over his own cash. The pirates responded by tearing apart the *George,* leaving once they found the gold in the rudder case.[23]

Though nothing attributed to Jeffers refers to open-boat attacks, given the life of sea crime to which he confessed, anything is possible. An open boat was present on the pirate side in the one episode Jeffers mentioned that can be satisfactorily documented elsewhere—a mid-October 1821 run-in with Kearny's *Enterprise.*

Recounting this incident involves synthesizing and interpreting a number of sources, all of which are flawed. Kearny's terse report to the secretary of the navy was written almost a month after the event, once the *Enterprise* had docked in Charleston, and lacks detail. Accounts printed in the era's newspapers are garbled or confusing. Then there is Jeffers himself, who must be treated with caution at the best of times.

With such caveats in place, the story began off Cape Antonio on October 13, 1821, when the schooner *Combine* happened on a pirate flotilla. The *Combine*'s captain, a Connecticut native named Jacob Dunham, later wrote that "we discovered three small schooners, one small sloop, and a large open boat lying at anchor about two miles from the land. In about the space of fifteen minutes the whole fleet got under weigh [*sic*] and bore down for us."

The pirates who boarded the *Combine* carried muskets, cutlasses, and knives, and while abusing Dunham and others gave commands in broken English. Their tactics included calling victims out of the hold one at a time for mock executions, terrifying not only the immediate targets but also those below who heard but could not see the proceedings. Nothing in Dunham's account singles out anyone who might have been Jeffers. Nor was an American or Englishman in charge of this band, for Dunham wrote that "an old Spaniard was pointed out to me who they said was the commodore." The pirates eventually released Dunham and his ransacked, damaged vessel. The next day, October 14, the *Combine* met a Spanish Navy brig, whose officers refused to pursue the pirates or even share provisions. Dunham steered toward Havana seeking relief.[24]

On that note, the *Combine*'s role in the story ended. But on the same day that Dunham had his disappointing encounter with the Spanish navy, a schooner flying red and gold Spanish colors near Cape Antonio stopped the Boston-registered brig *Aristides,* carrying dry goods. The Spanish flag was a ruse; the schooner might have been the *Picciana* that Jeffers mentioned in his confessions, but by his account he was on board its consort schooner the *Margaretta* during this episode. The boarders first knocked down the *Aristides*'s captain, Joseph Couthouy, taking his watch, then forced its crew to turn the vessel toward land. The *Aristides* eventually ran aground in shallow water, the collision shearing off its rudder and stern post. With water seeping into the hold, the pirates made the captives unload cargo onto another craft that came alongside. They punctuated their orders with beatings and threats to kill Couthouy and his entire crew.

They might eventually have done so. The next day, October 15, south of Cape Antonio, the crew of a pirate schooner took a French brig bound for Campeachy. Their association with Jeffers and his comrades is unclear, but they shared his gang's reputed style and killed all on board and presumably scuttled the prize, which was never heard of again.[25]

———————

Kearny had yet to learn of this horror when, at dawn on October 16, the *Enterprise* was cruising off Cape Antonio and stopped a suspicious vessel, the Colombian privateer *Centella*. Described as a large schooner, and carrying at least one 24-pounder, it was commanded by Charles C. Hopner, presumably another American in foreign service, whose commission papers were in order. While Hopner was answering questions put to him by the *Enterprise's* officers, another merchant brig, the Charleston-registered *Lucies,* captained by James Misroon, rounded the Cape. At 5 A.M. by Misroon's watch he spotted Couthouy's vessel in distress and Misroon bravely or foolishly headed toward the grounded *Aristides.* When the *Lucies* came abreast, Couthouy— probably at his captors' orders—hailed his visitor, identified his craft, and added that it had been taken by pirates. "At that instant," Misroon recorded, "we were fired at by a pirate, and shortly after was [*sic*] boarded by her, three others in company, all under Spanish colors."

Presuming Jeffers to be credible, the vessel whose crew boarded Misroon's craft was the *Margaretta.* Captain Samuel Jeffers's son would turn twenty-three the next month, and while James Jeffers claimed to have served as a captain among the pirates, his actual role on that schooner and in the outlaw flotilla itself is impossible to ascertain. What is documented is that the *Margaretta's* crewmen brandished cutlasses and blunderbusses, and they drove the *Lucies's* officers, crew, and passengers below decks. They then called their prisoners out in groups, pointed cocked blunderbusses at each person's breast, and demanded their valuables. This ritual over, some pirates began to break open trunks and cargo boxes in the hold. Others forced some of Misroon's crew to sail the *Lucies* closer to shore, eventually anchoring in three fathoms. Then they were again banished below decks along with the rest of the vessel's company.

The pirate colony's score kept going up. The brig *Larch,* registered in St. Andrews, New Brunswick, and traveling from Kingston to Havana, happened on the scene at about the same time the *Lucies* was being stopped. The pirates who halted it on that remarkable morning may not actually have boarded the *Larch,* as their luck had run out and events began moving fast.

There were now at least four pirate craft—three 40-ton schooners and a 25-ton sloop—swarming around three prizes, all close in to the Cape Antonio shore. Observers aboard the *Enterprise* spotted this herd of masts, and Kearny understood what was unfolding. With the legitimately commissioned *Centella* nearby, either Kearny sought Hopner's help, or else the privateer captain—with reason to be on his best behavior—volunteered it. Kearny, who must have recognized the irony of accepting aid from an insurgent privateer, did not mention Hopner or *Centella* in his brief report.[26]

They were soon under way toward the nest of vessels, the *Enterprise* heading for the *Aristides,* the *Centella* for the *Lucies.* Kearny ordered a cannon fired to signal the warship's presence, prompting one pirate craft to run up a red flag. The show of defiance was brief, however, for most of the pirates panicked. On the *Lucies* with the boarding party from the *Margaretta,* Jeffers recalled that the warships began their attack "before we had a chance of taking any thing out of" Misroon's ship. Misroon's account affirms his story, noting that after the single cannon shot, the pirates "precipitately left us, and began to tow and sweep their vessels in shore." The *Enterprise*'s gunfire had the same

U.S. Brig *Enterprise* and Pirate Schooners, October 16, 1821. *Watercolor by Irwin John Bevan. Courtesy of the Mariners' Museum, Newport News, Virginia*

effect aboard the wrecked *Aristides,* whose captors scrambled over the side to their own schooner, full of dry goods taken off the prize, and headed for shore with all sails set.

The *Lucies's* crew watched through the cabin windows as the *Enterprise* removed the crew of the grounded *Aristides,* which must have been done by boat as the warship could not safely venture so close to land. Once aboard the *Enterprise,* Couthouy reported what had taken place during the last two days. At about the same time, *Centella,* flying the Colombian flag, came within hailing distance of the *Lucies.* Misroon wrote that Hopner "enquired if we had been taken by the pirates, and being answered in the affirmative, instantly opened a well-directed fire upon them from a 24-pounder. When the firing had ceased, she again hailed us to say if the brig astern [the *Enterprise*] did not prove to be an American man-of-war, on our hoisting our signal, she would immediately come to our assistance—she then hauled off."

Red flag notwithstanding, the retreating pirates did not fire at the *Enterprise* or *Centella.* On the *Margaretta* Jeffers and the rest of the crew readied themselves to go over the side once it grounded. They left a pot of poisoned coffee on the galley stove, hoping their pursuers would drink it once they boarded the craft. No reports suggest anyone did. Jeffers mentioned the coffee episode when Kearny visited him in his cell in 1831 and it appears to have been an authentic detail.

The USS *Enterprise* now came within hailing distance of the *Lucies.* According to Misroon, Kearny "inquired if we had not possession of our ship again?" When Misroon answered affirmatively, Kearny "demanded all the boats and men we could spare, to go in pursuit of the pirates." Within ten minutes, according to Misroon, a five-boat flotilla was assembled. Three were loaded with marines and sailors, commanded by a Lieutenant McIntosh. The *Enterprise's* purser, named Perry, commanded the other two, made up of rescued merchant crewmen. Shortly after 9 A.M., with all aboard heavily armed, they headed for the pirate vessels congregating near the shore.[27]

<hr />

It was a daring assault. Open boats offered little protection from gunfire, and Kearny must have been counting on the pirates' utter disorganization. The St. Andrews *Herald* praised the venture's boldness given that "the most fatal consequences might reasonably have been expected in an attack by five open boats, of [on?] such an imposing force, in shoal water, where the *Enterprize* could not have assisted the assailants." Misroon observed in his log that at about 11 A.M., six hours after the *Lucies's* ordeal began and two hours after the task force had been launched, he could see that the pirate schooner that had plundered the *Aristides* was on fire. Couthouy wrote that the pirates had laid "a train of powder to blow up the vessel on the approach of the boats." Within half an hour, Misroon noted, the pirate craft was engulfed in flame "to the mast-head, all sail being set. At meridian she blew up." What happened when the boats landed? On the pirate side, Jeffers would maintain that "we had a fight with them, some of our men were killed, and I believe some of theirs." He claimed moreover that he and his comrades—in a journalist's words—"defended themselves for some time behind a 4 gun battery, but in the end, were defeated with considerable loss, and compelled to abandon their vessels and booty, and fly to the mountains for safety." But the St. Andrew's *Herald* reported that "no blood was shed" during Kearny's open-boat assault; Kearny's November 12 report made no mention of contact ashore, pirate fortifications, or American casualties, though it mentioned a need to replace, among other items, "a Launch lost at Cape Antonio." Kearny's account of the drama was, in fact, brief in the extreme: "The pirates ran their vessels on shore when pursued by our boats and made their escape except one man now a prisoner aboard this vessel." Kearny did not record the prisoner's name or fate.[28]

Kearny, in fact, may have been elsewhere when his boats hit the beach. Misroon's log stated that "after Capt. Kearney [*sic*] had dispatched the boats after the pirates . . . he stood round the Cape, with the brig [the *Enterprise*] to the southwest, and there captured another of the robbers." According to what Kearny later told Misroon, the crew of this roughly 40-ton schooner had massacred the crew and passengers of the Campeachy-bound French brig the day before. As Kearny retrieved this final schooner without its crew, its company probably escaped as had Jeffers and associates. Somehow Kearny learned of the French vessel's fate, perhaps by finding papers or other items from it aboard the pirate prize, evidently from which his men also recovered a woman's bloodstained dress.[29]

When Kearny returned to the Cape Antonio beachhead, he put the *Larch* back on its way, its time spent in captivity brief. (It would return to St. Andrews early in November.) With one pirate schooner smoldering at the shoreline, Kearny ordered a second burned "for want of men to man her." His remaining haul—two schooners and the sloop, their holds still containing stolen dry goods, coffee, and tobacco—received prize crews. Kearny ordered them to stop at Havana and then make for Charleston to be condemned and sold. The *Enterprise*, he knew, was entitled to a share of salvage proceeds. (A Charleston judge later awarded "one half of the net proceeds of

the vessels, and one quarter of the proceeds of the cargo" to Kearny, his officers, and his crew.)[30]

Kearny additionally had to tend to the shattered *Aristides* and the luckier
Lucies. Aboard the latter, Misroon wrote in his log that October 17 started
"with heavy squalls, thunder, lightning and rain." At about 4 P.M. he spotted
Kearny's three prizes "coming round the Point (Mangrove Point on the
chart)." At 9 P.M., *Centella*, which after its early intervention on October 16
seems to have played only a passive role in the episode, came alongside the
Lucies and Captain Hopner came aboard. His Colombian privateer needed
provisions, and he was willing to pay "even more than was demanded for
them," Misroon recorded. An hour later, the *Enterprise* joined them. Kearny
reported on the *Aristides*'s essentially wrecked state, told Misroon of the
French brig and of the taking of its captors' vessel. Given the *Aristides*'s situation, Kearny placed Couthouy and the rest of his crew on the *Enterprise*,
which also took aboard the *Lucies*'s mate, named Stackpole, who must have
been worse for wear after his adventures off Cape Antonio.[31]

<hr />

The *Lucies*'s saga was not yet over. By virtue of retaking it from the pirates,
Kearny felt within his rights to claim part of its cargo as a prize. Kearny
placed a midshipman and several sailors aboard and had Misroon sign
an agreement to take the *Lucies* to its Havana destination, where he would
demand from its cargo's consignees a third of its value as salvage. If not
allowed, Misroon was to head for Charleston, where Kearny would be waiting for him. When the *Lucies* arrived at Havana a day or so afterward, the
cargo owners balked at Kearny's proposal, and Spanish marines seized the
vessel, anchored in range of *El Morro*.

Waiting for the *Lucies* to show up, Kearny stayed in Charleston long
enough to refit the *Enterprise*. Before leaving, he reported that he intended to
cruise "along the South Half of Cuba where a number of Piracies are committed." But Kearny's initial destination was Havana to check on the *Lucies*.
There, Kearny, who blamed Misroon for the situation, was so adamant about
getting back his prize and its cargo that Spanish officials threatened to sink
the *Lucies* should Kearny try to take it. Havana's captain-general eventually
resolved the situation by promising the Americans their share from a Spanish prize court.[32]

Kearny was lucky at such a peaceful solution, as the *Enterprise*'s success
had made Americans unpopular with the pirates' connections in Havana.
Authorities there were accused of refusing to protect American citizens, while

merchants still angry at earlier crackdowns on slaving applauded robberies committed against U.S. shipping. Kearny himself reported that many on the island were "particularly inimical to Americans. My life and all my Officers lives are openly threatened at Havana for having interfered with their speculations." Anticipating a return visit by the *Enterprise,* some of the Cape Antonio pirates began building fortifications.[33]

———— •◦•◦• ————

The raiders continued to strike, and one November report claimed there were eleven pirate vessels cruising off Cuba. On December 12, pirates stopped and boarded two schooners, the *Emily* and the *Mary Rose,* the pursuit starting about ten miles from Matanzas. The heavily armed men who took over the coffee-laden *Emily* were described as Spaniards. One spoke good English, which he used in demanding money from the *Emily*'s captain, named Robbins. The pirates treated all the *Emily*'s crew roughly and hanged Robbins twice by the neck trying to get him to produce more than the $344 they found. They also beat him with swords, giving similar treatment to the cook and the mate. Besides ripping apart the ship and taking, among other things, rigging, an anchor, and some cable, they forced the crew to unload most of the *Emily*'s cargo onto their schooner. They finally released the vessel with the warning, a survivor recalled, "to steer to the northward, for if we returned to Matanzas, and were again captured by them, death should be our portion."[34]

On about the same day on Cuba's west coast, two schooners took and burned the brig *Alexander,* of Greenock, England, killing its captain and steward but bringing the rest of the crew alive aboard one of their craft. A few days later, on December 16 off Cape Antonio, they stopped the *Liverpool Packet,* of Portsmouth, on its way from Rio de Janeiro to Havana. After taking off $60,000, the pirates sent their *Alexander* captives aboard the new prize and ordered one of its boys to fill their water barrels. He was left stranded aboard their vessel when the pirates spied another sail and quickly cut their lines to the *Liverpool Packet.* The new victim was the schooner *Planet* of Portland, from which the raiders stole coffee, cider, and $300, and then flogged the captain to find out if more cash was aboard. Eventually they left, putting the young *Liverpool Packet* captive on the *Planet.*[35]

———— •◦•◦• ————

Kearny would hit the Cape Antonio "brotherhood" again before the end of the year, the impetus for his second attack being tips picked up about two months after the October 16 raid. While cruising off Havana in mid-December and scrutinizing all passing craft, Kearny reported on December 18 that he was sailing in pursuit of several vessels and was particularly interested in one which had been outfitted at Regla Bay inside Havana Harbor for a cruise near Cape Antonio. Three days later, the *Enterprise* swooped again onto that West Cuban pirate rendezvous. Kearny described the site of this raid as being "about four or five miles north of the Cape around a point easily discerned when passing that headland." Close to the shore—near a "reef, behind which these Villains make a harbour" wrote Kearny—the Americans found their suspect: a 35-ton schooner carrying about two dozen men. As had happened in October, the pirates immediately turned toward land, and once they crashed near the beach they clambered over the side. Again, Kearny launched men in small boats. This time the pirates were prepared to make at least a brief fight ashore.[36]

By that token alone, this December 21 raid sounds closer to the "serious engagement" Jeffers claimed to have been present at two months earlier at Cape Antonio against the *Enterprise*. (It is worth asking if he "improved" that story using details gleaned of the December attack.) That said, Kearny's report of the December 21 assault mentioned no protracted battle, but he did note that the pirates "made a stand on shore protected by a Bank [a good, natural breastwork], until our party got within musket shot when they deeming 'prudence the better part of Valor' took to their heels thro' the well known intricate paths of the thick woods of the Cape and effected their escape."

Keeping the captured schooner as a tender for the *Enterprise*, Kearny took note of a pirate settlement next to the makeshift harbor. With high winds halting any more sailing for the moment, Kearny and his men went ashore to explore it. Along with bits of bloody clothing and stores of coffee and cigars, they found personal letters and other documents taken from ships and victims.

They also found a fresh grave. Inside was the body of an American or European, Kearny reported, who had been stabbed in the chest. He was also missing the fingers from one hand, perhaps a defensive wound as he tried to shield himself from a cutlass. Before leaving, Kearny ordered the settlement burned.[37]

There were other naval successes against Caribbean pirates in late 1821 and early 1822. In October, the 18-gun USS *Hornet* stopped the schooner *Moscow* while it was chasing a merchant brig off St. Domingo. The *Moscow* carried a single 2-pounder cannon and nineteen men, and on board the schooner the

Hornet's crew found watches and clothing marked with former owners' initials. Between November and January the 12-gun schooner USS *Porpoise* snared seven pirate vessels off the Cuban coast. In March Kearny continued his successes at Cape Antonio by capturing seven raiding craft of assorted sizes.

But pirates were still loose in and around Caribbean waters. Off the east Cuban coast on April 30, 1822, the 12-gun schooner USS *Alligator* captured the *Cienaga,* a schooner that carried a single, long-barreled 12-pounder and four carronades. It had been a Colombian privateer before its crew—to quote *Niles' Weekly Register*—"mutinied at Ragged Island" and went on the account. Not far from where it captured the *Cienaga,* the *Alligator* found a sloop bobbing in the waves. It had "only a dog on board, and marks of blood on her deck."[38]

8

Shadow Years

SPEAKING A DECADE AFTER KEARNY's raids, Jeffers said that he and others who in late 1821 fled Cape Antonio headed "to the mountains, where we remained some days. We then separated; some got to Trinidada, south side Cuba; others got to the Havana." Unfortunately, Jeffers confessions include next-to-nothing about his subsequent life until his alleged appearance in Buenos Aires in 1826. Jeffers either gave out little about the intervening years, or else those who chronicled his admissions deemed them unimportant. He was close enough to Havana in 1822 to learn of reports made there by the crews of two Dutch vessels, a "ship and a bark" robbed off the Bahamas by a schooner mounting a single large cannon and carrying a privateer commission as a formality.[1]

It is possible that he participated in one of two independently reported actions involving the Beverly, Massachusetts-owned brig *Belvidere*. Yet while Jeffers recalled capturing and burning a *Belvidere*, which he identified as hailing from Boston, the documented vessel in question survived each encounter, an issue for which there is no convenient answer. The first episode involving the 150-ton *Belvidere*, which regularly worked the New Orleans cotton-trading route, came on December 9, 1821, when it was stopped and boarded by a schooner carrying fourteen men—all Spanish and Portuguese save for one American. While the pirates let the brig continue, the ugly experience prompted its captain, Zachary G. Lamson, to arm the *Belvidere* should pirates call again.

That occurred the following May 2, when the *Belvidere* was out of Port au Prince headed to New Orleans. Again a suspicious schooner gave chase and fired warning shots meant to coerce the *Belvidere* into stopping. This time Lamson kept all sails set, prompting the pursuer to run up "a red flag, with death's head and cross under it." The schooner came close enough for Lamson to count twenty-two men on deck, some firing muskets and pistols. Men on the *Belvidere* replied with their own small arms and two larger pieces: a 24-pound carronade and a "brass 3-pounder" charged with a cannon ball topped by eighty musket shot. Their fire chased the attackers off, and as the vessels separated Lamson—one of whose crew was killed—saw only a handful of men left standing on the schooner. If Jeffers was aboard the latter on this occasion, it was not as master, for Lamson reported that "the captain I saw distinctly laid on deck."[2]

Lamson was prudent in fighting back because surrendering did not guarantee safety. Two weeks after the second *Belvidere* episode, about thirty miles north of Cuba, two schooners halted and boarded four merchant vessels. A published extract from the logbook from one victim, the *Aurilla* of New York, detailed how its captors at first "behaved politely, encouraged us not to feel alarmed, as they intended us no injury." Their mood changed when they found no money. As with the raiders who took the *Combine* off Cape Antonio the previous October, their tactics included beatings and mock executions. Having finished the day by raping the women on board, at dawn they sent the ransacked *Aurilla* on its way. But they suddenly turned back, came aboard, and demanded the vessel's carpenter. The *Aurilla* had none, but to avoid more horrors "some person said that an old Negro man by the name of Simon, was the carpenter: they [the pirates] fell to beating him, drove him into the boat and took him off."[3]

That August a Kingston, Jamaica, newspaper reported on an affidavit sworn out detailing the mid-July boarding of the English ship *Blessing*. It had been stopped by a black schooner with *Emanuel* painted on its stern, "commanded by a white man, with a mixed crew of color and countries, among whom were English and Americans." Finding no money on board, the pirates performed what may be the first documented case of making a captive walk the plank. Having taken the *Blessing*'s captain, son, and crew aboard the *Emanuel,* and having failed to get money from the captain: "A plank was run out in the starboard side of the schooner, upon which he [the pirate leader] made captain Smith walk. . . . As he approached to the end, they tilted the plank, when he dropped into the sea, and there, when in the effort of swimming, the [pirate] captain called for his musket, and fired at him therewith, when he sunk, and was seen no more!" Smith's fourteen-year-old son watched his father's killing and dissolved in an "agony of tears and crying." The pirate chief responded by cracking a musket butt over the boy's head, then "took him by the foot and hove him overboard." The robbers eventually torched the *Blessing* and set the survivors adrift. A merchant schooner picked them up a few hours later.[4]

In 1822 Washington created a new force, the West India Squadron, to deal exclusively with Caribbean piracy. Commanded by Captain James Biddle, by the end of the year it was built around the 36-gun frigates *Congress* and *Macedonian*. Though too large for coastal pursuits, their presence fulfilled a suggestion Lawrence Kearny made in a report written from Havana the year before: "I would respectfully suggest to you the propriety of a vessel of war of the United States of a more considerable force than the *Enterprize* [*sic*] occasionally touching at this Port. In my several visits here I have found that the commercial interest is much benefited by the presence of the government vessels, as they possess more weight with the government here than the commercial agents who are not acknowledged."[5]

The squadron's workhorses were its smaller vessels, whose commanders on occasion matched Kearny's daring at Cape Antonio. For their part, the pirates were putting up harsher resistance. In June, off Sagua la Grande on Cuba's north coast, the 12-gun schooner USS *Shark,* commanded by Matthew Perry, launched boats to attack a pirate schooner. William Lynch, then a midshipman, later wrote that "with courage equal to our own, the pirates rushed forward to repel us, and a desperate hand-to-hand conflict ensued." His account of what followed could describe any epic fight in the wooden-ship era: "The musketry had now ceased, and a pistol shot was but occasionally heard, but the clash of steel was incessant, and the silent but deadly thrust became more frequent. The shout of an officer as he cut down the swarthy pirate with whom he was engaged, was responded to by a wild cry of exultation from the men, and animated as by one spirit, we bounded forward with a cheer. A better cause and far more numerous force, could not have withstood our charge. The pirates gave way, slowly at first, but when our leader called out 'push home, men! and no quarter!' and the cry 'no quarter! no quarter!' was fiercely repeated, they turned, and springing to the side, leaped overboard and endeavored to escape by swimming." Lynch recalled some of his comrades shooting at the swimmers, others getting into boats to pursue them in the water. Some even "plunged after them sword in hand." He added, "On the part of those wretches, not a cry was raised—not a supplication uttered. When too hotly pursued, they turned to grapple where they could, and in silence they received the death wound, and in silence they sunk, their throats gurgling the water which was deeply crimsoned with their blood."[6]

About five months later, the USS *Alligator* also encountered spirited opposition when it tried rescuing two American vessels pirates were holding for $7,000 ransom in a bay about forty miles from Matanzas. The operation turned into a running battle against three armed pirate craft, the crew of one defiantly nailing a red flag to its mast. As with the *Enterprise*'s raid at Cape Antonio a year earlier, the *Alligator* launched boats against its quarry. While ultimately the pirates were routed, the action cost the navy several killed and wounded.[7]

Factoring the stiffer resistance alongside yellow fever outbreaks and uncooperative Spanish officials, the West India Squadron still tallied an impressive number of captures by the end of 1822. A new commander, David Porter, early in 1823 added a "Mosquito Fleet" of shallow-draft schooners to aid in coastal operations. That July Kearny, now on the schooner *Greyhound*, led a raid on Cuba's Cape Cruz, where he took eight suspect craft and burned another pirate settlement.[8]

Raiders who survived American efforts also faced the British Jamaica Squadron. In February 1823, ten pirates captured by the HMS *Tyne* were hanged at Kingston's Port Royal Point. A few weeks later the British cutter *Grecian* forced ashore on the Isle of Pines a pirate vessel carrying eight guns and a crew of about one hundred, thirty of whom were killed and three captured. The following year HMS *Icarus* and supporting craft discovered the pirate schooner *Diableto* anchored in an inlet near Trinidad on Cuba's southern coast. After routing its crew, the British found aboard the *Diableto* nine captives from the American brig *Henry,* who had been anticipating their execution until the *Icarus* arrived. Their vessel was recovered about a mile away, a deserted sloop alongside containing some of its cargo.[9]

—◆•◆•◆—

Jeffers's assertion that he captured a barque called the *Transit* circa 1824–1825, destroying the crew and vessel, which had carried a cargo of molasses, marks the last dated prize of his admitted Caribbean pirate career. Jeffers and his mates were literally being chased out of their livelihood, though they did not necessarily go meekly. One historian who went through the records of the *New York Shipping and Commercial List* found dozens of instances of piracy between 1824 and 1830. (The *Transit,* which Jeffers after all said was made to disappear, is not among them.) However, several took place far from the Caribbean, and the total was still a drop from the days when *Niles' Weekly Register* feared that documenting recent captures alone would require a whole page of its tightly spaced text.[10]

According to maritime historian Basil Lubbock, "With the Jamaica Squadron on one side of Cuba and the American Mosquito squadron on the other, piracy from the old Cuban hiding places had become a difficult business by 1826, and most of the freebooters were turning to the slave trade as being much more profitable game." The practice still thrived despite regulation and growing social abhorrence. For some Cape Antonio veterans it might have been a return to the fold, because according to Lubbock, "In the nineteenth century the true pirate had generally served an apprenticeship in a slaver."[11]

Indeed, a contemporary editorial made slave-running sound like an easy career change for a pirate. "Slavers are generally fast sailing craft," it read in part, "manned with a motley mixture of all nations, of unprincipled characters and piratical dispositions; and already exiled from the society of honest men, and desperadoes by profession, they are reckless of consequence. If they chance to meet any unarmed vessel, with specie, they have no objection to making her a prize. They are well armed and full of men, so that resistance in case of such an attempt would be useless. The crime once committed, they are off in a moment—they paint their sides of a different stripe, and if the same ship should meet again it would be impossible for her to identify them."[12]

If Jeffers ever indulged in slaving, he kept it to himself. Whatever path he took, by his account he was back in the United States in late 1825 or early 1826, when word arrived of a new Latin American conflict brewing where his privateering past would be useful. This involved Brazil and the United Provinces of the River Plate, modern Argentina. The "Cisplatine War" between them centered over possession of territory that became modern Uruguay and would last about two years.

Jeffers was presumably then living and traveling under another name, for he was not far from his native Rhode Island and the family that still believed him dead. In its account of his confessions, the *Journal of Commerce* reported that Jeffers "sailed from Boston in the brig *Hitty* of Portsmouth, with a determination, as he states, of trying his fortune in defence of a republican government," that is, Buenos Aires. But as River Plate commerce was worth millions, Jeffers more likely had profit on his mind.[13]

Self-interested mariners were welcome in Buenos Aires, which when war started, reactivated its 1817 privateering legislation and printed up 118 letters of marque. Though England was neutral, one of its officials was concerned about British shipping given the "swarm of privateers (many of a piratical nature) which were likely to appear." Another expected them to be "blackguards of the most cut-throat description and the most proper fellows for the purpose."[14]

While the job description fit Jeffers, he would maintain that he began Argentinean service not as a privateer but as a regular naval officer. Upon arrival in Buenos Aires—the date is unclear—he either sought out or was directed to the office of the head of the United Provinces navy, Admiral William Brown. About two decades older than Jeffers, Irish-born Brown had risen from cabin boy to shipowner in the first phase of his career. He ran a packet service in South American waters until revolution struck, at which time he gave his services to Buenos Aires's bid for independence. In 1813 his motley fleet defeated a Spanish squadron on the River Plate. Remaining an active privateer, at one point he ignored instructions to return home in favor of cruising against Spanish shipping in the Caribbean.

Brown was a larger-than-life sea figure—he became well known to American newspaper readers—and even innocuous items about him appearing in the era's periodicals need to be read with caution. Brown's biographer noted that stories about the admiral included "exploits that never took place, but of which he was evidently believed capable by shipowners, harbour masters and government officials." What is certain is that in 1818 he returned to Buenos Aires and was tried for disobeying orders. Humiliated, Brown stayed in strictly commercial ventures until war with Brazil was formally declared on New Year's Day 1826. On January 12 the United Provinces government gave him command of the navy.[15]

Jeffers would have arrived after that date because by his version of events he met with the famous admiral and discussed a commission as a naval officer rather than a privateer. Brown had, in fact, been given fourteen letters of marque to distribute personally, but issued few at the start of the war as Buenos Aires placed early emphasis on building a regular fleet. Continuing with Jeffers's account, Brown subsequently took the former pirate to see the man whom Jeffers named only as the governor. In Buenos Aires, this was Juan Gregorio de Las Heras, who had authorized the privateering decree, but whose authority was shifting because the United Provinces was undergoing a political change. While Buenos Aires's governor hitherto ruled the country, a new constitution transformed that post into an actual presidency. Hence on February 6, 1826, Las Heras gave way to a legislature-elected president, Bernardino Rivadavia.[16]

The commissioning role of the governor rather than the new president in this alleged episode suggests it occurred prior to that transition. At this reception, Jeffers claimed, he found old shipmates who had also flocked to

Buenos Aires. One was named Dodge, about whom Jeffers said nothing more. Jeffers and Dodge received commissions as lieutenants, a rank which existed in two grades: *teniente* (or *capitan teniente*) and *sub-teniente* receiving respectively 75 and 60 pesos per month. Jeffers recounted that "when the Governor gave me the commission, he told me they wanted no cowards in their Navy, to which I replied that I thought he would have no apprehension of my cowardice or skill when he became acquainted with me. He thanked me, and said he hoped he should not be deceived; upon which we drank to his health and to the success of the Republic. He then presented me with a sword, and told me to wear that as my companion through the doubtful struggle in which the Republic was engaged. I told him I never would disgrace it, so long as I had a nerve in my arm."[17]

As with everything attributed to Jeffers, plausibility is mixed with little corroborative evidence. Both sides in the Argentine-Brazil conflict relied heavily on foreign-born sailors and officers. Americans and British made up more than half the Argentine navy's allotment of 56 officers, who oversaw 40 lesser-ranking noncommissioned personnel such as surgeons and pursers, and 1,300 seamen and marines. Anglo-American sounding names appear frequently in published collections of contemporary Argentine documents and more recent secondary sources. But there are no references to a Jeffers, or a Gibbs for that matter. Nor is there mention of an officer named Dodge. As that word itself is a synonym for "ruse," the man's choice of last name hints—assuming Jeffers's story is true—that aliases were common.[18]

Whether or not Jeffers himself used an alias in Buenos Aires, he was on firm ground in naming the *Veinticinco de Mayo* (May 25) as his new vessel. It began the war as the merchantman *Comercio de Lima,* an aging craft but one that Brown deemed the best available at the time. It was purchased, renamed for the 1810 date from which Argentineans marked their independence, then became Brown's flagship. Jeffers described it as a "ship of 34 guns," and Argentine naval documents do describe *Veinticinco de Mayo* as a *fragata* (frigate) or *corbeta* (corvette) carrying 28–36 cannon at different times.[19]

Again, the voice of caution needs to be heard. While Jeffers's statements about *Veinticinco de Mayo* refer to a real ship, so too did his recollections about the *Hornet* and the *Chesapeake.* And the "Twenty-fifth of May," celebrated in at least one English-language song, would have been as known in sailing circles outside Buenos Aires as was Admiral Brown.[20]

Aboard *Veinticinco de Mayo* Jeffers claimed to have served "in the capacity of 5th Lieutenant for about four months." Assuming Jeffers was there in early February when its cruises began, he would have been aboard until May.

An Argentine navy statement of May 13, 1826, numbers personnel aboard *Veinticinco de Mayo* at 275, with 171 being *marineros* (sailors). Unfortunately the document does not name officers or itemize their ranks.[21]

How does Jeffers's account square with the ship's documented history? According to Jeffers, during his period aboard *Veinticinco de Mayo* "we had a number of skirmishes with the enemy." His terminology might apply to the battle of Corales in February, a long-range cannon duel in which both sides shared a total of six dead and twenty wounded. But unless he had learned the art of understatement, "skirmish" hardly applies to the water-borne siege of the Brazilian-held city of Colonia. This action began in late February and lasted until Brown withdrew with heavy losses in mid-March.[22]

Repaired and refitted, the *Veinticinco de Mayo*'s next actions were off Montevideo. On April 10, Brown's force captured a Brazilian schooner, and the next day saw it take part in a running battle with the Brazilian frigate *Niterói* and other craft. Darkness ended the engagement, which again involved long-range gunfire. Brown reported nine killed and fourteen wounded aboard *Veinticinco de Mayo* and another of his vessels, *República Argentina*. Brazilian casualties were five killed and five wounded.[23]

The last action occurring in Jeffers's specified period aboard the *Veinticinco de Mayo* was another engagement at Montevideo. Brown planned a night operation for April 27, using his flagship aided by another craft, the *Independencia,* to board the *Niterói* and carry it off. But the attack nearly ended in disaster, the Argentine sailors mistaking the 50-gun *Imperatriz* for the smaller *Niterói*. After an hour and fifteen minutes of cannon and small-arms fire, and with nearby Brazilian ships alerted by the noise of battle, Brown withdrew, his men having never set foot aboard the *Imperatriz*.[24]

The *Veinticinco de Mayo*'s career in Buenos Aires's service ended with its being shot to pieces and run aground on July 30, 1826, at the Battle of Lara-Quilmes. Brown, rowed to another ship mid-battle, survived to fight again. The 1831 stories include no reference by Jeffers to this event. But he would have missed it because, Jeffers said, he had gained enough of Brown's confidence during his time aboard *Veinticinco de Mayo* for the *almirante* to offer him "command of a privateer schooner," a model known in Spanish as a *goleta*. This is plausible, Brown having been given the letters of marque to distribute. As about a quarter of all Argentine privateer captains were Americans, Jeffers would have been in good company.

At a later point in the conflict Argentine privateers employed a thousand sailors from a wide range of nations. But relatively few privateers were active in early 1826 so Jeffers should be traceable. Unfortunately, he cited neither the name of his new vessel, nor the *armadore* who owned and equipped it. He recalled that it had a crew of forty-six and carried a pair of long-barreled 24-pounders, and with it he "made two good cruises." One successful operation recorded that June involved the Argentine privateer *Hijo de Mayo*, manned by three dozen American and British sailors, which took a pair of Brazilian transports. But as a 17-ton *lanchón* or lugger, the *Hijo de Mayo* does not easily pass for Jeffers's privateer schooner. Moreover, its captain is well established as Englishman James Harris.[25]

Any prizes Jeffers took must have been worth significant cash, for he purportedly earned enough in the prize courts to enable him to buy "one half of a new Baltimore schooner," on which he would again embark against Brazilian shipping. Moves from master to shipowner did happen during the Cisplatine War. As their purchases were often modestly sized, Jeffers's claim to buying 50 percent of one of the highly regarded and premium-priced *goletas de Baltimore*—the era's fast "Baltimore clippers"—suggests success.[26]

But as with his earlier reputed command, the name of Jeffers's newly bought *goleta* did not see publication; nor did the name of the man who shared ownership. Reporters may have deemed such data unimportant, because Jeffers's first admitted cruise as part-owner of a legitimate ship of war ended quickly, a Brazilian warship capturing his schooner a week out of Buenos Aires.

There were twenty-seven Argentine privateers taken during the war, prisoners on both sides faring relatively well. Certainly Jeffers's description of his captivity belies any drama. He is recorded as saying simply that he was "carried into Rio [de] Janeiro, where the Brazilians [he probably meant Argentines] paid me my change"—evidently a form of ransoming. Jeffers claimed that "I remained there until peace took place, then returned to Buenos Ayres [*sic*], and thence to New York." When did peace take place? Negotiations began as early as mid-1827, but it was not until late the next year that formal ratification occurred. As one historian of Argentina wrote: "The war with Brazil simply petered out, with Uruguay established under British mediation as an independent nation."[27]

It might still be possible to draw parallels between some details Jeffers gave out about this period and certain examples documented in published Argentine sources. But the indistinct timeline and lack of names would reduce such analysis to conjecture. Certainly the unexciting finale to his Buenos Aires career must have disappointed the writers of 1831, especially when it was placed alongside Jeffers's tales of blood, horror, and Dutch females.

That said, one more woman now enters Jeffers's story, her presence mysteriously underdeveloped. Jeffers said he married her in Buenos Aires, the year unspecified (1827? 1828?), and that the marriage produced a child. By the time Jeffers gave out these details in 1831, he maintained that the woman was dead, the child still living. How the former died and who was taking care of the latter was left unstated. Even less was said of Jeffers's subsequent trip back to the United States, which marked the start of "about a year . . . passed in traveling from place to place." No reason is given for his roaming, which ended in early 1830 with Jeffers's reputed attempt to become a Barbary corsair.[28]

Piracy had been practiced by North African mariners long before Jeffers's day. Like many marauders in Europe and the Americas, Barbary corsairs insisted that they were privateers, often giving a percentage of their takings to local rulers in return for harbor rights and other protection. They usually made three annual Mediterranean cruises, avoiding the stormy summer and autumn months, hunting alone and preferring deception and stealth to battle. As with some earlier European military orders, such as Malta's Knights of St. John, Barbary corsairs saw captives not as witnesses to be eliminated but as slaves, not necessarily a better fate. Their captures of U.S. citizens at the turn of the century prompted action by the navy, but their effect on American shipping was minimal compared to that of the Caribbean pirates. Over one three-decade period, during which Barbary corsairs captured twenty-two American craft, their Caribbean-area counterparts took five hundred.[29]

What brought them to Jeffers's attention as potential employers was the conflict between Algeria and France. It began in April 1827, when the Dey of Algiers ended an interview with the French consul by striking him with a fly swatter. The insulted diplomat's country responded with a blockade, and Jeffers eventually sensed opportunity. As the *Journal of Commerce* expressed it in 1831, "Knowing that the French commerce presented a fine opportunity for plunder, he determined to embark for Algiers and offer his services to the Dey." From New York in the spring of 1830, Jeffers said, he took "the Sally Ann, belonging to Bath, landed at Barcelona, crossed to Port Mahon [Mahón, on the Spanish island of Minorca], and endeavored to make his way to Algiers." (Another version had him pass through Gibraltar.) However, the French blockade kept him from that destination, though Jeffers would claim that he did make it to Tunis, toying with but finally rejecting the idea of making a desert crossing to the Dey's besieged city. While in Tunis, in the reporter's words, Jeffers "amused himself with contemplating the ruins of

Carthage, and reviving his recollections of her war with the Romans," a state-ment implying that Jeffers's education included some classical history. But he gave up any plans of making war on France, and his next stop was that coun-try's southern port of Marseilles. Jeffers's travels from here would eventually take him back to America and his last cruise, aboard a New Orleans brig called the *Vineyard*.[30]

9

The *Vineyard*'s Last Voyage

IT IS UNKNOWN WHEN HE FIRST used that particular alias, but when James Jeffers arrived in New Orleans in the fall of 1830 as a mere sailor on the *Lexington,* he was known to all on board as "Charles Gibbs." Two of his *Lexington* shipmates would play roles in the final act of his maritime career. One was Aaron Church, about whom little is known. A sharper picture exists of Robert Dawes, who gave the fullest account of their subsequent voyage together on the merchant brig *Vineyard.*[1]

Born in December 1812, Dawes was the son of a Lancaster, England, shoemaker. He was sandy haired and of below-average height; one observer described him as "a good looking young man." In 1826, aged thirteen and with his father's permission, he went to sea. Dawes first set foot in the United States in 1829, arriving aboard the Boston-based *Lagoda,* a 340-ton, 107-foot long, 26-foot broad ship built three years earlier in Scituate, Massachusetts. It routinely traveled between Boston, New Orleans, and Liverpool, and Dawes likely signed aboard in that English port. Dawes remembered it as being captained by one Bradford, but the name John Bradshaw appears in its registration documents.

Dawes left the *Lagoda* at Duxbury, Massachusetts, and must have come under somebody's wing there for he spent three months going to a Cape Cod school. Either the urge to go back to sea struck or else he had to get out of town quickly, for in the late summer or early fall of 1830 the seventeen-year-old signed aboard the aforementioned *Lexington* at the boy's rate of $8 per month. The *Lexington* followed the *Lagoda*'s same Boston-New Orleans-Liverpool route, and Jeffers may have joined it in either Boston or Liverpool.

However and wherever their voyages started, Jeffers, Church, and Dawes quit the *Lexington* together when it docked in New Orleans, apparently in late October. Dawes left—deserted actually—in part because of the low pay. The circumstances of Jeffers's and Church's departures are unrecorded, though the Louisiana port would have been a logical stop for Jeffers were he headed back to South America.

But the craft that Jeffers and his two *Lexington* shipmates joined there was the brig *Vineyard,* headed for Philadelphia. For Jeffers, the destination was far from both his old Caribbean pirate haunts and Buenos Aires where he had a child waiting. Moreover, he would again go as a seaman, paid $16 a month like Church and Dawes, the latter having earned a raise. A journalist in 1831 wondered why Jeffers, "who had been accustomed to command, should enter as a common sailor on board the *Vineyard.*" Jeffers explained "that he sought employment to assuage the horrors of reflection."[2]

Another reason suggests itself. The *Vineyard* was carrying a load of Mexican silver.

————————

It is unclear when Jeffers learned this, but his source was the then-twenty-two-year-old man with whom he ultimately shared the gallows, Thomas J. Wansley. According to an autobiographical account later attributed to Wansley, his mother's first husband was a sailor who fathered her first two children while they lived in New Bern, North Carolina. When he died, she moved to Delaware, apparently returning to the vicinity of her family. She and her sister, who were both white, later married or otherwise became pregnant by men of African heritage, Wansley's mother bearing several children in the relationship.

Born on December 8, 1807, as the eldest offspring of his mother's second marriage, Thomas Wansley went to work at a young age. He grew to be an admitted "seducer . . . gambler, and Sabbath-day breaker," and was also "undutiful to his mother," who was still alive at the time of the subsequent *Vineyard* trial. An observer deemed Wansley handsome, "a light mullatto" [*sic*] whose features "approach but little towards those which distinguish the African race." The description continued, "He is about five feet ten inches in height—his well knit limbs convey the idea of great personal strength, and I have no hesitation in saying that I have seen but few persons of any colour who to my mind bear a more striking resemblance to the statue of the Apollo Belvidere, which . . . has been considered as the most perfect model of manly beauty." His various jobs included work as a servant for a chaplain named McGlaughlin, who provided him with religious instruction, and about a year spent aboard the 74-gun USS *Delaware.* Wansley joined it in early 1828 in Norfolk, Virginia, and was paid off and discharged on February 6, 1830, in

Contemporary woodcut of Thomas J. Wansley, from The Confession of the Terrible Pirate Charles Gibbs. *Courtesy of the Harry Ransom Humanities Research Center, University of Texas at Austin*

the same port. The *Delaware*'s muster rolls and payrolls list Wansley as ordinary seaman, but he later said he had served as steward or servant to the *Delaware*'s purser, Silas Butler.[3]

Aboard ship, the steward was both privileged and isolated. Writing of life on merchant vessels, on which only the captain might have such a worker in his employ, Richard Henry Dana wrote, "The steward is the captain's servant, and has charge of the pantry, from which everyone, even the mate himself, is excluded. These distinctions usually find him an enemy to the mate, who does not like to have anyone on board who is not entirely under his control. The crew do not consider him as one of their number, so he is left to the mercy of the captain."[4]

Wansley would double as steward and deckhand while serving aboard the *Vineyard*. How he got from Norfolk to New Orleans between February and October 1830 is undocumented. But he knew former *Lexington*-hand Church from earlier travels to Boston, and it is possible that through him Wansley met Jeffers and Dawes.[5]

Built at Kennebunk, Maine, in 1822 and originally owned by Bostonian Tobias Lord, the *Vineyard* was brig-rigged with two masts, a single deck, and a square stern. Surviving registration data list it as 159 tons, 85 feet long, and 23 feet wide at its broadest point. In October 1829, Lord sold it to two other Bostonians, Francis Watts and Isaac C. Pray, who in turn sold it to a third man, George Callander (or Callender). When registering his vessel, the new owner listed its master as John Ward of Kennebunk.[6]

By early November 1830, when Wansley became the first crewman to sign on the *Vineyard* in New Orleans, its new master was William Thornber. Engaged to a woman who lived on New York City's John Street, Thornber was a freemason, as was his first mate William Roberts. For its next voyage, their brig would bring a load of cotton, sugar, and molasses to Philadelphia.

But another, more valuable cargo was coming. Not long after signing the brig's articles, steward-sailor Wansley helped bring aboard a consignment of fifty thousand Mexican silver dollars, then worth approximately the same as their American counterparts. Jointly insured by the Ocean and American insurance companies, the specie shipment was probably delivered on November 6, 1830, for a bill of lading of that date was introduced at the subsequent trial. Written by Thornber, whose handwriting was identified by a witness, it listed ten ironbound barrels, each holding five thousand dollar coins. The shipment belonged to Philadelphia businessman Stephen Girard and was destined for the United States Bank in that city. As the only crewman aboard at the time, Wansley stowed the heavy barrels inside a hatch located under a ladder, which had to be held back for the money compartment to be opened. Its exact location was never specified, but it was probably in the companion way that linked the captain's cabin with the quarterdeck, a place Thornber and Roberts could easily watch.

How and when Jeffers learned what Wansley knew is significant. Did he sign on the brig *because* of the money, Wansley's knowledge perhaps passed via mutual acquaintance Church? If so, then Jeffers's presence aboard, even as a common sailor, fits the swashbuckler he later claimed to be. But if only accident put him aboard a Philadelphia-bound brig carrying a small fortune, then the self-proclaimed former pirate chieftain, privateer, and Argentine naval officer was aimlessly drifting. Regardless, some *Vineyard* crewmen were ignorant of the silver on board until almost a week at sea. By that time, those who enlightened them of its existence also had a plan to take it.[7]

On or about November 7, 1830, Thornber and Roberts got the *Vineyard* off on what would be its last trip. Some molasses and cotton was stowed on deck, which also contained a hencoop and two boats: a longboat and a smaller yawl or "jolly boat," each equipped with a mast and sail. Jeffers later described the jolly boat as "being rather a stout boat of from 12 to 15 feet keel, painted black, with a white streak running on both sides six or eight inches below the gunnel [that is, gunwale]." The *Vineyard's* only arms were a few boarding pikes and a small cannon probably used as a signal gun.[8]

The plot to take the *Vineyard* developed quickly and Jeffers was involved from the start. Dawes first heard about the money and the conspiracy about six days into the journey, as he sat on deck crafting rigging pins. Nearby was sailor Henry or Harry Atwell (or Atwood) who, along with John Brownrigg and James Talbot, rounded out the *Vineyard*'s crew. Testimony during the trial assigned Atwell—Jeffers knew him as Harry Atwood—a prominent role in the mutiny, but as he did not survive the *Vineyard* episode he may have made a convenient target in court.

With Jeffers at the tiller, Wansley approached Dawes, sat down on a box, and told the young Englishman about the money. Atwell probably kept an eye out for Roberts, elsewhere on deck at the time. According to Dawes, "Wansley said he helped put the money away," the steward exaggerating the ten-barrel load into "fifteen or sixteen kegs." The conversation lasted an hour, Atwell testing Dawes by telling him they planned to kill Thornber and Roberts and take the money, enough to last the rest of their lives. Atwell, who Dawes believed to be the conspiracy's leader, justified the plan by telling him that "the captain and mate were both old men, that it was time for them to die, and that the mate was a peevish fellow." The plotters then told the uneasy Dawes to keep silent or be killed. Dawes agreed and stayed alive, but the conspirators treated him as a very junior partner. When they met on one side of the deck to make plans, they sent Dawes to stand in view of the captain. It was thought that having a sailor in sight would keep Thornber from thinking the entire watch was off plotting against him.[9]

Five of the brig's nine personnel—Atwell, Church, Dawes, Jeffers, and Wansley—now formed an uneasy faction against Captain Thornber and First Mate Roberts. Brownrigg and Talbot appear to have played no role in the mutiny, though both were sounded out about joining the conspiracy.

By his own account, Brownrigg was born in Cumberland, England, circa 1789, went to sea in 1802, and first visited America in 1817. His career included stints forced aboard three British warships (HMS *Gloucester*, HMS *Dreadnought*, and HMS *Thames*), each of which he deserted. He had come to New Orleans in 1830 via Savannah, where he had "left an English vessel." An observer described him as having "a rather heavy and lugubrious countenance, though expressive of a degree of honesty. . . . He is rather under the middle size, and muscular, has light hair and bushy whiskers, yet, in his general appearance, there is nothing to distinguish him from the usual ordinary seamen." His *Vineyard* shipmates called him "Jack" or "the old man," and he sometimes acted in capacity of second mate.[10]

That position was, according to Richard Henry Dana, "proverbially a dog's berth."

> He is neither officer nor man. He is obliged to go aloft to reef and furl the topsails, and to put his hands into the tar and slush with the rest, and the men do not much respect him as an officer. The crew call him the "sailor's waiter," as he has to furnish them with spun-yarn, marline and all other stuffs that they need in their work. He is one to whom little is given and of whom much is required. His wages are usually double those of a common sailor, and he eats and sleeps in the cabin; but he is obliged to be on deck nearly all his time, and eats at the second table, that is, makes a meal out of what the captain and chief mate leave.[11]

Although not enviable, the post still put Brownrigg in Thornber and Roberts's confidence, and Jeffers took care when baiting him. Brownrigg recalled an occasion when Jeffers approached him. "Jack," he said, "there is money in the ship." Brownrigg said he did not believe it. "Wansley told me so," Jeffers replied, "when I shipped on board the brig to go to Philadelphia." If Jeffers hinted at more, Brownrigg either did not understand it or else pretended not to comprehend. He insisted later he was unaware of the situation until the mutiny occurred. On Talbot's part, little is recorded about the man except that when approached, he took Brownrigg's line and tactfully said he did not believe the story of money being aboard.

As the plot progressed, Thornber and Roberts may have picked up some warning signs. Dawes recalled "a dispute between the captain, mate, and the men." He left its origins unstated, but noted that "the captain told Atwell if he did not be quiet, he would 'still' him—and he was going to flog the steward." The conspirators themselves were unsure about how to proceed. There were at least two aborted attempts at putting the mutiny into motion. Some asked whether Brownrigg and Talbot would need to be silenced as well. Dawes would testify that Jeffers was unenthusiastic about killing the captain and mate, something unexpected in a man who claimed such a violent past. Perhaps the reputed time spent in Argentine naval uniform changed his attitude toward those in authority.[12]

Yet Jeffers was indeed able to kill when the mutineers finally acted, at about 12:30 A.M. on Wednesday, November 24, as the *Vineyard* was plowing through a sudden squall off North Carolina's Cape Hatteras. All hands were on deck, with Dawes at the tiller steering north-northwest. Thornber and Roberts went below as the storm abated, but the captain came back up in response to Brownrigg's shout that the wind had shifted. Thornber ordered Church, Talbot, and Wansley aloft to further secure the yardarms, and he sent Brownrigg forward and aloft to repair starboard-side rigging that had broken in the rough weather.

Brownrigg stayed aloft and at work while Church, Talbot, and Wansley clambered down and joined Atwell and Jeffers aft. Thornber was about two paces from the tiller, illuminated by light emanating from inside the binnacle, the box or cabinet that housed the compass in view of the helmsman. That aboard the *Vineyard* appears to have had only a single lantern, and with Thornber standing nearby, Dawes called to Wansley to trim the lamp wick. Wansley approached, knife in hand.

Dawes later denied having summoned Wansley for any reason other than servicing the light. "I did not call him to give him an opportunity of killing the captain," Dawes maintained. "I knew he was to be on deck to lend a helping hand; [I] did'nt [sic] know he was to dispatch him." But he conceded knowing that the conspirators would kill Thornber and Roberts "if a convenient opportunity occurred" that night.

With Thornber's back to him, Wansley sensed the time was right. He trimmed the lamp, but instead of using the knife on his nearby target, Wansley picked up the heavy lever or brake from the ship's pump. Dawes guessed what was about to happen, but did not avert his eyes. "I looked, feeling some curiosity to see how a man looked when he was being killed," he later admitted.

The steward raised the lever and struck. But the rolling sea, or perhaps his own nerves, affected his aim. The blow missed the captain's head, landing instead on the back of Thornber's neck. The captain fell forward yelling "Oh" once or twice—despite the weather Brownrigg heard it high above the deck —then he added the cry of "Murder!"

Under the quarterdeck, in the captain's cabin, Roberts also heard Thornber's screams, and bellowed, "What is the matter?"

Wansley struck again and Thornber made no more noise. Jeffers and Wansley lifted the captain's body by its head and feet and heaved it overboard.[13]

————◆·┼┼·●————

In the immediate aftermath of the attack on Thornber, Talbot fled to the forecastle in panic while Roberts, at the other end of the *Vineyard*, charged minus his weather gear up the companion way. At the door to the quarterdeck he

A nineteenth-century illustrator's depiction of the mutiny aboard the Vineyard: *Wansley and Jeffers are throwing Captain Thornber's body overboard while Atwell and Church prepare to strike the mate, coming up from below; Dawes is at the tiller. From* The Pirates Own Book, *1859 edition. Courtesy of the Mariners' Museum, Newport News, Virginia*

met Atwell and Church, the second murder team. Atwell struck Roberts with a club—later indictments would allege that a hatchet was actually used—sending the mate reeling down the stairs wounded but ready to fight for his life.

In the cause of murder, Jeffers showed coolness and courage. Needing light to find their quarry, he grabbed the binnacle lantern and started down the companion way ladder, followed by Atwell and Church. Without light to see the compass, Dawes abandoned the tiller and looking down the hatchway the seventeen-year-old watched the fight underway in the eerily lit, claustrophobic passage.

With the *Vineyard* presumably rolling in rough water, Church yelled for someone to grab Roberts. When Jeffers succeeded in pinioning the mate, Atwell struck him again and Church soon joined in, one of the attackers wielding the same pump lever Wansley had used on Thornber. The mate cried out as the blows landed home, blood spattering on the ladder.

The beating continued after Roberts was dragged on deck, the mate at one point getting hold of Dawes's wrist in what the young man later described as a death grip. Eventually his assailants broke the mate loose and heaved him overboard. Roberts retained consciousness, and in court Dawes testified that the mate "swam after the ship as long as he could, shouting as loud as he was able." Then his pleas faded into the darkness, leaving only waves in the *Vineyard*'s wake.[14]

———————

Brownrigg remained aloft during the few minutes this took, hearing nothing after the captain's shout but the sound of canvas flailing. When he nervously came down he encountered Atwell, who told him, "Jack, we have taken charge." When Brownrigg asked where the captain and mate were, Atwell told him, "They are overboard."

The British navy veteran went aft and found the steward, who told him about the killings. Brownrigg later testified that "Wansley had a little tub of water, and a rag in it: he was wiping the blood up from off the quarter deck and the cabin ladder. He said he had heard it asserted that murdered blood could not be wiped up, but that he could wipe it up."

Now back at the tiller, Dawes was steering north-northeast as the other mutineers broke into Thornber's liquor supply. Invited for a drink, Brownrigg joined them briefly in sampling some grog. Someone asked about Talbot, and Atwell fetched him from the forecastle where he found him praying. On deck, Talbot exchanged a few words with Brownrigg. "Oh dear, Jack, what's this," Talbot said. "It's bad work."

"I don't know," Brownrigg replied. "Go down and take a glass of grog, I have just been down and got one." Talbot did so.

By now Atwell had found among the ship's papers a receipt for the shipment of Mexican coins, and Wansley revealed the money compartment's location. The steward held back the ladder while other hands opened the hatch and retrieved one of the kegs. Brownrigg was there long enough to see them knock off the barrel's top to inspect its contents. Then they put it back; the share-out would be done later. It may have been at about this time— drinks in hand, the killing done—that Jeffers told Dawes and Brownrigg that they and Talbot owed their lives to his control over the others. For his part, Wansley told Brownrigg that he (Wansley) had saved him and Talbot from Jeffers. Whatever Atwell's role in the conspiracy, to Brownrigg from this point the man he knew as Charles Gibbs was in command of the *Vineyard*.[15]

———————

A day later, on Thursday, November 25, the seven survivors divided the fifty thousand Mexican dollars equally between them. Nonconspirators Brownrigg and Talbot drew full one-seventh shares, presumably either to buy

Detail from a map of Long Island by John Calvin Smith, 1844. Courtesy of the Lionel Pincus and Princess Firyal Map Division, New York Public Library, Astor, Lenox, and Tilden Foundations

silence or ensure guilt by association. With Roberts's murder under his belt, Atwell especially intimidated Dawes, who was kept working hard on deck and aloft while many of the others stayed below drinking and eating the *Vineyard's* stock of nuts and oranges.

According to Dawes, before the division of spoils, Atwell asked him, "Bob, what are you going to do with your money?" When Dawes replied that he did not know, Atwell said the mutineers would "give me $1,000 to let them take my share." Likely frightened, Dawes agreed to this trade, a deal so bizarre that Atwell cautioned him not to mention it. But Dawes related the story to Jeffers, who he may have regarded as a protector.

"No, No," he quoted Jeffers as saying, "you must take your share."

When he received his portion—a seven-way split would have netted each about 7,140 Mexican dollars—Dawes stowed it in bags he and others made especially for the purpose, usually with a thousand of the silver coins in each.

Brownrigg put a portion of his money, about 170 Mexican dollars, into a money belt he crafted himself—the others made similar ones—and 900 more in what he called a "clothes bag." The mutineers also divided up about $40 of Thornber's own money; one conspirator got the captain's gold watch while Wansley took some of his clothing. From Cape Hatteras, Jeffers kept the *Vineyard* headed for New York. Why he opted for that destination was never revealed. But the mutineers said among themselves that they now had enough so they would never have to return to the sea for a living—and all a landsman's pleasures were for sale in New York.[16]

With Jeffers as master and Atwell as mate, the trip up the eastern seaboard passed without incident, the *Vineyard* meeting one vessel but not communicating with it. Yet Jeffers must have been aware of several potential problems onboard. According to Dawes, among the killers "one of them got drunk, and one became crazy." No further details emerged on this statement, but regarding the *Vineyard*'s rum supply, Brownrigg did testify that "we drank three or four bottles of grog, the remainder was thrown overboard." If an executive decision was made to jettison the rum, there must have been a serious reason. Another concern lay in the two nonmutineers Jeffers had argued against killing: Brownrigg and Talbot. The pair, Brownrigg later related, "privately agreed to discover the criminals as soon as they could get ashore and do it in safety." Dawes, who owed his life to Jeffers, would maintain that he, Brownrigg, and Talbot even spoke of trying to retake the *Vineyard*. Jeffers, who claimed to have served among pirates who left no witnesses, would have cause to regret leaving them alive.[17]

<hr />

Late on Monday, November 28, the crew spotted a lighthouse on eastern Long Island. An estimated fifteen miles from the shoreline—the exact point in relation to Long Island is unclear—Jeffers anchored the brig for the last phase of the *Vineyard*'s ill-fated cruise, which was ending under cloudy, moonless skies, and in rough water.

The men had divided into two groups, one for each of the *Vineyard*'s boats. Into the long boat went Jeffers, Brownrigg, Dawes, and Wansley with what must have been many pounds of Mexican dollars. Similarly laden, Atwell, Church, and Talbot took to the jolly boat. Since it could not be sold and its appearance would require explanation, the *Vineyard* had to be scuttled before the mutineers could think of the future. After launching both deck craft, the jolly boat's occupants maneuvered alongside. With an axe Atwell chopped at the waterline, but was unable to produce a suitable hole in the thick oak planking. Showing considerable trust in his companions in the long boat, Jeffers climbed back aboard, went below to the captain's cabin, and set the *Vineyard* ablaze. It was about midnight, going into Tuesday, November 29.

Only the men in the longboat had a compass, which meant those in the jolly boat would follow them. The wind increased and the seas became worse, and a trip that started slow became terrifying. The craft were separated by a half mile or more, and those in both boats struggled to keep from going over. Brownrigg would claim that in the long boat, despite the distance and the noise of waves and wind, he could hear the men in the distant jolly boat crying for help. Accounts and testimony differ as to whether those in the long boat actually saw the end of the jolly boat, but they were convinced it did indeed founder off the New York shore. It would later be found, according to the *New York Daily Advertiser,* "with a small sum of money in her."

With their companions apparently drowned and their own situation desperate, Brownrigg, Dawes, Jeffers, and Wansley began to lighten the craft. A chest containing clothes was probably the first thing overboard, but as the seas closed in, the occupants panicked and did the unthinkable: they began to jettison their load of heavy Mexican dollars.

How much was consigned to the deep? Assuming the four men had each kept their seventh of the original amount, the longboat contained more than twenty-eight thousand Mexican dollars when it set off from the burning, sinking *Vineyard.* Brownrigg would testify that "the greater part of it [the loot] was thrown into the sea to save the boat." His own losses included his self-made money belt, which Dawes in his terror threw overboard. When the long boat's occupants eventually staggered ashore, Brownrigg had only thirty-seven dollars left on his person and the nine hundred in the clothes bag. Exhausted and poorer by many thousands of ill-gotten silver coins, they would eventually bury, in Brownrigg's words, only "four or five thousand dollars."[18]

It is unclear exactly where the men came ashore. They rested until they spotted a hunter passing by in a small boat. The former *Vineyard* men told him that they were castaways from the brig *William,* with Jeffers identifying himself as its mate. The hunter told them they had landed on Pelican Island, but it was actually what contemporary maps called Pelican Beach, part of Barren Island, located inside the Jamaica Bay between the Brooklyn and Rockaway coasts (today attached to the New York mainland). In 1831 Barren Island was home to a man named Johnson, and the hunter directed them to his home, where the *Vineyard* survivors stayed overnight on Tuesday, November 29. Somewhere nearby they buried most of the remaining money, marking the spot with clothing that may have included Thornber's.

Brownrigg was becoming bolder, because when left alone with Johnson that night he—by Brownrigg's own version—"told him all about the affair of the ship." What he hoped to gain is unstated, and any response by Johnson is unrecorded. Next morning Johnson accompanied Wansley when he went to fetch clothing at the money cache. Then Johnson led or helped convey the four to Gravesend—they brought the *Vineyard*'s longboat with them—where he left his charges at a tavern run by Samuel Leonard. In return for his services, the sailors paid Johnson using eleven of the *Vineyard*'s Mexican dollar coins and an American five-dollar bill. They also gave him a sword cane and the *Vineyard*'s telescope, and Jeffers handed him the silver watch that had belonged to William Roberts.[19]

Besides the landlord himself, there were two men present at Samuel Leonard's place when the *Vineyard* sailors arrived on Tuesday, November 30. Brownrigg, Dawes, and Wansley settled into the barroom while Jeffers, who the innkeeper later identified as Charles Gibbs, arranged transportation from Gravesend to Brooklyn. According to Leonard's later testimony, Jeffers agreed to pay $3 for the group to get a ride there in Leonard's wagon.

The negotiations took long enough for Brownrigg to down three glasses of grog and turn feisty. He later denied that the alcohol had affected him, and it may have been that with others around—several more people entered the tavern after the *Vineyard* shipmates came in—his fear of the mutineers waned. Whatever the reason, when Jeffers said they would be leaving soon, Brownrigg refused to come along.

"You may go on as soon as you have a mind to," Brownrigg said loudly enough for Leonard and probably everybody else present to hear. "You have murdered the captain and mate and I will go no further with murderers."

Jeffers, whose feelings can be imagined, responded by telling Leonard that Brownrigg was drunk, adding, "Don't mind him." The innkeeper feigned agreement. But he managed to tell one Robert Greenwood, who was either an employee or a customer, to go for the law.

Jeffers must have sensed danger, for a few minutes later he asked Leonard to step outside with him. Leonard agreed, but wary of this customer especially, he beckoned for others to accompany him. Once outside, Jeffers upped his offer for transportation. If Leonard would take them immediately to Brooklyn, Jeffers would give him $100, a sum that betrayed Jeffers's panic.

Again the landlord agreed, but Leonard also said that he had to wait for the return of his son, sent out earlier for a basket of eggs. "I said this to gain time till the arrival of the squire," he later explained in court, by which he apparently meant the local lawman.

Indeed, the squire arrived shortly after, accompanied by Greenwood now armed with a pistol. Wansley fled, but with Leonard's help the pair arrested Brownrigg, Dawes, and Jeffers. None offered any resistance; Leonard felt a need to tie up Jeffers but not the other two.

Soon after, Greenwood caught up with Wansley in some nearby woods. According to his later testimony, Greenwood told Wansley that "there was such a complaint against him, and that he must go before the squire." Wansley was unenthusiastic at the idea, but the armed Greenwood was persuasive. "I will not detain you long," he told his captive, "and if you can clear yourself of the charge, we want nothing with you."[20]

———————

Leonard and Greenwood helped convey the prisoners from the Gravesend tavern to the jail at Flatbush, where keeper Peter P. Whykoff relieved the *Vineyard* crew members of some of their belongings. Wansley, whose name was initially recorded as Thomas Williams, was wearing a money belt containing 259 Mexican dollars and had a few additional dollars and smaller coins in his pockets. Brownrigg had about ten dollars left in his clothing. The next day, Wednesday, December 1, Leonard swore out a complaint before King's County magistrates Elias Hubbard Jr. and John Terhune, relating Brownrigg's outburst at his tavern and the references to murder at sea. Brownrigg was then deposed, and he gave an account of what had happened since the *Vineyard* left New Orleans.

Brownrigg's testimony caused the others to collapse, momentarily at least. Someone asked Whykoff for a Bible—the request probably came from Wansley, who appears to have been the most religious of the three. One was provided, and the prisoners were reported to have been "reading or praying nearly all of Wednesday [December 1] night." That Wansley feared the game was up became clear in his conversations with Whykoff. The jailer later testified that while in his brief care the steward seemed depressed. Wansley discussed not only a fear of drowning, Whykoff claimed, but also volunteered "that his master often told him that he was born to be hanged, and it was very likely he would be."

Wansley's fears came closer to reality at 10:30 A.M. the next morning (December 2), when Dawes began a two-hour long statement before Hubbard and Terhune. His remarks supported Brownrigg's version of events and included details of the *Vineyard* conspiracy, in which Dawes maintained he had been a very unwilling participant. He described Wansley striking down Captain Thornber, then throwing his body overboard with aid from Charles Gibbs. Of the latter, he told how he aided Atwell and Church once they had wounded the mate, Roberts, but failed to kill him outright.

Wansley's own questioning before Hubbard and Terhune followed. He refused an offer of legal representation, maintaining, in a reporter's words, that "all the counsel he wanted was conscience." While Wansley acknowledged telling the others about the money on the *Vineyard*, he admitted little about his own role in the murders. He refused to say who threw the bodies overboard, for example, or who commanded the brig after the mutiny. Many of his answers were ambiguous; some seemed self-defeating. Admitting only to having witnessed the captain's murder, Wansley said he did not go to his assistance because Thornber did not call for him. Wansley was apparently still being questioned when U.S. Marshal Thomas Morris interrupted the proceedings. He carried a court order to have the prisoners taken to New York City proper, to be housed in the Bridewell prison.[21]

<hr>

Any reaction by Jeffers—whose examination was postponed—to Dawes and Wansley's remarks went unrecorded. But observers were startled to see Wansley smiling during the hearing. As for Dawes, the same journalist who found him "well dressed and his personal appearance altogether in his favor," noted that the young Englishman also exhibited "an air of *sang froid*—an unfeeling levity in his demeanor, which was truly surprising." The suspects also showed signs of fatalism. Being readied for the trip to Bridewell, one unnamed prisoner asked when they would be tried. The onlooker's curt answer—that it would be just before they were hanged—elicited no response: "To the reply they merely silently assented as a matter of no importance."

Their police escort consisted of officers Henry W. Merritt, who was also Bridewell's deputy keeper, and William F. Stephenson. Wansley asked Stephenson to help recover items left behind at Johnson's and Leonard's houses, the collection including clothing marked with Thornber's name. It is unrecorded if they, or Johnson, retrieved the buried cash, but insurance agents found no money when they later visited the cache site. It is unclear how much was ever actually recovered. The two policemen also formally interviewed Wansley, who according to Merritt kept talking of the incident even after all had crowded into a carriage bound for Bridewell. During the ride, as Wansley told his story, he was "occasionally prompted by Gibbs." It is possible to see Jeffers trying to lead Wansley's incriminating ramble into safer directions, but he acknowledged having had a role in the attack on Roberts.

For the moment, the pair declared Brownrigg guiltless. However, a newspaper cited Merritt stating that both Jeffers and Wansley "averred . . . that the boy, Robert Dawes, aided and assisted in the scheme, and helped to throw Capt. Thornby [*sic*] overboard." Perhaps it was at this point that Dawes—so Merritt would later testify—"protested his innocence." Wansley rebuked him. "Bob," Wansley said, "God knows you have got enough to answer for."[22]

10

"Adjudged a pirate and a felon"

DAWES, JEFFERS, AND WANSLEY APPEAR to have arrived at the Bridewell prison late on December 2, 1830. The next afternoon they were brought individually to the Pine Street office of Judge Samuel Rossiter Betts, who would sit on their trial on federal charges, to be heard by the U.S. Circuit Court for the Southern District of New York.

Then about forty-four, Betts was a Massachusetts native and Williams College graduate who had studied law in New York and been admitted to the bar there in 1809. Following War of 1812 army service, he was elected to Congress but declined reelection in 1817 to go back into the legal profession. Described as genial, logical, and hard-working, Betts became a New York judge in 1823; three years later President John Quincy Adams elevated him to the federal bench. He would serve the circuit court for New York's southern district for more than four decades. Betts' interest in maritime law ensured the *Vineyard* trial would take place under the eyes of a man later acknowledged as an expert in the field.

During their examination before Betts, the three prisoners "were duly and fully cautioned, as to their situation." With Dawes and Wansley adding nothing to their statements, Jeffers, still known as Charles Gibbs, was formally questioned for the first time. Perhaps with an eye on the sensation already brewing in the local press, the judge directed the journalists present to refrain from publishing any details Gibbs mentioned about the murders themselves. They followed his request, printing little besides Jeffers's description of the jolly boat, which was then being looked for along the New York coast. Betts was quoted telling Wansley "that his case seemed a pretty hopeless one, and that the trials would take place in a few days."[1]

*Samuel R. Betts, circa 1853.
Courtesy of the Collection of
the New-York Historical
Society, Image 78570d*

In reality, they would not begin for four months. Until then the suspects
would stay in the Bridewell prison. It had been built in 1775 a short distance
west of city hall, which housed the district's courtrooms. It was "a cheerless,
graystone edifice, two stories high, with basement, [and] a front and rear
pediment."[2]

The *Vineyard* suspects would receive lawyers only on the eve of trial, so
there was plenty of time for anxiety and a lack of counsel to affect their men-
tal state. By February the prisoner known as Charles Gibbs was seeking a
well-positioned legal confidante via Henry Merritt, the deputy keeper. Of
Merritt, a little survives in New York City records. Common Council Minutes from June 24, 1822, note that Henry W. Merritt, then a clerk living on
Chatham Street, was appointed a fireman in Fire Engine Company No. 15.
He resigned from the fire department about three years later, on July 18,
1825. His police career may have begun at that date.[3]

It is unclear what, if anything, Jeffers told Merritt about his maritime
past. But the approaching impanelment of a grand jury to hear the *Vineyard*
case probably sparked his February remark to Merritt that he wanted to talk
privately to a judge.

The official charged with prosecuting Jeffers and the others, District Attorney James A. Hamilton, was about a year younger than Betts and equally eminent. A Columbia University graduate and third son of Alexander Hamilton, he was, like his famous father, gifted and politically well connected. Later described as "facile, smooth-tongued and ambitious," James Hamilton had grown up amid his country's founders—his obituary would observe that he "had seen President Washington, and knew all the mythology of the heroes of the Revolution by heart." In 1829 President Andrew Jackson made Hamilton acting secretary of state for a few months and subsequently appointed him to the New York position in which he would try the *Vineyard* suspects.[4]

On Wednesday, March 2, the grand jury began returning a series of indictments in the *Vineyard* case. The "true bills," each bearing the required endorsement from jury foreman Hector Craig, provided the basis for trying Charles Gibbs, Dawes, and Wansley for the murder of Thornber and Roberts, as well as crimes such as mutiny, stealing cargo, destroying a vessel, and "robbery on the high seas"—in other words, piracy. The grand jury accepted the idea of a larger conspiracy, for Henry Atwell/Atwood, otherwise presumed drowned, was among those indicted for Roberts' murder. At 11 A.M. the next day—Thursday, March 3—with Judge Betts presiding, the three *Vineyard* mutineers pleaded not guilty to each count. Only now did the trio receive lawyers, Betts appointing two for each defendant. Wansley received Henry E. Davies and Charles C. King; the latter would be replaced by N. B. Blunt. Dawes was represented by Robert H. Morris and L. Sherwood. Still using the Charles Gibbs alias, Jeffers was assigned Joseph H. Patten and Seth P. Staples. Jury selection was to start Monday. The attorneys had the rest of Thursday and exactly three more days to prepare their clients' defenses.[5]

———◆•❖•◆———

Merritt by now had relayed Jeffers's request for a conference with a judge to police magistrate James Hopson. Born circa 1773, Hopson now lived at a Vandewater Street address, where he would remain until his death in 1854, aged eighty-one. An 1831 directory listed him as one of three police court judges. New York then had about two hundred thousand inhabitants, and a report for 1833 itemizes the crimes of about three thousand people "committed to the City Prison and Bridewell" over that year, more than one-third for assault and battery. To deal with what was likely an expanding workload a fourth judge appears in an 1835 register, at which time Hopson was still hearing police cases.[6]

Police magistrates were appointed by the city's Common Council, and, in a modern historian's words, "issued warrants, arraigned suspects, granted bail, and in lieu of bail committed arrested individuals to jail pending trial." An 1872 description of New York City police court business might still convey an idea of Hopson's workday when he met James Jeffers: "The business at the Police Courts . . . is dispatched with wonderful rapidity. . . . The Justice hears the charge of the officer, the explanation of the prisoner, and decides without counsel or jury whether he shall be discharged, fined, or detained for trial at the Court of Sessions. The vast majority of all arrested are discharged after spending a night in the station-house."[7]

The veteran jurist visited Jeffers on Sunday, March 6, 1831, the day before the trial was to start, and to him Jeffers made his initial revelations about his criminal past (detailed in this book's introductory chapter). Jeffers's request that Hopson keep their talk secret, should he be cleared in the *Vineyard* case, reflected remarkable optimism or naïveté. Against him stood not only Brownrigg's anticipated testimony but also the earlier statements of Dawes and Wansley, as well as Jeffers's and Wansley's own remarks to Merritt and Stephenson. Then there was Dawes himself.

Police officials took Dawes and Wansley from Bridewell to nearby city hall, which housed the room assigned the Circuit Court, at about 10 A.M. on Monday, March 7. Robert Greenwood had already helped transport the *Vineyard*'s longboat from Gravesend Cove to a location on South Street. It was on hand presumably to serve as evidence in the trial, scheduled to begin at 11 A.M. As that hour approached city hall was packed with citizens hoping to watch the proceedings. Given the crowd size, officials decided to hold the trial in the larger room reserved for the Superior Court. When Judge Betts took his seat and the doors were opened, the throng burst inside, some fighting for a place to sit. Betts's first order of business was to deal with a spectator, William T. Boyle, who struck an officer trying to restrain him in the rush. Betts sent Boyle off in police custody, his case referred to another venue.[8]

The court would first try Wansley for Thornber's murder. Seated near his attorneys, he watched closely while jurors were impaneled. Betts told press representatives that while they might publish verdicts, they should refrain from printing details that could influence jurors selected for future trials related to the *Vineyard* affair. The *Journal of Commerce* described this as an "injunction," but no reference to a formal order appears in the court minutes. The same document lists potential jurors called, a dozen of whom were finally sworn.[9]

New York City Hall, site of the courtroom where Jeffers and Wansley were tried. Courtesy of the Picture Collection, Branch Libraries, New York Public Library, Astor, Lenox, and Tilden Foundations

The trial began with the borrowed Superior Court venue filled to capacity with onlookers. Hamilton opened the proceedings by establishing the legal basis for the charges set forth in the indictment. He explained that the circumstances of the case against Wansley—and Jeffers as well—involved "willful, deliberate murder on the high seas." A prisoner being so-convicted, he said, would be "adjudged a pirate and a felon, and should suffer death." His first witness, Brownrigg, detailed the *Vineyard* mutiny and the subsequent trip to the New York coastline. The published transcript of his testimony makes him—and other witnesses—appear to ramble, probably because the writer tracked answers but not the questions that prompted them. Wansley, sullen but composed, looked on as his attorney Blunt put up a fight on his behalf. Judging from Brownrigg's replies, the cross-examination first tried to paint Brownrigg as a willing participant for having received a share; then assailed his credibility, by challenging impressions of happenings on deck gleaned while aloft on a stormy night. Any points Blunt scored may have dissolved when Hamilton followed Brownrigg with a surprise witness: Dawes. The young Englishman's appearance against him may have come as a shock to Wansley. The co-defendants had, a journalist noted, "appeared to be engaged in conversation about different matters, while the preliminary arrangements were making," but nothing unusual had been noted.[10]

Decades later, Hamilton detailed the circumstances behind the move to enlist Dawes for the prosecution. According to his *Reminiscences,* "The evidence of guilt [that is, Brownrigg's anticipated testimony and the various statements made months earlier] was not so full as to insure a conviction, unless one of these parties should be made State's evidence, which would discharge such one from trial." It fell to Hamilton to decide whom to offer a deal. After much deliberation, "I selected the boy as the witness, as probably the least guilty."[11]

Now the eighteen-year-old Dawes went from the prisoners' dock to the witness stand to speak freely as a member of the conspiracy itself. Amplifying points Brownrigg had established, he gave his eyewitness account of Wansley's attack on Thornber using the pump lever. He named Wansley the captain's sole assailant, observing that "no one else struck him." As to the immediate aftermath, Dawes suddenly pulled his punches. The previous December, he had told justices Hubbard and Terhune that "Charles Gibbs and the cook seized the captain, one by the head and the other by the heels, and threw him overboard." But now in court he said: "I do not know whether Wansley helped to throw him overboard; two persons did it."[12]

The assertion that Jeffers and Wansley heaved the captain over the side was made some other way during the proceedings, for later newspaper summaries of the evidence included this point. Dawes was in fact giving evidence while still a prisoner facing charges on capital crimes. Reporters "understood the district attorney intends to enter a *nolle prosequi*" (a dropping of charges) on all indictments on Dawes's behalf, but that would wait a day.[13]

What happened next in court may have convinced Hamilton that he had been right to make a deal with Dawes. Hamilton tried to enter into evidence the defendants' statements made before Hubbard and Terhune, but after hearing from the magistrates themselves and Flatbush jail keeper Peter Whykoff, Betts ruled that Wansley's had to be excluded. (The reason for this is unrecorded in the published transcript.) Hamilton patiently followed with witnesses who recounted the arrest at Gravesend and its aftermath: tavern owner Samuel Leonard; Robert Greenwood, who captured Wansley at gunpoint; and policemen Henry Merritt and William Stephenson, with whom Wansley and Jeffers chatted damagingly during the ride from Flatbush to Bridewell.[14]

As the case progressed, Wansley—who did not testify in his own defense —remained visibly calm and frequently conferred with his lawyers. His attorney Henry Davies, only twenty-six but destined to be a distinguished judge himself, cross-examined Dawes. To judge from the recorded responses

Davies tried to establish that Wansley participated in the mutiny only out of fear of Atwell.

While there is no record of closing statements by Hamilton or Wansley's lawyers, the published transcript paraphrases Betts directly addressing the jury: "Most of the evidence was recapitulated and commented upon, and the inquiry which the Jury were left to make, was First, whether there had been a murder committed on the high seas; Secondly, whether the prisoner was concerned in it or not?"

So instructed, they needed only twenty minutes to find Wansley guilty of Thornber's murder. Observers disagreed on how he took the news. To one, he "appeared to receive the verdict with perfect indifference." Another felt that "when the verdict was given he appeared slightly moved." A third described Wansley as agitated, noting that he "trembled visibly when he rose to hear the verdict of the Jury."[15]

Aware of Wansley's verdict, Jeffers's tension showed in varying degrees as proceedings against him for Roberts's murder began at 11 A.M. on Tuesday, March 8. By one account, Jeffers "appeared to be much agitated previous to, and during the progress of the trial." Another journalist wrote that "the iron visage of Gibbs was occasionally darkened with a transient emotion, but he had evidently abandoned all hope of escape, and sat the greater part of the time with his hands between his knees, calmly surveying the scene before him."[16]

After the jury was sworn, Hamilton first called U.S. Marshal Thomas Morris, whose recorded remarks in front of the still closely packed courtroom simply established the prisoner's admissions as to his native state and age. Morris gave Jeffers's age as thirty but other sources would establish it as thirty-two. Hamilton then called Dawes to the witness stand, simultaneously entering the *nolle prosequi* on the prisoner's behalf. Dawes began by again recounting Thornber's murder, and then shifted to the attack on Roberts. He testified as to having seen the man he knew as Gibbs take the binnacle lantern to use in the search below decks for the wounded man, and that he looked down the companion way hatch long enough to see the prisoner hold Roberts while Atwell and Church administered a beating. After Roberts was dragged on deck and pitched overboard, Dawes said, "Charles Gibbs then navigated the vessel, he being the only person on board who understood navigation."[17]

Under cross-examination by Jeffers's attorney Seth Staples, Dawes recounted his going to sea and how he came to sign aboard the *Vineyard*.

Staples pressed him on how he came to leave the *Lexington* in New Orleans to join the *Vineyard*. "I left the ship because I was not well treated, and did not get wages enough—had only eight dollars a month," Dawes replied. Staples then asked Dawes if he had not, in fact, run away from the *Lexington*. Dawes replied: "I left her, in plain sailing then I ranaway." Jeffers had almost certainly supplied this point. Staples may have used it to muddy Dawes's character.

Dawes's subsequent responses still affirmed Jeffers's guilt but also painted a complex picture of him. Holding Atwell to be the ringleader, Dawes noted that Jeffers limited the killing to the captain and mate, sparing himself and nonparticipants Brownrigg and Talbot. Moreover, Dawes called Jeffers "down-hearted about killing," and added that "he [Jeffers] did not like to do it." He also told the story of Atwell bullying him about giving over his share in return for a thousand dollars, and how the defendant told him to stand his ground.[18]

Brownrigg followed Dawes on the stand, again recounted the facts of the mutiny, and observed how the accused claimed to have intervened to save Brownrigg's life. Again in cross-examination Staples pressed the witness on his history of running away from vessels; Brownrigg admitted to having deserted several British ships but insisted he had been impressed onto each. When policeman-jailer Merritt testified, he made no mention of any of Jeffers's autobiographical remarks made in Bridewell, but detailed that in the carriage on the way from Flatbush to Bridewell "Gibbs said he and the mate had a scuffle." Merritt's colleague Stephenson recalled more damning words: "Gibbs said he dragged the mate out of the cabin, with the assistance of another person."[19]

<hr />

As with Wansley's trial, the accused did not testify, nor did Jeffers's lawyers call witnesses on their client's behalf. Accounts of the closing arguments have survived. For the defense Joseph H. Patten, whose office was located on Pine Street, began by broadly attacking the testimony from Dawes and Brownrigg, calling the jurors' attention "to the circumstances under which the former had been admitted a witness against Gibbs and Wansley." Patten claimed "there were no facts directly charging this man with the murder. There was not one fact against him but what might be reasonably accounted for." He told the jurors that "if they doubted the credibility of the witnesses, as they could not help doing . . . they were bound to acquit him." But the bulk of Patten's recorded argument on Jeffers's behalf centered on the theme of guilt—that of the jurors if they returned the wrong finding. Conviction would mean death, he noted, and should their guilty verdict be undeserved "they would themselves become the murderers."[20]

In contrast, Jeffers's other attorney, the fifty-four-year-old Staples, a Yale graduate and direct descendant of Miles Standish of *Mayflower* fame, focused on evidence and interpretation. Staples's strategy seems to have been to try to shift a larger share of the blame for the *Vineyard* mutiny on the steward—"a coloured man by the name of Wansley, who has since been convicted in being the actor in this scene, who appeared from the beginning to the end to have taken a very conspicuous part." Staples argued that his client was at most an unwilling conspirator, not to be put in the same category as Wansley, already bound for the gallows; and Atwell and Church, both beyond calling. Nor, Staples charged, had Dawes "said one word that would implicate Gibbs in acquiescing to the proposal to murder the officers of the ship." Then he posed a rhetorical question that is intriguing given the background Jeffers claimed: "Would Gibbs, being conscious that he was an actor in the affair, and one of the conspirators, have come to New-York? Would he have ran [*sic*] into the jaws of the enemy? Why, no, he would have made for one of the West India Islands, burnt the vessel and got off with the money." After Hamilton summed up for the prosecution, the case went to the jury at 9:45 P.M. Two and a half hours later—at a quarter past midnight on Wednesday, March 9—they returned a guilty finding. "Several hundred persons remained to learn the result," a reporter wrote, and Jeffers "was evidently affected on hearing the verdict."[21]

When proceedings resumed at 11 A.M. that day, Wansley's attorney Blunt moved for arrest of judgment, which would prevent sentencing from going forward. Hamilton spoke in opposition and Betts ruled against Blunt's motion. The judge then approved Hamilton's motion that Wansley and the prisoner still known as Charles Gibbs be sentenced Friday. The guilty verdicts on capital charges, coupled with the dropping of charges against Dawes, dissuaded Hamilton from pursuing the other indictments, and Betts lifted his request that the newspapers refrain from publishing testimony. The Thursday, March 10, *Journal of Commerce* summarized the *Vineyard* trial and its findings, observing that "the evidence of the guilt of the prisoners was full and conclucive [*sic*]."[22]

On Friday, March 11, Betts opened court at 11:30 A.M. The first item concerned one Bartimeus Colburn, convicted the day before of larceny. Betts deferred passing sentence for now and remanded Colburn to prison. Despite his destination, Colburn may have left with a song in his heart compared to Wansley and Jeffers, whose sentencing hearings followed his.[23]

Betts asked the former steward if there was any reason why he should not suffer death for the crime for which he had been convicted. Wansley took out a prepared statement and in a steady voice began to read it. Beginning with, "I will say a few words, but it is perhaps of no use," half-African Wansley accused the court of racism.

Coming in 1831, this defense strategy seems ahead of its time. Yet Wansley did not argue that he was innocent; merely that neither was Dawes, with whom the prosecution made a deal. He also took a shot at Brownrigg going free, contradicting his statement on the ride from Flatbush affirming the man's innocence. Said Wansley:

> I have often understood that there is a great deal of difference in respect of color, and I have seen it in this Court. Dawes and Brownrigg were as guilty as I am, and these witnesses have tried to fasten upon me greater guilt than is just; for their life has been given to them. You have taken the blacks from their own country, to bring them here to treat them ill—I have seen this.
>
> The witnesses, the jury, and the prosecuting Attorney consider me more guilty than Dawes—to condemn me, for otherwise the law must have punished him; he should have had the same verdict, for he was a perpetrator in the conspiracy.
>
> Not withstanding my participating, they have sworn falsely for the purpose of taking my life . . . they had the biggest part of the money, and have sworn falsely.

Wansley stopped, saying "I have said enough—I will say no more." But Betts invited him to continue. Wansley, who continued to pin the idea of mutiny on Atwell, stressed that "the conspiracy was known to the whole company, and had I informed, my life would have been taken . . . so I did not inform."

Despite this argument, his next words were a confession. "I have committed murder," Wansley said, "and I know I must die for it." He fell silent. Betts said, "If you wish to add any thing further you will still be heard." Wansley replied, "No Sir, I believe I have said enough."[24]

———◆••◆———

James Jeffers now came before Betts, who as with Wansley asked the prisoner if he had anything to say before sentence was passed. Jeffers responded with his version of the conspiracy story. Like Wansley, he carried himself well and spoke clearly and firmly. Also like Wansley, he now assigned Brownrigg and Dawes more active roles.

> It was off Tortugas that Atwell first told me there was money on board, and proposed to me to take possession of the brig. I refused at that time. The conspiracy was talked of for some days, and at last I agreed that I would join. Brownrigg, Dawes, Church and the whole agreed that they would. A few days after, however, having thought of the affair, I mentioned to Atwell what a dreadful thing it was to take a man's life, and commit piracy—and recommended him to "abolish" their plan.

In speaking of murder and piracy, was Jeffers acknowledging familiarity with the subjects? Even so, he claimed that he had "told Atwell that if ever he would speak of the subject again, I would break his nose." But he conceded lacking the character to hold to this: "Had I kept to my resolution I would not have been brought here to receive my sentence."

In Jeffers's version of events, "Brownrigg agreed to call up the Captain from the cabin, and [Wansley] agreed to strike the first blow. The Captain was struck and I suppose killed, and I lent a hand to throw him overboard. But for the murder of the mate, of which I have been found guilty, I am innocent—I had nothing to do with that. The mate was murdered by Dawes and Church."

Having arguably admitted to an accessory role in the murder of Thornber, Jeffers was adamant that he was blameless in that of Roberts. He finished with: "That I am innocent of this I commit my soul to that God who will judge all flesh—who will judge all murderers and false swearers, and the wicked who deprive the innocent of his right."[25]

Assured Jeffers had nothing to add, Betts remarked that neither man had said anything to dissuade him from sentencing them to death. He dismissed Wansley's racism argument, and he told Jeffers that even if he had not fatally struck the mate, he had done nothing to prevent the man's murder. If they had not been convicted on murder indictments, he said, they would surely have been found guilty on others that also warranted the death penalty.

There was more admonition directed at the pair, who Betts noted "now stand here [as] convicted murderers and pirates." But the essential detail of his sentencing was that the two would hang on April 22, between 10 A.M. and 3 P.M. Their bodies would be given to a medical college for experimentation.

Wansley wept. Jeffers was indifferent. He had already told his handlers he would not allow himself to be hanged.[26]

11

The Arch-Pirate Emerges

I T HAD BEEN WITHIN JUDGE BETTS's power at the March 11 sentencing to schedule immediate execution for Jeffers and Wansley. But Betts gave them several more weeks of life—until April 22—his stated intention being to allow the prisoners to prepare themselves spiritually for death. He cautioned that they should not "indulge in the slightest hope or expectation that the sentence can be revoked." That Betts was not a sadist can be seen in one of his actions in the 1840s. Still sitting in the Southern District of New York, he successfully solicited President James K. Polk to pardon a young postal carrier, James Bilyou, awaiting sentencing for mail theft. Betts wanted to spare Bilyou, apparently mentally disabled, a criminal record. But in passing judgment on Jeffers and Wansley in 1831, he dwelled on a vision of the pair suffering psychologically. "You will think it is a dreadful thing to die," he told the condemned killers at one point, adding that each would expire "in the prime of your manhood, without a friend to pity or console you, without one to shed a tear over you . . . on the public scaffold." The time allotted each was solely to "afford you an opportunity of consulting with pious men, who will no doubt converse and condole with you."[1]

As the execution date drew closer, clergymen would indeed be visiting Jeffers's and Wansley's cells. But by then a larger story than the *Vineyard* mutiny was making the rounds.

The Saturday, March 12, *Journal of Commerce* reported the sentencing hearing's details. It closed with two elements not previously reported: that "Charles Gibbs" was an alias and that the man's pre-*Vineyard* past involved privateering.

We are credibly informed that Gibbs is not the real name of the prisoner who passes by that name. He admits this, and further states, that he formerly commanded a Buenos Ayrean privateer, in which he made several cruises. During the last Spring he took passage for Gibraltar, and thence for Algiers, in the hope of procuring a situation on board some of their corsairs; but he found it impossible to elude the vigilance of the French blockading squadron, and proceeded to Tunis. His attempt was unsuccessful there, and he was compelled to return to Gibraltar. He sailed then for Boston, and afterwards to New-Orleans, where he shipped as one of the crew of the *Vineyard*.[2]

As yet there was no mention of Caribbean pirating. The writer's source was probably Henry Merritt, though Jeffers's sole confidante regarding his piratical career may still have been police magistrate James Hopson. The court having convicted Jeffers, the conditions had been met whereby Hopson could do what he wished with Jeffers's March 6 confession. The judge consulted with Amos Butler, a Murray Street resident then about fifty-two, who was proprietor of the Wall Street–based *Mercantile Advertiser*. He asked Hopson to question Jeffers about specific lost vessels.[3]

On Saturday, March 19, Hopson returned to Bridewell with Butler's list, which focused on losses between 1822 and 1829. In most cases Jeffers provided no information. But he acknowledged that he had robbed the Providence-based *Providence*, sparing its crew because of their Rhode Island connection. He also volunteered secondhand knowledge about Dutch vessels taken in 1822 while heading for Curaçao.

Upon leaving, Hopson promised to come back in a few days. He presumably again conferred with Butler and others, who must have deemed the man's story incredible. When Hopson visited Jeffers on Wednesday, March 23—by which time the convicted pair had been moved to the Bellevue prison—he told Jeffers he had doubts about his truthfulness. Brandishing his earlier list of the craft Jeffers claimed to have personally assisted in robbing and in some cases destroying, he asked the prisoner to repeat the details. Hopson presumably did this thinking inconsistencies in the two lists would reveal Jeffers as a liar. Those that were subsequently published are conveyed in tables 1 and 2.

The *Jane* of Liverpool is missing from Jeffers's second list, on which the hailing port of the *William* has shifted from Salem to New York. Jeffers was presumably not referring to the *William Dawson* of New York, which in the first list he recalled boarding and allowing to proceed. He did not mention the *William Dawson*'s vessel type, but records show that a ship by that name,

Table 1: Jeffers's March 6, 1831, list of captures

Vessel Name	Type	Where taken or sailing from	Nationality or Hailing port	Cargo/items stolen	Notes[4]
Jane	Brig		Liverpool	Dry goods	"Crew destroyed, vessel burnt"
	Brig	"from the Spanish Maine [*sic*]"	New York	Money	"Crew destroyed, vessel burnt"
Belvidere	Brig	Gulf of Mexico	Boston		"Crew and vessel destroyed"
	Brig	Gulf of Mexico	French	Money	"Crews and vessels destroyed"
	Brig	Gulf of Mexico	French	Money	
Providence	Ship		Providence	$10,000	"suffered to pass, as Examinant could not consent to destroy his own townsmen"
William	Ship		Salem	Dry goods and money	"Crew and vessel destroyed"
Dido	Bark		Bremen	Dry goods	"Vessel and crew destroyed"
Larkin	Bark		London	Dry goods	"Vessel and crew destroyed"
	Brig		Genoa	Plate, gilt-edge paper, 20–30 pianofortes	
William Dawson	Ship		French New York	Wine	"vessel and crew destroyed" "boarded her and let her pass"
Earl of Moria	Ship		London	Dry goods and money	"Vessel and crew destroyed"

Table 1: Jeffers's March 6, 1831, list of captures (*continued*)

Vessel Name	Type	Where taken or sailing from	Nationality or Hailing port	Cargo/items stolen	Notes
Indispensable	Ship		London	Dry goods and money	"Vessel and crew destroyed"
	Ship	"from Curaçao bound to Holland"	Dutch	Plate	"destroyed the vessel, and all on board except a young girl"
Caroline	Ship	Cape Antonio	American	Dry goods	Recaptured by USS *Enterprise*

Table 2: Jeffers's March 23, 1831, list of captures

Vessel Name	Type	Where taken or sailing from	Nationality or Hailing port	Cargo/items stolen	Year	Notes[5]
William	Brig		New York			"vessel and crew destroyed"
Larkin	Bark		London			"do" [ditto]
Belvedere [sic]	Brig		Boston			"do"
Indispensable	Ship		London			"do"
Earl of Moria	Ship	"on Bahama Banks"	London			"do"
	Brig		French			"do"
	Brig		French			"do"
	Brig	"from Straits"	Genoa			"do"
	Brig		New York			"do"
	Ship	"from Europe"	French			"do"
	Ship	"South Cuba"	Dutch	Dry goods		"do"
Dido	Ship		Dutch			"do"
	Brig	"from Europe"	"do" [Dutch]			"do"
Providence			Providence	$10,000		"let her pass because the crew were his townsmen"
Transit	Bark			molasses	"1824 or 25"	"vessel and cargo ['crew' was probably intended] destroyed"
	Ship	"from Curaçoa"	Dutch		1819	"vessel and cargo ['crew' was probably intended] destroyed"

Table 2: Jeffers's March 23, 1831, list of captures (*continued*)

Vessel Name	Type	Where taken or sailing from	Nationality or Hailing port	Cargo/items stolen	Year	Notes
Caroline	Ship	Cape Antonio, bound from Liverpool	Charleston			Gibbs afterwards recollected that "this ship was the *Luciur* [*sic*]"

its home port unspecified, visited New York Harbor on June 18, 1827, which might help date an encounter to Jeffers's late period. He was reasonably consistent in his recollections of the *Belvidere; Providence*—which on March 19 he told Hopson he had stopped twice: once from Liverpool–New York and once from New York–Mobile; the *Dido;* the *Larkin;* the *Earl of Moria* (*Earl Moira*?); the *Indispensable;* the *Caroline* (later assigned a variant of the *Lucies*'s name); and the two unnamed French and one unnamed Genoese brigs. Presuming the *Belvidere* to have been Captain Lamson's vessel out of Beverly, Massachusetts, he was demonstrably wrong both times about its fate. Interestingly, on March 23, Jeffers added the reference to the "Bark *Transit,* in the year 1824 or 25." Four days' earlier Hopson had asked him if he knew anything of a brig of that name, its master named Ellet, taken between Trinidad and New York in 1829. Jeffers professed ignorance on that occasion, but the question may have jogged his memory about an earlier incident involving an identically named vessel of a different design.[6]

Jeffers, who was apparently shackled in his cell, had another visitor at Bellevue on March 23: former governor William Channing Gibbs of Rhode Island. The governor's trip came in part, a New York newspaper reported, to help put an end to "the idle reports, which were in circulation, that a relationship existed between him and the convict Gibbs." The same source observed that the prisoner himself had "repeatedly declared since his conviction that the name of Gibbs is acquired. He is however a native of Rhode Island and lived for some time in the vicinity of Newport." Whatever passed between them was not revealed.[7]

Slightly more was recorded about another person with whom Jeffers made contact in his final weeks. The *Journal of Commerce* would report, "By a singular occurrence of circumstances, the woman with whom he became acquainted in Liverpool, (and who is said, at that time to have borne a decent character,) is now lodged in the same prison with himself." If this referred to Bellevue, she was presumably kept in its women's section. Why she was in jail was left unreported, as was how and why she crossed the Atlantic. Jeffers wrote the woman two letters, one of which the *Journal of Commerce* published after cleaning up the grammar and spelling. Jeffers signed it with his alias.

Bellevue Prison, March 20, 1831

It is with regret that I take my pen in hand to address you with these few lines, under the great embarrassment of my feelings, placed within these gloomy walls, my body bound with chains, and under the awful sentence of death. It is enough to throw the strongest mind into gloomy prospects, but I find that Jesus Christ is sufficient to give consolation to the most despairing soul. For he saith that he that cometh to me I will in no wise cast out.

But it is impossible to describe unto you the emotions of my feelings. My breast is like the tempestuous ocean, raging in its own shame, harrowing up the bottom of my own soul. But I look forward to that serene calm when I shall sleep with kings and counsellors of the earth. There the wicked cease from troubling, and there the weary be at rest. There the prisoners rest together; they hear not the voice of the oppressor.

And there I trust my breast will not be ruffed by the storm of sin,— for the thing which I greatly feared has come upon me. I was not in safety, neither had I rest; yet trouble came. It is the Lord, let him do what seemeth to him good.

When I saw you in Liverpool, and a peaceful calm wafted across both our breasts, and justice no claim upon us, little did I think to meet you in the gloomy walls of a strong Prison, and the arm of justice stretched out with the sword of the law, awaiting the appointed period to execute the dreadful sentence. I have had a fair prospect in the world, at last it budded and brought forth the gallows. I am shortly to mount that scaffold, and to bid adieu to this world, and all that was ever dear to my breast.

But I trust when my body is mounted on the gallows high, the heavens above will smile and pity me. I hope that you will reflect on your past, and to fly to that Jesus who stands with open arms to receive you. Your character is lost it is true. When the wicked turneth from the wickedness that they have committed, they shall save their soul alive.

Let us imagine for a moment that we see the souls standing before the awful tribunal, and we hear its dreadful sentence, depart ye cursed into everlasting fire. Imagine you hear the awful lamentations of a soul in hell. It would be enough to melt your heart, if it was as hard as adamant. You would fall upon your knees and plead for God's mercy, as a famished person would for food, or as a dying criminal would for a pardon.

We soon, very soon, must go the way whence we shall ne'er return. Our names will be struck off the records of the living, and enrolled in the vast catalogues of the dead. But may it ne'er be numbered with the damned. I hope it will please God to set you a [*sic*] your liberty, and that you may see the sins and follies of your life past.

I shall now close my letter with a few words which I hope you will receive as from a dying man: and I hope that every important truth of this letter may sink deep in your heart and be a lesson to you through life.

> Rising griefs, distress my soul,
> And tears on tears successive roll.—
> For many an evil voice is near,
> To chide my woes and mock my fear;
> And silent memory weeps alone,
> O'er hours of peace and gladness flown.

I shall remain your sincere friend.

Charles Gibbs[8]

A fragment of another reputed Charles Gibbs letter also appeared, allegedly written by Jeffers "after his condemnation to one who had been his early friend."

Alas! it is now, and not until now that I have become sensible of my wicked life, from my childhood, and the enormity of the crime, for which I must shortly suffer an ignominious death!—I would to God that I had never been born, or that I had died in my infancy!—the hour of reflection is indeed come, but come too late to prevent justice from cutting me off—my mind recoils with horror at the thoughts of the unnatural deeds of which I have been guilty!—my repose rather prevents than affords me relief, as my mind, while I slumber, is constantly disturbed by frightful dreams, of my approaching awful dissolution![9]

A journalist who had "seen two letters from him [Jeffers] to a friend, since sentence was passed upon him" observed that the missives "evince some anguish of spirit, but there is no reason to conclude that he is so thoroughly penitent that he would not, by the recovery of his liberty, rush again, if he had an opportunity, into the perpetration of similar acts of atrocity."[10]

—•◦•◦•—

In spite of Amos Butler's *Mercantile Advertiser* connections, to judge from surviving periodicals the story of Jeffers's confessions of piracy may have broken in a Rhode Island paper. Its source was reportedly Jeffers's "junior counsel"—was this Patten or Staples, or a muddled reference to Hopson?—

to whom the prisoner had recounted his life of maritime atrocity. The source related some details to a friend, who in time-honored tradition told a newspaperman, in this case from the Providence *Literary Subaltern.*

The subsequent article in its Friday, March 25, issue took the lid off a tale even darker than the *Vineyard* story: "Gibbs the pirate now under sentence of death in the city of New York . . . has made to his council since his condemnation, a confession fraught with horrible and frightful atrocities." Its account of Jeffers's piracy career included a version of the "Dutch Girl" story. The writer concluded that "the story of this man[']s life stands unsurpassed in the black catologue [*sic*] of crime, and it will be remembered long after the histories of Pierre Le Grand, and Kidd are forgotten."[11]

The *Literary Subaltern* also commented on the pirate's background: "The man who goes by the name of Gibbs, is not entitled to that name. We understand, that he is a native of Newport, and is attached to one of the most wealthy and respectable families of that city. He was formerly the commander of a ship; and, is represented to be a man of talents and genius. If we are not altogether in error as to the man and his story, and if our information can be depended upon, Gibbs, as he is called, was formerly well known in this town [Providence], and was once the cock of the walk of good society."[12]

It took several days for the New York *Journal of Commerce* to catch up. On March 30, exactly a week after the third Hopson-Jeffers interview, it printed its first take on the prisoner's pirate career: "The confessions of this wretched being, now on the confines of eternity, to one of the Police Magistrates, unveil a career of long and desperate crimes, and they bring the varying torments of his partially awakened conscience into an existence that is almost visible upon his agitated brow while he recites the horrible catalogue. He has been familiar with scenes of blood and carnage, even from his boyhood, and an active participator in the commission of crimes that are stamped with the most shocking barbarity."

Though "unable to obtain the entire confession" made to Hopson, the newspaper related bits of the story, including that of the Dutch captive and her fate, and the encounter with the USS *Enterprise.* It also added elements that did not appear in Hopson's notes, such as the *Hornet/Chesapeake* and Boston grocery fictions, which must have originated from Jeffers himself, possibly being conveyed through Merritt.[13]

Now with a public to oblige, Jeffers relayed a request to the magistrate asking him to give Merritt the notes of their interviews. He complied and the text arrived the day after the *Journal of Commerce* story ran, somebody writing on it that it had been "delivered to Mr. Merritt, March 31st, 1831, at the request of Gibbs." The jailer duly passed it on to the *Journal of Commerce,* which incorporated it into a longer, fuller, and in some cases "corrected" story about Charles Gibbs, which ran on April 7. The reporter presumably interviewed the prisoner, for parts of the story are fleshed out with first-person quotes from Jeffers. The transcript of Hopson's notes received one significant cut: the editors—or Hopson—had removed "a long statement given of the monies taken, and where secreted," which might have dealt with the *Vineyard* loot, or perhaps involved other *Treasure Island*-type tales.

Overall, the reporter admitted skepticism on some points. Hopson's caution was clear from his own notes, particularly his March 23 remark to Jeffers that "I expected all he had told me could not be true." Regardless, the long April 7 *Journal of Commerce* article remains the closest thing to a comprehensive source on the man's alleged career. Several hundred extra copies were printed to meet demands from readers, who began their own debate over the subject.[14]

———————

Jeffers's earlier vow to avoid the gallows had prompted the *Journal of Commerce* to urge his keepers "to take such precautions that he cannot add the crime of suicide to the already black catalogue of his offences." At that time Jeffers and Wansley either shared a cell or were at least "allowed communication," but in Bellevue, where they were transferred on or before March 20, they were separated. Jeffers was kept isolated after publication of the confession, the move intended to make him more talkative on certain points. The *New York Sentinel* reported, "It is thought that by solitary confinement he will be induced to make further confessions, and disclose the names of some of his accomplices in various scenes of blood, who are yet at liberty."[15]

The atmosphere at the "Bellevue Establishment" adjacent to the East River at 26th Street and First Avenue, likely contributed to the pressure. The prison there was a 50-by-150 feet rectangular stone building dating to 1816. It shared the 20-acre, stonewall-enclosed plot with an almshouse and hospital—which would take over the entire site in 1848. Its correctional innovations included a grain-processing treadmill known as a "stepping wheel," on which both male and female inmates toiled. The entire complex was known for disease and overcrowding. Of the prison, a modern historian noted that "for the most part, its cells were really just large rooms holding a dozen or so prisoners. So many would be packed into the rooms that sometimes there was hardly enough floor space for the inmates to sleep." Awaiting execution, Jeffers and Wansley were each given a separate narrow cell, which a visitor "could not help regarding as a living grave."[16]

Under any circumstances the strain inside Jeffers became more apparent as the execution date drew near. According to one report, "He often asks if he should not be murdered in the streets, if he had his liberty, and was recognized, and frequently exclaims, 'Oh, if I had got into Algiers, I never should have been in this prison to be hung for murder.' . . . Since his trial, his frame is somewhat enfeebled, his face paler, and his eyes more sunken; but the air of his bold, enterprising and desperate mind still remains. In his narrow cell, he seems more like an object of pity than vengeance; is affable and communicative, and when he smiles, exhibits so mild and gentle a countenance, that no one would take him to be a villain. His conversation is concise and pertinent, and his style of illustration quite original."[17]

Clergy besieged both him and Wansley, particularly in the days approaching the April 22 execution date. Some secular visitors, intrigued by Jeffers's confession, went hoping to get more details. An otherwise unidentified layman on his own fact-finding mission left an account of his April 19 visit to Jeffers and Wansley in their separate, claustrophobic cells in Bellevue. He found the recently baptized Wansley using "language at once, calm, modest, scriptural and consolatory." Amid hopes for pardon from God, Wansley "freely and frankly confessed that the sentence of the law, upon which he was to suffer, was just—and that he now calmly and patiently waited the near approach of that period, when it would be carried into execution. These admissions on his part were made with all the appearance of candour, and I doubt not with perfect sincerity." Jeffers was a harder case. His interviewer asked for additional information "respecting those guilty men with whom you have been associated." Concealing their names, he told the prisoner, would allow them to "go on to add murder to murder and crime to crime, after you have passed into an awful eternity." Jeffers briefly looked anxious but recovered himself and replied, "Sir, I have bound myself by the most awful and solemn obligations, and which, I have confirmed by an oath on the bible, that I never would disclose the names of my associates." His visitor withdrew but recorded his feelings about the pair. Wansley he deemed "a real and sincere penitent." In contrast, Jeffers was a "strange and singularly anomalous character. . . . I know not what opinion to form, and therefore shall not express any."[18]

Evidence exists that Jeffers rethought his silence. Just after his execution, it was reported that near his end Jeffers "made a full disclosure of all the accomplices, aiders and abettors in his piracies." The person who received it told the *Journal of Commerce* that he would take it directly to the president. Its publication, the man said, "will astound the people of this nation." Relating these details to its own readers, the *Charleston Mercury* commented that "the people expect, impatiently, the promised publication."[19]

Such a report was indeed prepared, though apparently never published. Its compiler was Newport native and career politician James Coggeshall, who also may have been the layman who penned the account of the visit to the condemned men's cells. Born in 1787, at various times in his life Coggeshall was involved in banking and manufacturing, and he once loaned $1,000 to Horace Greeley to help start the *New York Tribune.* "God bless his honored memory!" Greeley wrote of his benefactor, who in history's view is as obscure as Greeley is famous. Described in one genealogical study as "an ardent old-line Whig," he arrived in New York circa 1827, where prior to being named federal inspector of lights along the New Jersey coast he served as a senior official in the city's prisons. This was certainly the connection through which Coggeshall came into contact with Jeffers.[20]

Coggeshall had enough political clout to follow through on his promise to take James Jeffers's final confession to the White House. Shortly after Jeffers's hanging, Coggeshall obtained a private interview with President Andrew Jackson, who mentioned the meeting in his own letter to District Attorney James Hamilton:

Washington, May 4, 1831

DEAR SIR: Mr. James Coggeshall, of New York, has communicated to me in confidence the substance of certain disclosures made to him by the pirate Gibbs, also James D. Jeffrees, recently executed in New York. The facts as stated are of deep interest, and if Coggeshall is as honest and respectable a man as he is represented to be, the subject ought to be sifted to the bottom. I have informed him that I can take no steps in the matter until I hear from you, by whom the prosecution against the pirate was conducted, and have advised Mr. Coggeshall to return to New York and communicate the whole matter to you. You will please to send for him and receive his statement in form; and report it to me, with the best evidence you can upon a full and careful examination obtain, as to the credibility of Mr. Coggeshall, the probable character of his motives for making the disclosure to government, and the circumstances under which the confessions were made by the deceased pirate. Any suggestions you may think proper to make upon the subject will be thankfully received.[21]

Hamilton duly interviewed Coggeshall and passed on his own report to Jackson. In early June Secretary of State Edward Livingston informed the prosecutor that the president had read the document, which referenced a new source whose name Hamilton deleted when preparing his papers for publication. After redaction, Livingston's note read in part that Hamilton was "at liberty to employ **** in such a manner as you think will best attain the object of ascertaining the truth of the confession, and securing the proof necessary to convict those concerned in the transaction." So at this point the "truth of the confession" was still being assessed, and it is uncertain as to what use Hamilton, who resigned as prosecutor in 1833, made of it.[22]

Jeffers had at least one more interview with a government official: Lawrence Kearny. The former USS *Enterprise* commander, now holding the rank of master commandant, was among the last visitors to Jeffers's cell before the April 22 hanging, and Jeffers's credibility relies in part on an account of this meeting.

Kearny's Cuban-coast heroics brought fame, but his subsequent career tasks varied in their level of adventure. For a time he served in Boston, heading the Charlestown Navy Yard. In 1826 he was given command of USS *Warren*, in which he hunted Mediterranean pirates for the next several years. He had successes but also tired of extended life at sea, and late in 1829 Kearny was put in charge of recruiting in New York.[23]

National Archives documents give an idea of the pirate hunter behind a desk. On July 12, 1830, Kearny asked for leave, which his superiors denied because "your services are indispensably necessary at the Rendezvous." The administrative crush seems to have ended after the following January, his February 5 return noting that his office had sent on thirty-four ordinary and able seamen, two boys, one landsman, and one petty officer, their cash advances tallying $1,218. Nine days later Kearny asked the secretary of the navy for a three-week leave of absence "as I am desirous of making a visit to Boston." He noted that winter was a bad season for recruiting sailors—"not more than one or two some times in a week are entered"—and that another officer was willing to "attend in my absence and account for the necessary expenditures of monies which will be very small under the circumstances."[24]

Kearny's request was approved, and the period of leave kept him absent during the *Vineyard* trial, but he returned in time to read news reports about "Gibbs the Pirate" and its subject's experiences at Cape Antonio. Kearny sought an interview at Bellevue with Jeffers. According to the *Journal of Commerce*, Jeffers "in the course of their conversation referred to numerous incidents that occurred there [Cape Antonio], which none but a person present could have known. He enquired of Captain K. if he found some warm coffee on board of the ship when he took possession of her? which being answered in the affirmative, he added, with a half smile, 'you didn't drink any of it!' intending to convey the idea that it was prepared and poisoned for their destruction. We learn from a gentleman who was present at the interview, that Capt. Kearney [sic] was fully satisfied that he [Jeffers] had been a pirate, and a participator with the Cape Antonio free booters in the commission of many of their horrible outrages upon the lives of their fellow beings."[25]

Nothing contradicts this in the work of Kearny's biographer, who in writing of Cape Antonio piracy circa 1821 noted that "the directing genius was the notorious Charles Gibbs."[26]

A week before the hanging, the *Newport Mercury* reported,

> We learn, that a letter has been received by a Clergyman of this Town, from New York, in which the writer states, that the person who calls himself Charles Gibbs, now under sentence of death for piracy and murder on board the brig *Vineyard*, had disclosed to him his real name and family, and that it was the wish of the culprit, that the information might be communicated to his friends in this town. If this information should prove to be correct, the confessions of the professed Gibbs, which is now going the rounds of the Newspapers, must have been a sheer falsification, as the person alluded to sailed from this port on his first voyage in 1816, being then about 17 years of age. His family received 10 or 12 years since what they considered an authentic account of his death at New Orleans.[27]

Reprinted in New York the day before the execution, the piece stimulated further investigation. The *Journal of Commerce* reporter seems to have confronted the prisoner about his background and his piracy story. Jeffers stuck to his tale of infamy, but

> He admitted that what he had communicated in regard to his being on board the *Hornet* and *Chesapeake* was unfounded, and declared that his sole object in making such representations was to conceal his true name, and prevent his friends from being visited with the stigma that his crimes would cast upon them. He said if he had confessed that he first went to sea in the brig *Brutus* from Newport in 1816, that then he might easily have been traced and identified as James D. Jeffers.[28]

On the night before his hanging, a visiting clergyman baptized Jeffers under his real name. The clergyman was probably the Reverend Duncan Dunbar, a Washington Street resident who would the next day accompany Jeffers and Wansley to their hanging. Born in Scotland in 1791, in 1817 he moved to New Brunswick and became a Baptist. In 1823 he moved to America and five years later he became pastor of a church on Vandam Street in New York City. According to an 1878 biography by his son-in-law, Dunbar had a reputation for ministering in prisons and to convicts. A year before Jeffers and Wansley mounted the scaffold, Dunbar served as spiritual adviser to one Richard Johnson, sentenced to hang for murdering a woman "who had cruelly deceived and injured him." The description of Dunbar's ministrations to Johnson in 1830 might also have applied to the reverend's later efforts with Jeffers and Wansley: "Even down to the last hour, he [Dunbar] was with him [Johnson], spending the whole night preceding the execution in prayer and conversation in the cell, and rejoicing, when the sad scene was over, in the belief that one who was deemed by man unfit to live, was, by faith in the pardoning blood of Christ, made meet for heaven."[29]

As their last hours approached, Jeffers and Wansley would have been interested to learn that a Charleston newspaper had cited their case to argue against the death penalty's value as a deterrent. The *Charleston Courier* took its lead from Jeffers's remark to Hopson, reprinted from the *Journal of Commerce*, that he had eliminated victims "because a man has to suffer death for piracy; and the punishment for murder is no more. . . . I am sure that if the punishment was different, there would not be so many murders." From this, the *Courier* concluded that "the law . . . produces crime," a view the crosstown *Charleston Mercury* contested.[30]

Further north, not far from where James Jeffers grew up, the Providence *Daily Advertiser* was readying an article that compared pirates such as Jeffers to freemasons, an assertion the *Literary Subaltern* denounced for tarring "thousands . . . of the most unimpeachable reputation, as participators in the crimes perpetrated by Gibbs the Pirate!"[31]

Pirate executions traditionally stimulated ballad writers. Of unknown origin, lyrics to a song called "Charles Gibbs" survived in fragmentary form to be published a century after his execution.

> My bloody knife was always ready,
> Well he [be?] it understood.
> No god nor man I ever feared

Upon the briny flood.
No pitty have I ever shown,
Lord, who would pitty me?
By here I lie and long to die [...][32]

Wansley, who sent an "affectionate letter to his mother" in his last days at
Bellevue, was also said to have penned a farewell in the form of a personal
hymn, which was published after his execution.

When on this you do glance an eye
O let it Calm your breast
To think that Wansley has gone on high
with Jesus for to wrest

What weakness then it is of mind
to start or fear to die
Or dread to lieve this world behind
when Jesus is so nigh

But oh ef Christ is not our friend
well may we fear and start
For oh how retched is there end
that Jesus bids depart

But now you do your Jesus know
and you your Saviour love
So you will for sake all things below
and we shall meet above[33]

12

"A dreadful thing to die"

OWNED BY THE NATIONAL GOVERNMENT, Ellis Island was the death site for pirates condemned by New York's federal courts. The hanging of Jeffers and Wansley, scheduled there for 10 A.M., April 22, was to be the state's first execution of 1831. The previous one, at Batavia in November 1830, had ended the life of James Gray, convicted in the stabbing death of a Leroy tavern landlord.

Until Jeffers and Wansley mounted the scaffold, Ellis Island had not been the site of an execution since December 1826, when federal authorities hanged a black man named William Hill for mutiny and murder aboard the schooner *Decatur*. That vessel was taking convict slaves from Baltimore to a form of hard-labor exile in Louisiana. At sea, three prisoners broke loose, threw overboard the captain and mate, took over the craft, and, in the law's eyes, became pirates. The officials that eventually tracked them down could identify only Hill as a leader and brought him to New York for trial and conviction on federal charges.

The previous man hanged at Ellis Island for piracy-related charges was also black: forty-year-old Thomas Jones, executed in mid-1824. Captured after an international search, Jones was found guilty of being one of the mutineers on board the brigantine *Holker* in 1818, on a cruise to the West Indies. The all-black crew mutinied, using harpoons to kill their white captain, the white first mate, and a white passenger. They then sailed to Santo Domingo, destroying the *Holker* before heading into the wild.[1]

The last white man executed in New York as a pirate before Jeffers was George Brown, who in 1819 was mate aboard the schooner *Retrieve*. While sailing from Cadiz to Vera Cruz, Brown led a mutiny that resulted in his captain being thrown overboard. A shipmate tipped off authorities when the

Retrieve reached port, and a New York court found Brown guilty. In October the twenty-two-year-old was hanged aboard his former craft, docked in the East River.[2]

───◆◆◆───

As had been the case in the Old World, public executions, though meant to deter witnesses from a life of crime, were still a form of public entertainment. The children who witnessed them sometimes imitated them. In 1820 an eleven-year-old Baltimore boy named Christian Bitte died during a reenactment staged by his friends.[3]

Sometimes spectators witnessed more than one death, as happened at the December 28, 1827, hanging of Levi Kelly at Cooperstown, New York. About forty at the time, Kelly was condemned for fatally shooting a man who "came to the defense of a lame boy whom Kelly was scolding." The execution drew four thousand spectators despite a heavy rain, and a wooden grandstand holding six hundred people on it collapsed, resulting in dozens of deaths and injuries.[4]

As a result, and to stem the unwanted traffic high profile executions generated, an 1829 hanging was moved offshore to Blackwell's (now Roosevelt) Island. Yet the mass of would-be spectators simply rented or otherwise acquired boats, causing chaos along the river and several accidents. City officials responded by banning all public executions in the municipality. But this local ordinance did not apply to federally owned Ellis Island.[5]

───◆◆◆───

The double hanging of Jeffers and Wansley drew a crowd of thousands on April 22. Hours before the execution, Ellis Island was packed with people and its shoreline clogged with boats, some full of spectators unable to land. One person drowned when a small craft overturned. A clerk with permission to leave work to see the hanging did not return immediately, and the next day "apprehensions were excited for his safety."[6]

In front of this capacity crowd, Jeffers and Wansley faced an exotic variant on the traditional hanging. Post-Enlightenment authorities generally favored quick executions meant to minimize suffering. Historian Richard Marius noted that the era's "hangmen tried to kill their clients by a quick drop that broke the spinal cord with such rapidity that all muscular activity ceased in an instantaneous death." But on Ellis Island this morning, the thirteen-foot-high gallows had been so arranged, wrote a witness, "that the hanging of the Pirates should take place by slinging them *up*, instead of dropping them from a scaffold, as is most generally done with persons hanged."

The mechanism consisted of heavy weights attached via ropes and pulleys to a pair of 5/8-inch thick hemp nooses, dangling under the gallows crossbeam. When all was ready, by cutting a single control rope the weights would drop, and the resulting action would wrench the men swiftly into the air. The goal must have been to improve on the effectiveness of gravity as a propellant— a simple noose-and-trapdoor arrangement would have sufficed had the intention been otherwise. But it remained to be seen how it would work on Jeffers and Wansley.[7]

The condemned men had had little sleep, for it was reported that overnight "several clergymen visited both the convicts and prayed and conversed with them without intermission." Jeffers also received the woman from Liverpool, who "was admitted to see him, by her own request. She seemed greatly affected, and both embraced each other very tenderly."

Her former lover and his companion were well attired for their execution. A witness recorded that Jeffers, who was still Charles Gibbs to the crowd, "was dressed in a blue roundabout jacket, and blue trowsers and white cap, the jacket bearing on the left arm the figure of an anchor worked with white ribbon: Wansley wore a white linen frock coat, white trowsers and white cap, all trimmed with black ribbon."

At 8 A.M., escorted by U.S. Marshal Thomas Morris and a squad of U.S. Marines from the Brooklyn Navy Yard, they left Bellevue for their last voyage, aboard the steamboat *Bellona*. It arrived at Ellis Island by 9:30 A.M., the prisoners being escorted into its fort. While 10 A.M. was the appointed time for the execution, at some point during the journey the pair managed to convince the authorities that they needed more time to prepare themselves. The Reverend Dunbar, who said later that he was convinced of Jeffers's repentance, might have been influential in this, and it was agreed to postpone the hanging to noon.

There was one last meeting with their past. Inside the fort Jeffers and Wansley encountered Robert Dawes, who had not only had charges against him dropped but had been given a job at the Brooklyn Navy Yard as well. Now the British-born Dawes stood before his *Vineyard* shipmates wearing an American naval uniform; he may have been ordered to witness their execution. Notwithstanding their remarks at sentencing about Dawes, the condemned pair, a newspaper reported, now "gave him some sound advice, which, it is to be hoped, he will follow." But it was noted that when they shook hands for the last time, Dawes "seemed little moved by their situation."

The rest of the stay in the island's fort was, noted the *Journal of Commerce,* "wholly devoted to religious exercises, in which both the wretched criminals participated, with great apparent earnestness. They *seemed* penitent, particularly Wansley; and in their supplications to the throne of mercy, acknowledged that the punishment which awaited them, was justly due to the horrid crimes they had committed." At about 11:30 A.M., they were taken outside.[8]

----•◆•----

They marched toward the island's west side, where the gallows had been constructed near a lone tree. The huge crowd was orderly enough for a reporter to remark that "the whole scene was in the highest degree solemn and affecting." Wansley was shaking and needed to be supported. Jeffers, in spite of his earlier promise to not allow himself to be hanged, was calmer than some had expected. He "betrayed no marks of terror, although it was evident that he shrunk from death. When first brought out, he surveyed the gallows with an anxious eye, but seemed satisfied that there was no avoiding his fate."[9]

Under the gallows, a deputy federal marshal named Read placed the nooses loosely around the men's necks. This done, Jeffers addressed the crowd. His execution speech exists in different forms. One version quotes him as follows:

> Good people who surround me here, you behold me with this fatal
> cord around my neck, soon to appear before that just God whom I have
> so often offended. In youth I was on board a vessel of war, and took an
> oath that at any other time would seem horrible to me; I kept it, and
> was a murderer, and I hope you will all take warning by my fate. I was
> born of respectable parents, and received a good education, but I did
> not properly apply these advantages;—however, I hope that Christ will
> make my death as easy as if I had died on a downy pillow—I now con-
> fess as I have before confessed, that I have been guilty of shedding the
> blood of many of my fellow men, of which I humbly pray the forgive-
> ness of God.

Presumably "vessel of war" referred to the Cartagenian privateer *Maria* on which, he had told Hopson, he took his first steps toward piracy; the oath could have been that to keep secret the names of his comrades in mass murder.[10]

After Jeffers finished, Wansley asked a clergyman—possibly Dunbar, but others named Kent and Carter were also present—to sing a psalm with him.

Several people standing nearby joined in, though Jeffers was not specifically included among them in newspaper accounts. The singing calmed Wansley enough for him to make his own speech.

"Wansley's frame was visibly agitated," the *Journal of Commerce* reported, "though his voice was firm and his countenance composed. He clearly felt, as he was forewarned by Judge Betts in his impressive sentence, that it was a dreadful thing to die." Wansley's exact remarks were not transcribed but a witness recalled that he first "acknowledged the justice of his sentence." Though raised in a "pious and respectable family," he admitted erring when he "put entire confidence in his own power to avoid evil." Accordingly, "he warned all who were present to be diffident in themselves; and added, that although they might not be murderers nor robbers, yet they required penitence." Finally, he prayed for Jeffers and "requested the prayers of all around him."[11]

When Wansley finished, the final preparations were made, the nooses being drawn tighter. The prisoners kept their caps on. Their arms may have been pinioned at the elbows against their sides, for although bound Wansley "clasped his hands as if in attitude of praying," and Jeffers had finagled a last aspect of command: he was to drop a handkerchief from one of his restrained hands as the "signal that he was ready." No consideration seems to have been taken of Wansley's state of preparation.

Jeffers's last recorded words were to the doctor who was on hand to certify the convicts' deaths. Jeffers "asked him in a low tone whether he could die easier by holding his breath, or breathing out." The doctor "advised the latter mode."

Then, having presumably exhaled, Jeffers dropped the handkerchief. It was about 12:05 P.M.

An unnamed deputy marshal—it may have been Read—swung a hatchet through the crucial cord holding in check two sets of five 56-pound weights, which via the ropes and pulleys ultimately controlled the height of the nooses. The action whipped Jeffers and Wansley off the ground—the violent uplift also pushed Jeffers's cap forward across his face—and left them dangling in the air.

Neither received the hoped-for broken neck, but their exits were different. Wansley stopped twitching after a minute of strangulation. "He appeared to suffer but little bodily pain," wrote a witness, who attributed this to his being heavier than Jeffers, his weight making the noose's work of suffocation easier.

In contrast, Jeffers was denied the easy death for which he had prayed. The knot on the noose had somehow shifted from behind his neck to beside one ear. One reporter thought Jeffers did this himself in his final moments before the gallows mechanism was sprung. Whatever the cause, the noose's pressure was not directly on Jeffers's windpipe. He remained motionless during his first minute suspended in the air, and then began to writhe. The slowly smothering man was seen trying to lift his pinioned arms high enough to remove the cap from over his face. He must have succeeded, for he "raised his hand so as to open his lips." It took five or six minutes for his contortions to cease.[12]

The newspapers were discreet about other physical reactions. Addressing a suicide investigation in another century, historian Marius wrote that "well known to professional hangmen of all times was that a victim of slow strangulation was bound to bleed from the nose and the mouth and to discharge bowels and bladder in the struggle against the noose. But even the quick drop used by the nineteenth-century hangmen seldom succeeded in avoiding the mess. Suicides today who hang themselves are still almost always found in a fouled condition."[13]

The bodies of Jeffers and Wansley stayed on the scaffold for forty-five minutes before being cut down. Wansley's hands were still clasped in prayer.[14]

When sentencing Jeffers and Wansley to death several weeks earlier, Judge Betts had stipulated how the bodies were to be disposed. The authorities would "deliver the body of [each convicted man] after Execution shall have been done upon him to Doctor John Augustine Smith, Professor of Anatomy, in the college of Physicians and Surgeons of the University of the State of New York, provided that some person or persons appointed by the said Professor for that purpose shall attend to receive and take away the dead body at the time of the Execution."[15]

In doing this, Betts was being a good citizen. Condemned criminals were usually the era's only legally and socially acceptable specimens, and anatomists were chronically short of corpses for study and experimentation. Late-February newspapers reported that a medical professor and a student were arrested in western Massachusetts for allegedly digging up two recently interred bodies, which were recovered intact and reburied.[16]

The specified recipient of Jeffers's and Wansley's cadavers, Dr. John Augustine Smith, was then in the prime of a distinguished medical and academic career. Born in Virginia in 1782, the son of a clergyman, his first term of service at the College of Physicians and Surgeons began when the New York County Medical Society opened it in 1807. In 1814 he became head of

Contemporary woodcut of the double execution, from The Confession
of the Terrible Pirate Charles Gibbs. *Courtesy of the Harry Ransom
Humanities Research Center, University of Texas at Austin*

his Virginia alma mater, William and Mary, returning to the College of Physicians and Surgeons in 1825. He became its president in the same year Jeffers
and Wansley were hanged.[17]

As his presence at the Ellis Island execution would likely have been reported, Smith probably entrusted assistants with collecting the pirates' bodies. Writers did, however, note the presence of a different celebrity, the artist
and sculptor John Henri Isaac Browere, who also had a role to play in the
hanged men's final chapter. Born John Henry Brower in New York in 1790,
he set up as a portrait painter in 1815. An interest in sculpture stimulated
his experiments with "life masks," and his subjects included statesmen and
celebrities. Most of Browere's models found the process agreeable, though
Thomas Jefferson was a notable exception. Browere risked no complaints
when experimenting with a different type of artistry: death masks. To fulfill
a commission in 1830, he was said to have secretly exhumed the corpse of
Elias Hicks, a recently deceased Quaker leader, which he reburied after the
mask set.

Now on Ellis Island, before the dead pirates' bodies were taken away, he
applied the same process to the faces of Jeffers and Wansley. What befell the
masks is unrecorded. After Browere died of cholera in 1834, his collection
was put into storage. Many items disappeared over the following decades;

what survived was bequeathed to Cooperstown's New York State Historical Association. The collection does not include the masks of Jeffers and Wansley.[18]

Of the bodies themselves, few contemporary records still exist from the College of Physicians and Surgeons (located on Barclay Street in 1831, and part of Columbia University since 1860). None documents receipt of the corpses, which were probably used for dissection or demonstration. Nor did any nineteenth-century anatomical collection from the old college survive to the present within Columbia University Medical Center's holdings.[19]

That said, one physical relic of Jeffers still exists. A cranium, discolored with age, sawed off from the rest of a human skull, sits in the cabinet of curiosities held by New York City's General Society of Mechanics and Tradesmen. Written on it, in black ink, is "The scull of Jas. D. Jefferson The Pirate who went By the Name of Gibbs[.] Born in New Port, R.I."

It has been in the society's collection since at least 1891. It appears to have originally been part of a collection devoted to phrenology—study of the shape of the head as related to character. How it found its way into such an exhibition is unknown. The corpse's original recipient, Dr. John Augustine Smith, opposed such studies. Still, the skull portion made a fine example, and a reporter who saw it in 1891 described it in phrenological terms. After recounting the pirate's career, the writer observed that Jeffers "had a receding forehead, the seat of rash intrepidity being abnormally developed, with a total absence of the bumps of cautiousness."[20]

Epilogue

The Legacy of Charles Gibbs

WHEN HOLES WERE SHOT through some of his autobiographical stories in 1831, and when he admitted that the name he was being tried under was an alias, James Jeffers claimed that his goal was not to cover his crimes, but to shield his identity. If so, he succeeded. Today the Jeffers name is little known in pirate history while Charles Gibbs still catches enthusiasts' imagination.

In 1996 a piracy exhibition at New York City's South Street Seaport Museum featured a cutlass, on loan from a private collection, said to have belonged to Gibbs himself.[1] In 2003 Florida-based singer-songwriter Chris Foster copyrighted "Charles Gibbs," a song that recounted Jeffers's career as a cautionary tale, its last verse beginning: "To romanticize a pirate is to make a mockery of life."[2] At about the same time appeared a pirate-themed greeting card, blank inside, its cover an illustration from the *Pirates Own Book*. Originally captioned "Gibbs Carrying the Dutch Girl aboard His Vessel," the illustration now bore the legend: "Just a Pirate Chasing Booty."[3]

Modern double-entendre aside, the vintage drawing had turned rape and murder into a safely stylized tableau. Jeffers is a rakish Jack Tar–ype, hoisting the elegantly dressed, reluctant young woman from land into a rowboat, a brig visible in the distance. His eyes are closed, his mouth open anticipating a kiss. She looks merely uncomfortable; her stiff body and outstretched arms make it appear as if Jeffers is lugging a mannequin.

Similar artistic license clothes most nineteenth- and twentieth-century accounts of the man's life. They also started with a source that was unreliable, even untrustworthy. Evidence of his privateering career rests largely on his own testimony—and he also told excellent but false tales of service aboard the *Chesapeake* under James Lawrence. Of the crimes to which he admitted, Jeffers cannot be judged innocent, but more facts about the extent of his guilt are needed to determine his proper role in maritime infamy.

Yet there is no denying that in 1831 a New York jury convicted him of murder and, by the nature of the charge, of piracy as well. So the romanticized image of Charles Gibbs sweeping a "golden-haired virgin" into his arms under Caribbean skies gives way to a sharper one. It is of James D. Jeffers of Newport being cut down from an Ellis Island gallows on a somber April afternoon, having suffered the agonizing death of an authentic pirate.

ABBREVIATIONS

Holdings of the National Archives and Records Administration (Washington, D.C., and regional repositories)

NA-RG21
Record Group 21, Records of the U.S. Circuit Court for the Southern District of New York, Criminal Case Files, 1790–1853.

NA-RG24
Record Group 24, Records of the Bureau of Naval Personnel, M330 Abstracts of Service Records of Naval Officers ("Records of Officers"), 1798–1893.

NA-RG36
Record Group 36, Records of the U.S. Customs Service, Collector of Customs, District of Newport, R.I., Crew Lists, 1811–1826, Box 40 (NRAB 98–111), and Box #4 (E-662).

NA-RG41
Record Group 41, Bureau of Marine Inspection and Navigation Records relating to Vessel Documentation.

(Abbreviations beginning with "NA-RG45" refer to materials contained in Record Group 45, Naval Records Collection of the Office of Naval Records and Library)

NA-RG45-M124
Miscellaneous Letters Received by the Secretary of the Navy, 1801–1884.

NA-RG45-M125
Letters Received by the Secretary of the Navy from Captains, 1805–1861, 1866–1885.

NA-RG45-M147
Letters Received by the Secretary of the Navy from Commanders, 1804–1886.

NA-RG45-M148
Letters Received by the Secretary of the Navy from Commissioned Officers Below the Rank of Commander and from Warrant Officers, 1802–1884.

NA-RG45-M149
Letters Sent by the Secretary of the Navy to Officers, 1798–1868.

NA-RG45-P
Personnel Records, 1798–1890.

NA-RG45-SGIS
U.S. Navy Subject File, 1775–1910, file SG-Illegal Service, including blockade running, piracy, smuggling, and filibustering.

NA-RG45-T829
Miscellaneous Records of the U.S. Navy, 1789–1925.

Abbreviations pertaining to other sources

NHS-Jeffers
Application for membership (1912) by Susan Allen Croacher to the National Society of the Daughters of the American Revolution (referencing Samuel Jeffers as her ancestor), Jeffers file, Newport Historical Society Library, 82 Touro St., Newport, R.I.

NWR
Niles' Weekly Register

NYJOC
New York Journal of Commerce

SRE [followed by port name]
Works Progress/Work Projects Administration, *Ship Registers and Enrollments* (see bibliography for full citations).

NOTES

Preface

1. Hawes, *Off Soundings*, 79, citing Sheffield, *Privateersmen in Newport*; McKee, *A Gentlemanly and Honorable Profession*, 238.

2. A footnote to the article acknowledged, "It appears that the late pretended enumeration of captures by the pirates, was the mere coinage of the brain of one of our editors—as he himself has confessed!" See "History of the Pirates, &c," *NWR*, May 17, 1823, 163.

3. The materials are held in the National Archives Northeast Region (New York) repository, in Record Group 21 (Criminal Case Files, 1790–1853), hereafter NA-RG21.

4. Drake, *A Full and Accurate Record of the Trials of Wansley and Gibbs*. The author consulted a copy of the original held by the libraries of Brown University.

5. See the bibliography for further data on *Ship Registers and Enrollments of Boston and Charleston, Vol. I, 1789–1795*, and the WPA-compiled materials for 1821–1840 held by the Phillips Library of the Peabody Essex Museum in Salem, Massachusetts. Though this research was unable to turn up a source for New York ship registration data, two National Archives microfilm series (M237 and M1066) do list vessels arriving at that port, along with passenger names and cargo descriptions. These sources provide the basis for Steuart, ed., *Passenger Ships Arriving in New York Harbor*, in which they are discussed on 1:vii.

6. Correspondence (March 15 and November 3, 2004) from Kenneth R. Cobb, director, New York City Municipal Archives.

7. Cordingly, *Under the Black Flag*, 162. The author is grateful to Jeff Remling of the South Street Seaport Museum, New York, New York, for background on rigging types and terminology used throughout this work.

Chapter 1: "So mild and gentle a countenance"

1. Botting, *The Pirates*, 181.

2. "We understand that the real name of the person convicted of piracy and murder on board the brig *Vineyard*, under the assumed name of Charles Gibbs, is James Jeffreys." Untitled article, *Salem Gazette*, April 15, 1831, 2 (citing the *New York Daily Advertiser*). The spelling *Jeffreys* is also employed in "A visit to the

condemned criminals Gibbs and Wansley, by a Layman," in *The Confession of the Terrible Pirate Charles Gibbs*, 18. President Andrew Jackson referred to "James D. Jeffrees" in his May 4, 1831, letter to James A. Hamilton, printed in Hamilton, *Reminiscences of James A. Hamilton*, 218.

3. Coker, *Charleston's Maritime Heritage*, 161n7.

4. "Gibbs the Pirate," *Literary Subaltern*, March 25, 1831, 3; Gosse, *The Pirates Who's Who*, 134. For a recent critique of the *General History*, see Turley, *Rum, Sodomy & the Lash*, 3–91.

5. "Confessions of Gibbs the Pirate," *NYJOC*, April 7, 1831, 2 (emphasis in original). This important article—the most comprehensive surviving contemporary statement of Jeffers's admissions—appears to correct details, or at least convey another version of the Jeffers story originally given in "Gibbs the Pirate," *NYJOC*, March 30, 1831, 2.

6. *Mutiny and Murder*, title page (emphasis in original); Snow, *Pirates and Buccaneers*, 273; "Execution of the Pirates," *NYJOC*, April 23, 1831, 2; Konstam, *History of Pirates*, 163; "A visit to the condemned criminals Gibbs and Wansley," in *The Confession of the Terrible Pirate Charles Gibbs*, 17.

7. For congressional acts dealing with piracy and their legal interpretation, see Lenoir, "Piracy Cases in the Supreme Court," passim. The *Vineyard* episode is recounted in more detail in a later chapter; this summary draws principally on Drake, *Trials of Wansley and Gibbs*, passim; "Trial for Murder and Piracy," *NYJOC*, March 10, 1831, 2; and "Sentence of the Pirates," *NYJOC*, March 12, 1831, 2.

8. "Confessions of Gibbs the Pirate," *NYJOC*, April 7, 1831, 2, which includes Jeffers's remark about receiving a wound on his nose; "Trial for Murder and Piracy," *NYJOC*, March 10, 1831, 2; "Trial for Murder and Piracy," *Rhode Island Republican*, March 17, 1831, 2 (quoting "The *Commercial Advertiser* of Friday").

9. Drake, *Trials of Wansley and Gibbs*, 9; "The Pirates," *Rhode Island Republican*, March 24, 1831, 2 (citing the *New York Courier*); "Brief Notices," *NWR*, April 9, 1831, 94; Gibbs, *The Gibbs Family of Rhode Island and Some Related Families*, 57. The former governor did, in fact, have a son named Charles, but the births of all his children followed his marriage in 1822, a prohibitively late date. Mohr, *Governors for Three Hundred Years 1638–1954*, 130.

10. Drake, *Trials of Wansley and Gibbs*, 8, 13.

11. "Confessions of Gibbs the Pirate," *NYJOC*, April 7, 1831, 2. Hopson's approximate age can be inferred from his obituary in the *New York Times*, April 11, 1854, 8.

12. The trial is detailed in a later chapter.

13. "Confessions of Gibbs the Pirate," *NYJOC*, April 7, 1831, 2; Johnson, quoted in Bartlett, *Bartlett's Familiar Quotations*, 355.

14. "A visit to the condemned criminals Gibbs and Wansley," in *The Confession of the Terrible Pirate Charles Gibbs*, 17; "Confessions of Gibbs the Pirate," *NYJOC*, April 7, 1831, 2.

15. "Confessions of Gibbs the Pirate," *NYJOC,* April 7, 1831, 2; Lamson, *The Autobiography of Capt. Zachary G. Lamson,* 254–55, 260; "Insurgent Cruizers," *Lloyd's List,* May 16, 1817, 1.

16. Sugden, *The Complete History of Jack the Ripper,* 6.

17. Douglas and Olshaker, *The Cases That Haunt Us,* 187.

18. Correspondence from John Douglas, June 29, 2005.

19. "Confessions of Gibbs the Pirate," *NYJOC,* April 7, 1831, 2.

20. "Execution of the Pirates," *NYJOC,* April 23, 1831, 2; Alden, *Lawrence Kearny, Sailor Diplomat,* 62–63; Andrew Jackson to James A. Hamilton, May 4, 1831, and Edward Livingston to James A. Hamilton, June 7, 1831, in Hamilton, *Reminiscences,* 218, 249; G. F. Emmons, *The Navy of the United States, 1775–1853,* 77.

21. Alden, *Lawrence Kearny,* 62; "Confessions of Gibbs the Pirate," *NYJOC,* April 7, 1831, 2.

22. "Execution of the Pirates," *NYJOC,* April 23, 1831, 2; *Mutiny and Murder,* 5.

23. See Turley, *Rum, Sodomy & the Lash,* 44–61, for more on published piracy trial transcripts, ballads, and confessions. For contemporary New York examples, see the sources given in Hearn, *Legal Executions in New York State, 1639–1963,* 294–305.

24. A copy of this very rare pamphlet is held by the Harry Ransom Humanities Research Center, University of Texas at Austin.

25. *Mutiny and Murder,* 5–7, 29–35, and passim. The author consulted a copy of the original held by the Cornell Law Library. This monograph should not be confused with an article by the same name that appeared in the December 4, 1830, *Baltimore Patriot* and is cited in several places in this book.

26. Ellms, *The Pirates Own Book,* 97–98. See pp. ii, vi–viii, for the work's publishing history. In 1924 Ellms's chapter "Charles Gibbs" was condensed into a short entry for Gosse's *The Pirates Who's Who,* 133–34. Another version of the Gibbs tale appears in an 1836 work: Thomas, *An Authentic Account of the Most Remarkable Events.* It too had a long reprinting history, and one reader suggested that its version of the *Vineyard* mutiny influenced one of Edgar Allan Poe's works; see Huntress, "Another Source of Poe's *Narrative of Arthur Gordon Pym.*"

27. Snow, *Pirates and Buccaneers of the Atlantic Coast,* 273–74, 287; Beater, *Pirates and Buried Treasure on Florida Islands,* 27–38. Also worth mentioning is the chapter on Charles Gibbs in Seitz, *Under the Black Flag,* 320–28. Published in 1927, the work refutes the *Hornet/Chesapeake* tale but adds many unattributed details that have not been encountered in contemporary sources.

Chapter 2: Formative Years

1. "Execution of the Pirates," *NYJOC,* April 23, 1831, 2; "Gibbs, the Pirate," *Newport Mercury,* April 16, 1831, 3; "Confessions of Gibbs the Pirate," *NYJOC,* April 7, 1831, 2; "An interesting and correct account of the Execution of the

Pirates," in *The Confession of the Terrible Pirate Charles Gibbs,* 2. At the time of Jeffers's execution, the *Journal of Commerce* reported that his tale of robbing the *Providence* had "been fully confirmed to us" but offered no other details. See "Execution of the Pirates."

2. "Confessions of Gibbs the Pirate," *NYJOC,* April 7, 1831, 2; Drake, *Trials of Wansley and Gibbs,* 9, 10, 15; *Mutiny and Murder,* 5; "Trial for Murder and Piracy," *NYJOC,* March 10, 1831, 2.

3. NHS-Jeffers; Sheffield, *Privateersmen of Newport,* 33–34, 62–63.

4. Sheffield, *Privateersmen of Newport,* 33–34. Sheffield apparently had local sources and knowledge about Jeffers, for his account of Samuel Jeffers's career is not affirmed in the list of American Revolutionary War privateers contained in G. F. Emmons, *The Navy of the United States,* 140. Emmons lists eight vessels called the *General Green,* but none was commanded by a Jeffers or commissioned by Rhode Island. The same work's only reference to a *Trimmer* concerns a Pennsylvania-commissioned "boat" carrying ten men and mounting one gun (165).

5. Starkey, "The Origins and Regulation of Eighteenth-Century British Privateering," 69–81, Starkey, "Pirates and Markets," 107–24, and López Nadal, "Corsairing as a Commercial System: The Edges of Legitimate Trade," 125–36, all in Pennell, ed., *Bandits at Sea;* Frayler, *It's Only Money,* 4–5; Frayler, *Everybody Wants to Get in on the Act,* passim.

6. Cordingly, *Under the Black Flag,* 161–64; correspondence from Jeff Remling, South Street Seaport Museum, New York, New York, December 17, 2004; Davis, *Rigs of the Nine Principal Types of American Sailing Vessels,* passim; Kemp, *The History of Ships,* 108–9; Harland, *Seamanship in the Age of Sail,* 57, 62–63, 78; Lubbock, *Cruisers, Corsairs and Slavers,* 14–24; King, *Coast Guard Under Sail,* 66–67. Jeffers told Judge Hopson of one "privateer schooner, with a Big Gun amidships, which they had under cover" (from "Confessions of Gibbs the Pirate," *NYJOC,* April 7, 1831, 2).

7. MacLay, *A History of American Privateers,* 12–13, 40–41.

8. Petrie, *The Prize Game,* 69.

9. Schonhorn, ed., *General History of the Pyrates,* 4; Dow and Edmonds, *Pirates of the New England Coast,* 17; Hawes, *Off Soundings,* 68.

10. Dow and Edmonds, *Pirates of the New England Coast,* 9, 17, 30–43, 84–98, 346–47; Schonhorn, ed., *General History of the Pyrates,* 55–56, 419–39, 667–68, 684–85; Hawes, *Off Soundings,* 16, 17–23, 26–30, 36; Pérotin-Dumon, "The Pirate and the Emperor: Power and Law on the Seas, 1450–1850," in Pennell, ed., *Bandits at Sea,* 31.

11. Dow and Edmonds, *Pirates of the New England Coast,* 145–49, 288–308 (quoting the July 22, 1723 *New England Courant*); Schonhorn, ed., *General History of the Pyrates,* 318–36; Hawes, *Off Soundings,* 59, 61.

12. Hawes, *Off Soundings,* 78–101; MacLay, *History of American Privateers,* viii, 69, 77–78; Frayler, *Everybody Wants to Get in on the Act,* passim.

13. NHS-Jeffers; Ralph S. Mohr, *Governors for Three Hundred Years*, 130; Hawes, *Off Soundings*, 99, 211, 223, 228, 230; Copy of deed "received the 15th of January, 1799," Land Evidence, Book 8:77, and copy of deed "received April 29th 1803," Land Evidence, Book 8:410–11, Portsmouth (Rhode Island) Town Hall. Descendants of the Gibbs maritime clan had their own idea who "Gibbs the Pirate" was: "a mate on one of George Gibbs's vessels who assumed the name of Gibbs, organized a mutiny, turned pirate and committed numerous depredations." But the brief reference to this piratical "character, well-known at the time" appears alongside examples of George Gibbs's pre-1800 commerce, well before Jeffers's career. George Gibbs, *The Gibbs Family of Rhode Island and Some Related Families*, 12–13.

14. The June 10, 1815, customs list for the *Starling* is contained in the 1815 folder in NA-RG36 (box 40). According to the DAR application in NHS-Jeffers, Samuel Jeffers Jr. was born June 2, 1794. He may be the same Samuel Jeffers of Newport who died in January 1826 "at Valparaiso, aged 31 years," listed in Arnold, ed., *Vital Records of Rhode Island*, 18:518.

15. NHS-Jeffers; Arnold, ed., *Vital Records of Rhode Island*, 21:302 and 18:518; "Confessions of Gibbs the Pirate," *NYJOC*, April 7, 1831, 2; "An interesting and correct account of the Execution of the Pirates," in *The Confession of the Terrible Pirate Charles Gibbs*, 2.

Chapter 3: The *Hornet*, the *Chesapeake*, and the "Boston Grocery"

1. The muster rolls and payrolls for American warships of the era are in NA-RG45-T829. Also Record Group 45, box 565, of the U.S. Navy Subject File contains lists of prisoners exchanged from the USS *Chesapeake*.

2. Tucker and Reuter, *Injured Honor*, 191; NA-RG45-T829, roll 30, USS *Chesapeake*, and roll 90, USS *Constitution*; Martin, *A Most Fortunate Ship*, 74; correspondence from Jeff Remling, December 17, 2004, South Street Seaport Museum, New York, New York.

3. *Mutiny and Murder*, 6, 29.

4. Gibson, *Demon of the Waters*, 10–18, 43–47.

5. McKee, *A Gentlemanly and Honorable Profession*, 155; Dana, *Two Years before the Mast*, 17; Doyle, "The Adventure of the Sussex Vampire," 1025.

6. Gibson, *Demon of the Waters*, 66; Robson, *Boy Seaman R.N.*, 13.

7. Davie, "Observations and Instructions," in Lavery, ed., *Shipboard Life and Organization*, 266–67; MacLay, *History of American Privateers*, 127–28; Dana, *Two Years before the Mast*, 166; Gibson, *Demon of the Waters*, 66; Phillipson, *Band of Brothers*, 5–9.

8. The illustration is reproduced in, among other sources, Botting, *The Pirates*, 28–29.

9. Tucker and Reuter, *Injured Honor*, 1–17, 81–82, 191, 202–4; Guttridge and Smith, *The Commodores*, 111–12, 121–35, 147–71, 211–12, 289–99; NA-RG45-T829, roll 30, USS *Chesapeake*. For the term *frigate*, see "Definitions of Old Sea

Craft," in Schonhorn, ed., *A General History of the Pyrates*, xlvi, and Kemp, *The History of Ships*, 115–17.

10. Robinson, *Jack Nastyface*, 25–26, 28.

11. Dana, *Two Years before the Mast*, 5. For more on the purser's duties, see McKee, *A Gentlemanly and Honorable Profession*, 350–63.

12. Frayler, *Seaman's Clothing in* Friendship's *Era*, 2–4, and Frayler, *Shoes, Ships, and Survival*, passim.

13. Harland, *Seamanship in the Age of Sail*, 91–93, and passim; Dana, *Two Years before the Mast*, 8–9. For the British influence on American naval regulations, see Valle, *Rocks and Shoals*, 41.

14. Stephen Stewart and John Von Radowitz, "Skeleton Jigsaw Reveals Life of an Ancient Mariner," *Herald* (Glasgow), September 11, 2004, 28; Matt Joyce, "Remains of 17th Century Sailor Laid to Rest," Associated Press story released February 3, 2004.

15. Dana, *Two Years before the Mast*, 29–31; McKee, *A Gentlemanly and Honorable Profession*, 149.

16. Frayler, *Repeat Performance*, passim; Frayler, *Fire and Lights*, passim. Harlow, *The Making of a Sailor*, 150; Guttridge, *Mutiny*, 7.

17. McKee, *A Gentlemanly and Honorable Profession*, 170–77, 246–47; Dana, *Two Years before the Mast*, 11–12, 54–55; Bligh, quoted in Alexander, *The Bounty*, 94.

18. Valle, *Rocks & Shoals*, 3, 16, 18, 41–42, 81; Alden, *Lawrence Kearny*, 116; Langley, *Social Reform in the United States Navy*, 163; Guttridge, *Mutiny*, 8–9; McKee, *A Gentlemanly and Honorable Profession*, 264–66.

19. Quoted in McKee, *A Gentlemanly and Honorable Profession*, 240–41.

20. Quoted in Giovanni Bonello, *Histories of Malta*, 118 (citing Innes, *The History of Torture*, 97).

21. Harland, *Seamanship in the Age of Sail*, 93–94; Dana, *Two Years before the Mast*, 156; Lavery, ed., *Shipboard Life and Organization*, 183.

22. Dash, *Batavia's Graveyard*, 71–72; Dana, *Two Years before the Mast*, 154, 201; Frayler, *Rats*, passim; correspondence from John Frayler, Salem (Massachusetts) National Maritime Historical Site, January 11, 2005.

23. Harlow, *Making of a Sailor*, 147–49; Dash, *Batavia's Graveyard*, 73–74; Frayler, *Pickled Fish and Salted Provisions*, passim.

24. Dana, *Two Years before the Mast*, 208–9.

25. Frayler, *The Medicine Chest*, 4–9.

26. Martin, *A Most Fortunate Ship*, 75–76; Uden and Cooper, *Dictionary of British Ships and Seamen*, 404; Tucker, *Handbook of 19th Century Naval Warfare*, 10–13; Frayler, "Armed to the Teeth," passim.

27. "Sam" to "Honoured Father," quoted in Lewis, ed., *Life before the Mast*, 170–71 (citing Moorhouse, ed. *Letters of the English Seaman*).

28. Tucker and Reuter, *Injured Honor*, 191; NA-RG45-T829, roll 30, USS *Chesapeake*, and roll 90, USS *Constitution*; Frayler, *Seaman's Clothing in* Friendship's *Era*, 4.

29. Martin, *A Most Fortunate Ship*, 15, 127–30, and passim; NA-RG45-T829, rolls 72 and 73, USS *President*. National Archives materials checked for further reference to "Jefferies" include contemporary navy court-martial records in Record Group 125, microfilm publication 273.

30. "Confessions of Gibbs the Pirate," *NYJOC*, April 7, 1831, 2.

31. "A visit to the condemned criminals, Gibbs and Wansley," in *The Confession of the Terrible Pirate Charles Gibbs*, 17.

32. Guttridge and Smith, *The Commodores*, 170, 186, 205–6, 209–18; MacLay, *History of American Privateers*, 11; Miller, *Broadsides*, 345–46; Lambert, *War at Sea in the Age of Sail*, 193–98; Tucker and Reuter, *Injured Honor*, 82; Tucker, *Handbook of 19th Century Naval Warfare*, 13. In 1820 James Barron, senior officer on *Chesapeake* during the 1807 *Leopard* incident, restored his reputation by killing Stephen Decatur, his chief critic, in a duel. That same year the *Chesapeake*, then serving the British government as a Devon prison ship, was dismantled for its wood, some of which remains in the Chesapeake Mill in Wickham, Hampshire, England. As Guttridge and Smith relate, the mill is located "near a riverbank, with its joists and floor beams, portions of deck once paced by Barron, Decatur, and Lawrence, easily visible from within. . . . It is seldom visited by Americans" (*The Commodores*, 289–99, 322).

33. "Gibbs the Pirate," *NYJOC*, March 30, 1831, 2.

34. Guttridge and Smith, *The Commodores*, 212.

35. "A visit to the condemned criminals, Gibbs and Wansley," in *The Confession of the Terrible Pirate Charles Gibbs*, 17.

36. "Confessions of Gibbs the Pirate," *NYJOC*, April 7, 1831, 2. This article conveys a slightly different version of the "Boston grocery" story originally given in "Gibbs the Pirate," *NYJOC*, March 30, 1831, 2.

37. Ellms, *The Pirates Own Book*, vi–viii, 98.

38. *The Boston Directory* for 1816, 114; *The Boston Directory* for 1818, 99. Krieger, Cobb, and Turner, eds., *Mapping Boston*, 7, 120, 191, 193.

39. "Gibbs the Pirate," *Salem Gazette*, April 19, 1831, 4; Krieger, Cobb, and Turner, *Mapping Boston*, 193; Liberty Square—at the junction of Kilby, Water, and Batterymarch streets in Boston—was named in 1793 (Boston Board of Street Commissioners, *A Record of the Streets, Alleys, Places, Etc. in the City of Boston*, 220).

Chapter 4: Going to Sea in a Lawless Age

1. "One authority," quoted in MacLay, *History of American Privateers*, 31–32.

2. "Execution of the Pirates," *NYJOC*, April 23, 1831, 2; *SRE Newport* 1:81; correspondence from Jeff Remling, South Street Seaport Museum, New York, New York, December 17, 2004; crew lists and other customs documents in NA-RG36; and entries under the page 3 "Ship News" column of the *Newport Mercury* for the following dates in 1816: January 13, March 30, April 27, May 11, June 1, August 17, and August 24. Another candidate for Jeffers's *Brutus* (but less likely given its design) was a two-deck, three-masted ship built in Connecticut in 1806. It was

about 104 feet long and 28 feet broad at its widest point. It was registered in Providence in May 1815 and registered in New York in October 1817 by new owners, New York City merchants Charles C. and John Griswold, who named Barzilla Goodrich as the *Brutus's* captain. The approximately 372-ton vessel appears to have soon changed hands, for Robert Allen was listed as its "husband or managing owner" when it was "condemned as unseaworthy" at New York that December. NA-RG41, vol. 11964, book no. 148, Registers [of] Sail, September 27, 1815 to December 9, 1815; and NA-RG41, Master Abstract of Registers, 1815–1912, I:202 and I:223. While their holdings of customs records for Newport go back to Jeffers's era (and include documents for Newport-based ships filed in Charleston), according to National Archives officials their Charleston-specific collection starts in 1840. But it is possible that a crew list exists somewhere, for some port, that would show how James Jeffers got to the Caribbean.

3. Allen, *Our Navy and the West Indian Pirates*, 5.

4. Emmons, *The Navy of the United States*, 76–77; King, *The Coast Guard Under Sail*, 65; Allen, *Our Navy and the West Indian Pirates*, 6, 9; "Highly important law case," *NWR*, April 19, 1817, 114; Bradlee, *Piracy in the West Indies*, 17–19. For this spelling of Laffite's name, see John Smith Kendall, "The Successors of Laffite," 363.

5. Lubbock, *Cruisers, Corsairs and Slavers*, 59–66; Allen, *Our Navy and the West Indian Pirates*, 6–9; Bradlee, *Piracy in the West Indies*, 17–20; Emmons, *The Navy of the United States*, 76–77; Spain, "Flags of the Texas Revolution"; Vale, *War betwixt Englishmen*. Nothing suggests Jeffers ever sailed with Jean Laffite's crews from New Orleans; yet one likely apocryphal story holds that he was known to the smuggler boss. According to Lubbock (*Cruisers, Corsairs & Slavers*, 62), Laffite once "contrived to capture a Spanish Governor, along with his Confessor and secretary; and accused him of being in league with the American pirate Gibbs. Lafitte [*sic*] rove nooses from his yardarms, and stood the wretched Governor and his priest beneath them, whilst the secretary rushed ashore in search of the fifty thousand dollars ransom money. And when the secretary came off with the doubloons, Lafitte politely bowed his prisoners over the side." The tale probably evolved as stories about "Charles Gibbs" flourished in the nineteenth century. No date is given for the alleged episode, but as Laffite's career lasted until at least 1821 it is plausible that he and Jeffers crossed paths. Jeffers and associates almost certainly ran afoul of other gangs.

6. "More of legitimacy," *NWR*, November 25, 1815, 215; "Case of the *Romp*," *NWR*, December 28, 1816, 289 (citing the *Richmond Enquirer*); Bailey, *A Diplomatic History of the American People*, 167, 168n5.

7. "South America," *NWR*, September 5, 1818, 32. The *Louisa* "was a prize to the Buenos Ayrean privateer *El Congreso*, and was purchased by the claimant, Almeida, armed and equipped by him at Ensenada, and in April, 1818, came to Baltimore to be refitted. She was there refitted, and sailed from that port in August, 1818 under the command of the claimant, ostensibly bound on a sealing voyage to

the North West Coast of America, with a crew of ninety-six men, principally citizens of the United States; and armed with ten guns and some small arms." *The Arrogante Barcelones*, 20 U.S. 496 (1822) case text. Almeida later lost the *Louisa* to mutineers, whose subsequent robbery of an American vessel sparked another federal case. See Lenoir, "Piracy Cases in the Supreme Court," 546–47.

8. "Miscellaneous," *NWR*, December 5, 1818, 265; "Naval," *NWR*, November 19, 1814, 172; Emmons, *The Navy of the United States*, 76–77; "'Spanish' America," *NWR*, August 2, 1817, 365; "'Spanish' America," *NWR*, July 26, 1817, 346; "'Spanish America,'" *NWR*, March 7, 1818, 31; Faye, "Privateersmen of the Gulf and Their Prizes," 1071–72.

9. Allen, *Our Navy and the West Indian Pirates*, 9–10; López Nadal, "Corsairing as a Commercial System," in Pennell, ed., *Bandits at Sea*, 125; Faye, "Privateersmen of the Gulf and Their Prizes," 1092; "Case of the *Romp*," *NWR*, December 28, 1816, 290 (citing the *Richmond Enquirer*). For Civil War privateering, see Robinson, *The Confederate Privateers*. For more on the legalities of privateering when insurgencies are involved, though using later examples, see George A. Finch, "Piracy in the Mediterranean," 664–65.

10. Destefani, "Guerra de corso contra el Brasil," 6:261; Vale, *War betwixt Englishmen*, 96–97; "South America," *NWR*, October 16, 1819, 111.

11. Allen, *Our Navy and the West Indian Pirates*, 9–11; "The U.S. Ship Peacock," *NWR*, November 9, 1822, 148; "Expedition to Porto Rico," *NWR*, March 22, 1823, 48; Lubbock, *Cruisers Corsairs and Slavers*, 59.

12. Berckman, *Victims of Piracy*, 15; Exquemelin, *The Buccaneers of America* 74–97, and passim; Schonhorn, ed., *A General History of the Pyrates*, 326–27.

13. MacLay, *History of American Privateers*, 11–12; Petrie, *The Prize Game*, 19–30.

14. Faye, "Privateersmen of the Gulf and Their Prizes," 1043 (citing Corrales, ed., *Documentos para la historia de la Provincia de Cartagena*, 2: 296–98).

15. Ibid., 1043 (citing Corrales, *Documentos*), 1046; Untitled article, *NWR*, January 4, 1817, 312 (citing the *Baltimore Patriot*); "'Spanish' America," *NWR*, July 26, 1817, 346; "The Marine List," *Lloyd's List*, September 20, 1816, 1. For more on the wars ashore, see Harvey, *Liberators*, passim; Rodríguez O., *The Independence of Spanish America*, passim; and Burkholder and Johnson, *Colonial Latin America*, 304–49.

16. Patterson to Secretary Crowninshield, quoted in Allen, *Our Navy and the West Indian Pirates*, 9–10; "Gibbs the Pirate," *NYJOC*, March 30, 1831, 2; Cordingly, *Under the Black Flag*, 160.

17. Faye, "Privateersmen of the Gulf and Their Prizes," 1092 (citing the *Gazeta de Buenos Ayres*, December 13, 1817); Vale, *War betwixt Englishmen*, 97–98.

18. "Confession of Gibbs the Pirate," *NYJOC*, April 7, 1831, 2; Lane, *Pillaging the Empire*, 18, 27, 35, 37, 65; Hakluyt, *The Principal Navigations, Voyages, Traffiques and Discoveries of the English Nation*, 16:223.

19. "Confession of Gibbs the Pirate," *NYJOC,* April 7, 1831, 2.

20. *SRE New Orleans* (1804–1820), I:73–74; correspondence from Carey Lucas Nikonchuk, South Carolina Historical Society, September 2, 2004; *SRE Newport* I:337–38; 1811 folder, NA-RG36.

21. *SRE Newport* I:337–38 and forms in the 1815 and 1816 folders in NA-RG36.

Chapter 5: The Privateer *Maria*

1. Harvey, *Liberators,* 135–36, 142–43, 154; Faye, "Privateersmen of the Gulf and Their Prizes," 1039–1040, 1044. For a history of New Granada up to about this point, see Rodríguez O., *The Independence of Spanish America,* 150–59.

2. Schonhorn, ed., *General History of the Pyrates,* 203.

3. "Gibbs the Pirate," *NYJOC,* March 30, 1831, 2; "Confession of Gibbs the Pirate," *NYJOC,* April 7, 1831, 2; "Savannah, October 31," *Charleston City Gazette and Commercial Daily Advertiser,* November 3, 1821, 2 (citing the *Georgian*); Faye, "Privateersmen of the Gulf and Their Prizes," 1040, 1044–47, 1062. Regarding the *Maria,* the author is grateful to Mauricio Tovar (correspondence, June 23, 2005), head of la División de Servicios al Público, Archivo General de la Nacion, Colombia, who performed a cursory search of the relevant Colombian archives. He reported finding no matches for Captain Bell's *Maria* although several nineteenth-century privateers employed that title or variants of it. The archivist noted that future research along this line might examine the extensive files of "la secretaría de guerra y marina," which contain 1,619 unindexed volumes.

4. Faye, "Privateersmen of the Gulf and Their Prizes," 1073.

5. "Case of the *Romp,*" *NWR,* December 28, 1816, 289 (citing the *Richmond Enquirer*).

6. "Spanish America," *NWR,* April 5, 1817, 95–96; "Spanish America," *NWR,* April 26, 1817, 139. Though Hutchings was acquitted of piracy in the case of the *Romp/Santafecino,* the vessel apparently remained impounded. On April 11, 1817, a federal judge in Virginia announced that "the schooner *Romp,* with her tackle, guns, &c. were declared to be forfeited to the United States; for being employed in cruising against, and committing hostilities upon, the subjects of the king of Spain. . . ." Four days later one Thomas Taylor, through an attorney, "prayed an appeal from the decree, which was allowed, on or before the 1st of May, upon the security of 500 dollars." See "The *Romp,*" *NWR,* April 26, 1817, 143.

7. "Relations with Spain, *NWR,* September 12, 1818, 42–43; "Commodore Taylor," *NWR,* October 3, 1818, 89 (citing the *New York Mercantile Advertiser*); "Law Case—S.A. Patriots, &c," *NWR,* October 10, 1818, 103–4 (citing the *New York Evening Post*); "Judicial Report," *NWR,* November 7, 1818, 167–75 (citing the *National Advocate*); "Commodore Taylor—a law case," *NWR,* December 19, 1818, 290.

8. Patterson to U.S. Navy Department, April 24, 1816, quoted in Allen, *Our Navy and the West Indian Pirates,* 10; Faye, "Privateersmen of the Gulf and Their

Prizes," 1051–56; "New Orleans, Aug. 4," *NWR,* September 11, 1819, 31 (citing the *Baltimore Patriot*).

9. "Pirates," *NWR,* May 27, 1820, 240.

10. "Americans in prison," *NWR,* April 5, 1817, 82 (citing the *Norfolk Beacon*). George Little, writing of service aboard an American privateer during the War of 1812, alleged that its captain once proposed cruising under both American and Cartagenian flags "and this to be kept a profound secret from the crew until we had sailed from port" quoted in Lewis, ed., *Life before the Mast,* 402–3, citing Little, *Life on the Ocean.*

11. "Confession of Gibbs the Pirate," *NYJOC,* April 7, 1831, 2.

12. Ibid.; George Little, quoted in Lewis, ed., *Life before the Mast,* 398–99, citing Little, *Life on the Ocean.*

13. Konstam, *History of Pirates,* 184–85; "Piracy," *NWR,* September 15, 1821, 48.

14. Lubbock, *Cruisers, Corsairs and Slavers,* 26, 48.

15. Woodbury, *The Great Days of Piracy in the West Indies,* 95.

16. Frayler, *The Arms Chest,* passim; Held, *The Age of Firearms,* 103; Harvey, *Liberators,* 156–57.

17. Konstam, *History of Pirates,* 117; Woodbury, *The Great Days of Piracy,* 95; Correspondence from Jeff Remling, South Street Seaport Museum, New York, New York, December 17, 2004.

18. Lubbock, *Cruisers, Corsairs and Slavers,* 76.

19. Exquemelin, *The Buccaneers of America,* 14–15, 58.

20. R. Henley to secretary of the navy, October 30, 1821, printed in *Charleston City Gazette and Commercial Daily Advertiser,* December 8, 1821, 2; Lubbock, *Cruisers, Corsairs and Slavers,* 48–49; Smith, *The Atrocities of the Pirates,* 9, 11, 13, 26.

21. "Confession of Gibbs the Pirate," *NYJOC,* April 7, 1831, 2; "Spanish America," *NWR,* March 15, 1817, 47.

22. Held, *Age of Firearms,* 162; "Privateering—and Piracy," *NWR,* April 17, 1819, 129; "Savannah, Aug. 17," *NWR,* August 29, 1818, 9; "South America," *NWR,* September 19, 1818, 63.

23. "The Privateer *Gen. Rondeau,*" *Newport Mercury,* July 1, 1820, 3 (citing the *Boston Centinel*); "Piracies," *NWR,* June 24, 1820, 298; *Campañas navales de la República Argentina,* II:199.

24. "South America," *NWR,* September 12, 1818, 41.

25. "Confession of Gibbs the Pirate," *NYJOC,* April 7, 1831, 2; Smith, *The Atrocities of the Pirates,* 95–96.

26. Robert M. Harrison to John Quincy Adams, April 20, 1817, quoted in Allen, *Our Navy and the West Indian Pirates,* 11–12; "Case of the *Romp,*" *NWR,* December 28, 1816, 289 (citing the *Richmond Enquirer*).

27. Schonhorn, ed., *General History of the Pyrates,* 167; Cordingly, *Under the Black Flag,* 98; Smith, *The Atrocities of the Pirates,* 9; Dow and Edmonds, *The*

Pirates of the New England Coast, 354–55. A pirate quartermaster's tasks are detailed elsewhere, but on navy vessels, according to Martin, "The quartermasters were among the most experienced seamen aboard and had charge of signals, keeping a lookout, and steering the ship" (*A Most Fortunate Ship*, 73). For steering, see also under "Captain's Orders, HMS *Amazon*, 1799," in Lavery, ed., *Shipboard Life and Organization*, 133. The sailing master's job was "an honourable and responsible one," but its "responsibilities were endless." He "wore no uniform" but took charge of navigation, equipment, and general management of the entire ship (Beaglehole, *The Life of Captain James Cook*, 26). A boatswain (English sailors pronounced the title as *bo'sun*) oversaw rigging and canvas. See Harland, *Seamanship in the Age of Sail*, 18, 94; "Regulations and Instructions Relating to His Majesty's Service at Sea" and "Captain's Orders, HMS *Amazon*, 1799," in Lavery, ed., *Shipboard Life and Organization*, 27–28, 129, 155–57. Though boatswains were known for their traditional use of a pipe or whistle to call hands to work, surviving examples indicate that in the Dutch merchant service the instrument (known as a *sifflet*) was a nonworking item for ornamental purposes only (Harm Stevens, *Dutch Enterprise and the VOC*, 26–27). The gunner was in charge of all weaponry and powder stores aboard ship. See "Regulations and Instructions Relating to His Majesty's Service at Sea," and "Captain's Orders, HMS *Amazon*, 1799," in Lavery, ed., *Shipboard Life and Organization*, 29–37, 131.

28. "Confession of Gibbs the Pirate," *NYJOC*, April 7, 1831, 2; Smith, *The Atrocities of the Pirates*, 7–8.

29. Drake, *Trials of Wansley and Gibbs*, 10, 15.

Chapter 6: "Against all nations"

1. "Confessions of Gibbs the Pirate," *NYJOC*, April 7, 1831, 2. An earlier footnote refers to Joseph Almeida's loss of the *Louisa* to mutineers, who then robbed an American vessel. Lenoir, "Piracy Cases in the Supreme Court," 546–47. Other examples of privateers turning pirate might include the *Pelican*. In summer 1818 this five-gun schooner was apparently operating on a privateering commission when its forty-five-man crew mutinied, killed their captain, then robbed two vessels. "Ship News," *Newport Mercury*, September 26, 1818, 3. Another case involves the *Cienaga*, captured by the USS *Alligator* in 1822, discussed in a later chapter and documented in "Pirates, &c.," *NWR*, June 1, 1822, 221–22.

2. "Confessions of Gibbs the Pirate," *NYJOC*, April 7, 1831, 2.

3. "Shipping and Commerce," *NWR*, January 25, 1817, 353; "Shipping and Commerce," *NWR*, March 29, 1817, 69–70; "West Indies," *NWR*, June 7, 1817, 237; "Cuba," *NWR*, March 7, 1818, 31; "Negroes Imported," *NWR*, December 12, 1818, 269 (citing the *Dem. Press*).

4. "West Indies," *NWR*, June 14, 1817, 250; "From Havana," *Newport Mercury*, July 15, 1820, 3; "The Cuba Pirates," *NWR*, November 16, 1822, 164.

5. Exquemelin, *The Buccaneers of America*, 105. U.S. House of Representatives, 18th Congress, 1st Session, *Report of the Committee on Foreign Affairs*, 2.

6. "West Indies," *NWR*, May 10, 1817, 174; "Privateering," *NWR*, July 6, 1822, 289; "Pirates of Cuba," *NWR*, March 23, 1822, 49; "Boston, Nov. 5," *Charleston City Gazette and Commercial Daily Advertiser*, November 17, 1821, 2; Konstam, *The History of Pirates*, 163; "Confession of Gibbs the Pirate," *NYJOC*, April 7, 1831, 2; "Pirates, &c.," *NWR*, June 1, 1822, 221–22; Havana *Noticioso*, quoted in "Piracy," *NWR*, April 20, 1822, 114. For accounts of local expeditions against the marauders, see "The Pirates of Cuba," *NWR*, March 16, 1822, 34, and "Pirates of Cuba," *NWR*, March 23, 1822, 49.

7. Untitled item under "Editorial Articles," *NWR*, January 5, 1822, 290; "The Pirates of Cuba," *NWR*, March 16, 1822, 34; Smith, *The Atrocities of the Pirates*, 35–36; Alden, *Lawrence Kearny*, 40.

8. "A Card," *Charleston Courier*, November 13, 1821, 2.

9. "Confessions of Gibbs the Pirate," *NYJOC*, April 7, 1831, 2.

10. Schonhorn, ed., *A General History of the Pyrates*, 371; Botting, *The Pirates*, 48–49; Cordingly, *Under the Black Flag*, 114–19.

11. Lubbock, *Cruisers, Corsairs and Slavers*, 67, 76; Morison, "Old Bruin," 79; Smith, *The Atrocities of the Pirates*, 54–55, 73–74; Konstam, *History of Pirates*, 98–101; "West Indies," *NWR*, October 5, 1822, 69 (citing the *Kingston Chronicle*); Cordingly, *Under the Black Flag*, 130–31.

12. "Confessions of Gibbs the Pirate," *NYJOC*, April 7, 1831, 2. Jeffers is quoted as saying he made "an oath on the bible, that I never would disclose the names of my associates" ("A visit to the condemned criminals, Gibbs and Wansley," in *The Confession of the Terrible Pirate Charles Gibbs*, 18).

13. "The Pirate Gibbs," *Charleston Courier*, April 19, 1831, 2; More, *Utopia*, 33.

14. Hohnen, *Hamlet's Castle and Shakespeare's Elsinore*, 18; Cordingly, *Under the Black Flag*, 223–40; Schonhorn, ed., *General History of the Pyrates*, 451.

15. "Spanish America," *NWR*, March 7, 1818, 31; "Florida," *NWR*, June 7, 1817, 237.

16. "South America," *NWR*, May 17, 1817, 184; "South America," *NWR*, October 23, 1819, 128.

17. Quoted in *Mutiny and Murder*, 8–9.

18. "Confessions of Gibbs the Pirate," *NYJOC*, April 7, 1831, 2; Schonhorn, ed., *General History of the Pyrates*, 350–51; Langley, *Social Reform in the United States Navy*, ix, 209–41, and passim; Pack, *Nelson's Blood: The Story of Naval Rum*, 131–32, 135–36; Alden, *Lawrence Kearny*, 75; Valle, *Rocks and Shoals*, 200–211.

19. "Confessions of Gibbs the Pirate," *NYJOC*, April 7, 1831, 2; "I" entry no. 373 (Indispensable), *Register of Shipping* (1816); Lawrence Kearny to Commodore Patterson, December 28, 1821, NA-RG45-M124, roll 91; Lubbock, *Cruisers, Corsairs and Slavers*, 60.

20. Smith, *The Atrocities of the Pirates*, 36–40.

21. "Confessions of Gibbs the Pirate," *NYJOC*, April 7, 1831, 2; Botting, *The Pirates*, 178.

22. Dana, *Two Years before the Mast*, 16–17.

23. November 16, 1824, deposition by George Brown, contained in the report of John Mountain, vice commercial agent of the United States in Havana. U.S. Senate, 18th Congress, 2nd Session, *In Senate of the United States,* 1–2.

24. Bradlee, *Piracy in the West Indies,* 141 (quoting the *Marblehead Messenger,* January 21, 1881). The story of Zachary G. Lamson, who armed the *Belvidere* after that vessel's first experience with pirates, is detailed in a later chapter.

25. "Confessions of Gibbs the Pirate," *NYJOC,* April 7, 1831, 2.

26. Smith, *The Atrocities of the Pirates,* 29–32; *The History of the Lives and Bloody Exploits of the Most Noted Pirates,* 267.

27. Schonhorn, ed., *General History of the Pyrates,* 194–95, 244, 269, 281–82, 330.

28. Snow, *Pirates and Buccaneers of the Atlantic Coast,* 275.

29. Exquemelin, *Buccaneers of America,* 58; Schonhorn, ed., *General History of the Pyrates,* 138–39, 194–95, 213–14; Dow and Edmonds, *The Pirates of the New England Coast, 1630–1730,* 353–56; Cordingly, *Under the Black Flag,* 96–98.

30. Smith, *The Atrocities of the Pirates,* 43; Lubbock, *Cruisers, Corsairs & Slavers,* 48; "Piracy," *Charleston City Gazette and Commercial Daily Advertiser,* December 20, 1821, 2.

31. "Confessions of Gibbs the Pirate," *NYJOC,* April 7, 1831, 2.

32. "Piracy," *NWR,* October 20, 1821, 118–19; "West Indies," *NWR,* June 13, 1818, 271; "Pirates," *NWR,* September 29, 1821, 80; Robert S. Redmond, postscript to Smith, *The Atrocities of the Pirates,* 135–36; "West Indies," *NWR,* October 5, 1822, 69 (citing the *Kingston Chronicle*).

33. Untitled article in the "Chronicle" section, *NWR,* November 30, 1816, 223.

34. Don Luis de Onis, quoted in Allen, *Our Navy and the West Indian Pirates,* 10–11; Untitled article, *NWR,* January 4, 1817, 312 (citing the *Baltimore Patriot* and the *New Orleans Gazette*); "Spanish America," *NWR,* February 1, 1817, 380.

35. "Enforcement of Neutrality," *NWR,* February 1, 1817, 383–84; "Laws of the United States," *NWR,* March 22, 1817, 51–52; "West Indies," *NWR,* May 10, 1817, 174; "Proclamation," *NWR,* January 31, 1818, 376 (citing the London *Gazette*).

36. "Ship News," *Newport Mercury,* December 21, 1816, 3; "Case of the ship *Providencia,*" *NWR,* December 12, 1818, 269 (citing the *Norfolk Herald*). For an example involving Joseph Almeida and his taking of a Spanish ship in 1818, see the case text *The Arrogante Barcelones,* 20 U.S. 496 (1822), online at http://supreme.justia.com/us/20/496/case.html.

37. "Confessions of Gibbs the Pirate," *NYJOC,* April 7, 1831, 2; Allen, *Our Navy and the West Indian Pirates,* 14. In 1830, when Jeffers came ashore after scuttling the *Vineyard,* his original story was that he had been mate of a vessel called the *William.* "Mutiny and Murder," *Baltimore Patriot,* December 4, 1830, 2 (citing the *New York Commercial Advertiser*).

38. This section is based on relevant entries in the 1816 *Register of Shipping* and the following references from *Lloyd's List:* "Barbadoes" (*Earl Moira* as a troop transport), January 26, 1816, 2; "Barbadoes" (*Earl Moira*), March 8, 1816, 2;

"Guadaloupe" (*Earl Moira*), March 12, 1816, 2; "Baltimore" (*Earl Moira*), November 12, 1816, 2; "Insurgent Cruizers" (*Jane*), May 16, 1817, 1; and "Jamaica" (*Earl Moira*), May 20, 1817, 2.

39. "Confessions of Gibbs the Pirate," *NYJOC*, April 7, 1831, 2; Lubbock, *Cruisers, Corsairs & Slavers*, 31; Smith, *The Atrocities of the Pirates*, 92–93.

40. "Confessions of Gibbs the Pirate," *NYJOC*, April 7, 1831, 2; Lubbock, *Cruisers, Corsairs & Slavers*, 69.

41. "Pirates," *NWR*, November 30, 1822, 193.

42. Allen, *Our Navy and the West Indian Pirates*, 12–15; Faye, "Privateersmen of the Gulf and Their Prizes," 1044, 1045; Rodriguez, "Louis Aury: Héroe Naval de la Gran Colombia," passim; "Notice," *Boston Daily Advertiser*, September 19, 1816, 1.

43. "Florida," *NWR*, July 26, 1817, 347; "Florida," *NWR*, August 16, 1817, 397; "Florida," *NWR*, October, 25, 1817, 143; "Florida," *NWR*, November 8, 1817, 175; "Amelia Island," *NWR*, December 20, 1817, 267; "Amelia," *NWR*, January 24, 1818, 360; "Amelia Island," *NWR*, January 31, 1818, 375; Allen, *Our Navy and the West Indian Pirates*, 14–15; King, *The Coast Guard Under Sail*, 73. For more on Aury at Old Providence, see "Proclamation," *NWR*, October 3, 1818, 90–91.

44. "Gibbs the Pirate," *NYJOC*, March 30, 1831, 2; "Confessions of Gibbs the Pirate," *NYJOC*, April 7, 1831, 2. In the latter source the reporter's narrative places this episode "during the cruise which was made in the latter part of 1817 and the beginning of 1818." But the same article contains the transcript of Judge Hopson's notes, which includes Jeffers's reference on March 23, 1831, to the capture of a "Dutch ship from Curacoa in 1819, vessel and cargo destroyed." Like so much originally published about the Gibbs-Jeffers tale, there is no explanation for the discrepancy.

45. "West Indies," *NWR*, August 21, 1819, 430.

46. "Confessions of Gibbs the Pirate," *NYJOC*, April 7, 1831, 2; *Mutiny and Murder*, 12.

47. Jack Beater, *Pirates and Buried Treasure on Florida Islands*, 31.

48. Turley, *Rum, Sodomy & the Lash*, 28–29; Schonhorn, ed., *General History of the Pyrates*, 153–65, 212. For more on women pirates, see Cordingly, *Under the Black Flag*, xvi, 56–78; John C. Appleby, "Women and Piracy in Ireland: From Gráinne O'Malley to Anne Bonny," 283–98; and Rediker, "Liberty beneath the Jolly Roger: The Lives of Anne Bonny and Mary Read, Pirates," in Pennell, ed., *Bandits at Sea*, 299–320. U.S. Navy pirate hunter Lawrence Kearny reported that one Cape Antonio gang included "even a *woman* and *children* . . . belonging to the [then-imprisoned] captain of them," Kearny to David Porter, August 10, 1823, quoted in Alden, *Lawrence Kearny*, 59 (emphasis in original).

49. *Mutiny and Murder*, 12, 14; "Confessions of Gibbs the Pirate," *NYJOC*, April 7, 1831, 2; "Brief Notices," *NWR*, April 9, 1831, 94; "Gibbs the Pirate," *NYJOC*, March 30, 1831, 2.

Chapter 7: The Pirate Hunters and Their Prey

1. "Spanish America," *NWR*, December 20, 1817, 266; Frayler, *The Medicine Chest*, 9; "South America," *NWR*, October 31, 1818, 156.

2. "South American Affairs," *NWR*, July 11, 1818, 342.

3. "South America," *NWR*, August 1, 1818, 392; "South America," *NWR*, October 31, 1818, 156; "Miscellaneous," *NWR*, December 5, 1818, 265.

4. Bailey, *A Diplomatic History of the American People*, 163–74; Allen, *Our Navy and the West Indian Pirates*, 17, 97–98.

5. Kendall, "The Successors of Laffite," 363–66; King, *The Coast Guard Under Sail*, 69–70; Allen, *Our Navy and the West Indian Pirates*, 16–20; Emmons, *The Navy of the United States*, 76–77; Konstam, *The History of Pirates*, 162–63; "Chronicle," *NWR*, October 16, 1819, 111; "Chronicle," *NWR*, October 23, 1819, 128; "Piracies," *NWR*, December 25, 1819, 287; "Sixteen Pirates Condemned," *NWR*, February 5, 1820, 400; "Pirates," *NWR*, January 15, 1820, 335; "New-Orleans," *NWR*, June 3, 1820, 256; "Chronicle," *NWR*, June 17, 1820, 287; "New-Orleans," *NWR*, June 17, 1820, 288.

6. "Confessions of Gibbs the Pirate," *NYJOC*, April 7, 1831, 2; Snow, *Pirates and Buccaneers of the Atlantic Coast*, 278; Lubbock, *Cruisers, Corsairs & Slavers*, 73.

7. "Confessions of Gibbs the Pirate," *NYJOC*, April 7, 1831, 2.

8. Ibid.; Untitled item under "Providence," *Literary Subaltern*, March 25, 1831, 4.

9. Snow, *Pirates and Buccaneers of the Atlantic Coast*, 278; "Confessions of Gibbs the Pirate," *NYJOC*, April 7, 1831, 2.

10. Beater, *Pirates and Buried Treasure on Florida Islands*, 33–34.

11. "Confessions of Gibbs the Pirate," *NYJOC*, April 7, 1831, 2. After Jeffers's execution, it was reported that "his family received 10 or 12 years since what they considered an authentic account of his death at New Orleans" (see "Gibbs, the Pirate," *Newport Mercury*, April 16, 1831, 3).

12. "Confessions of Gibbs the Pirate," *NYJOC*, April 7, 1831, 2. Of the *Dido*, in late February 1815 the Newport-based schooner *Mars* encountered "the Bremen ship *Dido*, bound for the Virgin Islands" (MacLeish, "Portrait of a Yankee Skipper," 1, 38–43, 97). According to Kemp, *The History of Ships*, 153, the three-masted barque had square-rigged fore and main masts, and a schooner-rigged mizzen (rearmost) mast. Regarding Jeffers's mention of the *Larkin* in his confessions to Hopson, the 1820 edition of the London-published *Register of Shipping* includes a Whitby-based *Larkin* in its "L" section (entry 128), though it was not a barque. The *Journal of Commerce* writer ("Confessions of Gibbs the Pirate," April 7, 1831, 2) held that Jeffers's reference to the *Larkin* actually meant the *Larch*, captured at Cape Antonio in October 1821, but rescued soon after by the USS *Enterprise*. The writer was "doubtless" about this, even though the *Larch* was a brig, not a barque, and was of St. Andrews, not London.

13. "Chronicle," *NWR*, January 1, 1820, 304; *Dictionary of American Naval Fighting Ships*, 2:355–56, and 3:605; NA-RG45-P, entry 72, Statements of Service from Officers ("Returns of Services of Officers"), August 1842–August 1843, vol. 2 (containing the summary of Kearny's career).

14. Alden, *Lawrence Kearny*, 34–36; Lubbock, *Cruisers, Corsairs & Slavers*, 70.

15. Bailey, *Diplomatic History*, 303; Alden, *Lawrence Kearny*, 129–86.

16. Allen, *Our Navy and the West Indian Pirates*, 20; Konstam, *History of Pirates*, 154; "South America," *NWR*, July 29, 1820, 398; "Privateering or Piracy," *NWR*, May 19, 1821, 192; "Philadelphia, May 19," *NWR*, June 2, 1821, 224; "Chronicle," *NWR*, June 17, 1820, 287; "A Pirate," *NWR*, August 5, 1820, 416.

17. Allen, *Our Navy and the West Indian Pirates*, 20–21; Bailey, *Diplomatic History*, 173–74; Kearny to secretary of the navy, March 13 and 28, 1821, abstracts of which appear in "Letters written to the Department by Naval Officers concerning the suppression of piracy in the West Indies and Gulf of Mexico, 1821–25," a June 1937 document in NA-RG45-SGIS citing NA-RG45-M148.

18. Allen, *Our Navy and the West Indian Pirates*, 21–23; "Piracy," *NWR*, September 15, 1821, 48; "Piracies," *NWR*, September 22, 1821, 64; "Pirates," *NWR*, September 29, 1821, 80; "Piracy," *NWR*, October 20, 1821, 118–19.

19. Faye, "Privateersmen of the Gulf and Their Prizes," 1082 (citing the *Washington Gazette*, August 27, 1821).

20. Bradlee, *Piracy in the West Indies*, 51–57, 69–70; Lubbock, *Cruisers, Corsairs & Slavers*, 70–72; Gonzalez, *The Caloosahatchee*, 118–30.

21. "Piracies," *NWR*, September 22, 1821, 64

22. "Richmond, October 24," *Charleston Courier*, October 30, 1821, 2 (citing the [Richmond?] *Advertiser*).

23. "Piracy," *NWR*, October 20, 1821, 118–19; "From the New-York Gazette, October 20," *Charleston City Gazette and Commercial Daily Advertiser*, October 26, 1821, 2.

24. Dunham, *Journal of Voyages*, 172–79, quoted in Alden, *Lawrence Kearny*, 44–51.

25. "Pleasing Intelligence: Capture of the Pirates!" *Charleston Courier*, October 31, 1821, 2; untitled articles, *Charleston Courier*, November 13, 1821, 2; Alden, *Lawrence Kearny*, 51–52. Built in Quincy, Massachusetts, in 1820, the 97-foot long *Aristides* was listed at 291 tons with a breadth of about 26 feet. Registration data describe it as having "two decks, two masts, square stern, no galleries, a billethead." *SRE Boston and Charlestown, 1821–1830*, 37.

26. "Pleasing Intelligence: Capture of the Pirates!" *Charleston Courier*, October 31, 1821, 2; untitled articles, *Charleston Courier*, November 13, 1821, 2; "The Pirates," *NWR*, November 10, 1821, 162; "Report of the Secretary of the Navy for the year 1822. Statement of Captures of Piratical Vessels and Boats made by Vessels of the United States Navy in the West Indies," NA-RG45-SGIS; "Naval," *NWR*,

November 24, 1821, 204; Kearny to secretary of the navy, November 12, 1821, NA-RG45-M148, roll 27; "Gibralatar, 6th November," *Lloyd's List*, December 4, 1821, 2.

27. "Pleasing Intelligence: Capture of the Pirates!" *Charleston Courier*, October 31, 1821, 2; "Confessions of Gibbs the Pirate," *NYJOC*, April 7, 1831, 2; "Pirates Taken," *Charleston City Gazette and Commercial Daily Advertiser*, October 31, 1821, 2 (citing unspecified "Havanna [sic] papers received at this Office"); Alden, *Lawrence Kearny*, 52; Kearny to secretary of the navy, November 12, 1821, NA-RG45-M148, roll 27; "Ship News," *Charleston City Gazette and Commercial Daily Advertiser*, November 12, 1821, 2. The coffee episode is mentioned in "Execution of the Pirates," *NYJOC*, April 23, 1831, 2.

28. "Pleasing Intelligence: Capture of the Pirates!" *Charleston Courier*, October 31, 1821, 2; "The Pirates," *NWR*, December 1, 1821, 213, (citing the St. Andrews *Herald*); Kearny to secretary of the navy, November 12, 1821, NA-RG45-M148, roll 27; Alden, *Lawrence Kearny*, 52 (citing Dunham, *Journal of Voyages*, 182–85); "Confessions of Gibbs the Pirate," *NYJOC*, April 7, 1831, 2. When the *Enterprise* later docked in Charleston it had on board a "Mr. Vinro, of this city, cast away on the coast of Cuba." Was this the "prisoner" taken at Cape Antonio? "Ship News," *Charleston City Gazette and Commercial Daily Advertiser*, November 12, 1821, 2.

29. "Pleasing Intelligence: Capture of the Pirates!" *Charleston Courier*, October 31, 1821, 2; untitled articles, *Charleston Courier*, November 13, 1821, 2. Of the mysterious French vessel, the excerpt from Misroon's logbook for October 17, 1821 ("Pleasing Intelligence") states that "After Capt. Kearney [sic] had dispatched the boats after the pirates yesterday, he stood round the Cape with the brig to the southward, and there captured another of the robbers, who had taken a French brig the day before bound to Campeachy." According to one of the untitled November 13 *Charleston Courier* articles: "It was reported that the pirates had a short time before captured a French ship, and murdered all on board, including a lady passenger; and the fact of a lady's clothes being found on board of one of their vessels, stained with blood, is strong confirmation of the report." And Kearny, in referring to blood-stained clothing found after the December 21 raid at Cape Antonio, wrote on December 28: "It will also be recollected that on a former occasion a female dress was found in the same state among those infernal rascals." Kearny to Commodore Patterson, December 28, 1821, NA-RG45-M124, roll 91.

30. "The Pirates," *NWR*, December 1, 1821, 213 (citing the St. Andrews *Herald*); Kearny to secretary of the navy, November 12, 1821, NA-RG45-M148, roll 27; "Ship News" columns, *Charleston City Gazette and Commercial Daily Advertiser*, November 3, 12, and 14, 1821, all appearing on 2; "Ship News," *Charleston Courier*, November 12, 1821, 2; "Salvage," *NWR*, January 19, 1822, 335.

31. "Pleasing Intelligence: Capture of the Pirates!" *Charleston Courier*, October 31, 1821, 2; "Ship News," *Charleston City Gazette and Commercial Daily Advertiser*, November 12, 1821, 2. The latter source reported that on December 17 Kearny met up with the schooner *Bold Commander*, which had had its own adventures with

pirates, and the officer "put on board some coffee and dry goods, (taken from the prizes) together with an officer on board, and ordered for this port [Charleston]." See also the account under "Ship News," *Charleston Courier,* November 12, 1821, 2. Hopner's command may be the vessel referred to in a report contained in the *New York Shipping and Commercial List* of January 15, 1825: The "Spanish brig '*Maceas,*' from Gibara, Cuba, for Cadiz, with a cargo of tobacco, was captured on the 3d ult. by the pirate schooner '*Centella,*' formerly a Colombian privateer" (quoted in Bradlee, *Piracy in the West Indies,* 158).

32. "Extract of a letter from Havana, dated 24th October, received at Boston," in *National Intelligencer,* November 15, 1821, 3; Kearny to secretary of the navy, November 12, 19, and 23, 1821, NA-RG45-M148, roll 27; "Naval," *NWR,* January 5, 1822, 304.

33. "Havana," *Charleston City Gazette and Commercial Daily Advertiser,* December 18, 1821, 2; untitled item under "Editorial Articles," *NWR,* January 5, 1822, 290; Kearny to Commodore Patterson, December 28, 1821, NA-RG45-M124, roll 91; "From Havana," *Charleston Courier,* November 23, 1821, 2; Bradlee, *Piracy in the West Indies,* 22.

34. "The Pirates," *NWR,* November 10, 1821, 162; "Piracy," *Charleston City Gazette and Commercial Daily Advertiser,* December 20, 1821, 2.

35. "More Piracy, Norfolk, Jan. 10," *Boston Columbian Centinel,* January 19, 1822, 2.

36. Untitled article, *Charleston City Gazette and Commercial Daily Advertiser,* December 29, 1821, 2; Kearny to secretary of the navy, December 18, 1821, NA-RG45-M124, roll 91; Kearny to Commodore Patterson, December 28, 1821, NA-RG45-M124, roll 91; "Report of the Secretary of the Navy for the year 1822. Statement of Captures of Piratical Vessels and Boats made by Vessels of the United States Navy in the West Indies," NA-RG45-SGIS.

37. "Confessions of Gibbs the Pirate," *NYJOC,* April 7, 1831, 2; Kearny to Commodore Patterson, December 28, 1821, NA-RG45-M124, roll 91.

38. "Report of the Secretary of the Navy for the year 1822. Statement of Captures of Piratical Vessels and Boats made by Vessels of the United States Navy in the West Indies," NA-RG45-SGIS; Allen, *Our Navy and the West Indian Pirates,* 21; R. Henley to secretary of the navy, October 30, 1821, printed in *Charleston City Gazette and Commercial Daily Advertiser,* December 8, 1821, 2; Emmons, *The Navy of the United States,* 76–77; "Pirates, &c.," *NWR,* June 1, 1822, 221–22.

Chapter 8: Shadow Years

1. "Confessions of Gibbs the Pirate," *NYJOC,* April 7, 1831, 2.

2. Ibid.; Allen, *Our Navy and the West Indian Pirates,* 29–30, citing *Essex Institute Historical Collection,* October 1922; Bradlee, *Piracy in the West Indies,* 1–5; Lamson, *The Autobiography of Capt. Zachary G. Lamson,* 254–55, 260. For more on the cotton trade, see Frayler, *Mericani,* passim.

3. "A Tale of Terror," *NWR*, July 13, 1822, 309–10.

4. "West Indies," *NWR*, October 5, 1822, 69 (citing the Kingston, Jamaica, *Chronicle*).

5. Allen, *Our Navy and the West Indian Pirates*, 24; Kearny to secretary of the navy, December 18, 1821, NA-RG45-M124, roll 91.

6. Lynch, *Naval Life*, quoted in Morison, *"Old Bruin,"* 78–79.

7. "The Pirates of Cuba," *NWR*, December 7, 1822, 211–12.

8. Morison, *"Old Bruin,"* 81; Allen, *Our Navy and the West Indian Pirates*, 39–41; Emmons, *The Navy of the United States*, 76–79; Alden, *Lawrence Kearny*, 55–59 (citing Farragut, *The Life of David Glasgow Farragut*, 95–97). In early 1823 Kearny was transferred from the *Enterprise* to the USS *Decoy*, which was a larger vessel serving an inactive role as supply ship to Porter's fleet. Once Porter established a new base at Key West, Kearny was able to obtain command of the USS *Greyhound*. On July 9 the *Enterprise* was damaged beyond repair when it ran aground, without casualties, on the West Indian island of Little Curaçao. Alden, *Lawrence Kearny*, 54; *Dictionary of American Naval Fighting Ships*, 2:355–56.

9. Bradlee, *Piracy in the West Indies*, 47–51; *The History of the Lives and Bloody Exploits of the Most Noted Pirates*, 272–76; Lubbock, *Cruisers, Corsairs and Slavers*. 85–86. Jeffers referred to his crew having once "had a very narrow escape at one time, from the English man-of-war brig *Coronation*," probably a reference to HMS *Carnation*, which according to Bradlee (*Piracy in the West Indies*, 47) was a sloop that cruised off Cuba in the early and mid-1820s. "Confessions of Gibbs the Pirate," *NYJOC*, April 7, 1831, 2.

10. "Confessions of Gibbs the Pirate," *NYJOC*, April 7, 1831, 2; Bradlee, *Piracy in the West Indies*, 157–62.

11. Lubbock, *Cruisers, Corsairs and Slavers*, 86; Lubbock, *The Blackwall Frigates*, quoted in Bradlee, *Piracy in the West Indies*, 147.

12. *Salem Gazette*, December 18, 1829, quoted in Bradlee, *Piracy in the West Indies*, 138–39.

13. "Confessions of Gibbs the Pirate," *NYJOC*, April 7, 1831, 2; Vale, *War betwixt Englishmen*, 83; Levene, ed., *Historia de America*, 5:160–64. *Hitty* candidates might include a 101.5-foot-long, 337-ton vessel built in South Berwick, Maine, in 1812. "She sailed the triangular trade route with cargoes of rum from the Caribbean and cotton from the South." Owner John Lord imported various goods into Portsmouth, New Hampshire (from "The Counting House Rediscovers Local Maritime History").

14. Destefani, "Guerra de corso contra el Brasil," 258, 261–63; Vale, *War betwixt Englishmen*, 96–99.

15. Ireland, *The Admiral from Mayo*, 47, 52–56, and passim; Vale, *War betwixt Englishmen*, 25–27.

16. Levene, *Historia de America*, 5:139–43; Destefani, "Guerra de corso contra el Brasil," 258; Robertson, "South America and the Monroe Doctrine," 101; Barbara

A. Tenenbaum, chief ed., *Encyclopedia of Latin American History and Culture,* 1:148; Lewis, *The History of Argentina,* 43.

17. "Confessions of Gibbs the Pirate," *NYJOC,* April 7, 1831, 2; Vale, *War betwixt Englishmen,* 245; Carranza, *Campañas navales de la República Argentina,* 4:187.

18. Vale, *War betwixt Englishmen,* ix, 26–28. Other sources consulted include Carranza, *Campañas navales de la República Argentina;* Destefani's three chapters on privateering during the Argentine-Brazil war in volume 6 of the *Historia Maritima Argentina* collection; and correspondence from Benicio Oscar Ahumada, professor of history, Departamento de Estudios Historicos Navales, Armada Argentina, April 17, 2006.

19. "Confessions of Gibbs the Pirate," *NYJOC,* April 7, 1831, 2; Carranza, *Campañas navales de la República Argentina,* 2:263, 266, 277, and 4:178, 185, 186, 189. Ireland, *Admiral from Mayo,* 152, describes a corvette as "a flush-decked three-masted sailing ship smaller and normally less speedy than a frigate with about 20 or fewer cannon firing fairly light shot."

20. The song lyrics—credited to William Finney, who was wounded aboard the ship at its final battle on July 30, 1826—are reproduced on a plate in Carranza, *Campañas navales de la República Argentina,* 4: between pages 208 and 209, with Spanish translation on the obverse.

21. "Confessions of Gibbs the Pirate," *NYJOC,* April 7, 1831, 2; Carranza, *Campañas navales de la República Argentina,* 4:189.

22. Vale, *War betwixt Englishmen,* 29–39, 40–49; Carranza, *Campañas navales de la República Argentina,* 2: 277–93; Ireland, *Admiral from Mayo,* 57–59.

23. Vale, *War betwixt Englishmen,* 50–52.

24. Ibid., 52–59; Carranza, *Campañas navales de la República Argentina,* 2:295–307.

25. "Confessions of Gibbs the Pirate," *NYJOC,* April 7, 1831, 2; Vale, *War betwixt Englishmen,* 78–82, 92–93, 96–104; Carranza, *Campañas navales de la República Argentina,* 2:341–58; Destefani, "Guerra de corso contra el Brasil," 263–64, 286, 296.

26. "Confessions of Gibbs the Pirate," *NYJOC,* April 7, 1831, 2; Vale, *War betwixt Englishmen,* 97–98; Destefani, "Cruceros de Guerra y Corso de Brown en 1826 con la Sarandi y la Chacabuco," 309; Carranza, *Campañas navales de la República Argentina,* 2:263 and 4:185–86. For more on Baltimore clippers, see Peter Kemp, *The History of Ships,* 165–67.

27. "Confessions of Gibbs the Pirate," *NYJOC,* April 7, 1831, 2; Vale, *War betwixt Englishmen,* 93, 98–100, 207–17; Tenenbaum, chief ed., *Encyclopedia of Latin American History and Culture,* 1:148. For a detailed study of Argentine privateers in the 1827–1828 period, see Destefani, "Apogeo y decadencia del Corso en la Guerra Contra el Brasil," passim.

28. "Confessions of Gibbs the Pirate," *NYJOC,* April 7, 1831, 2. An untitled item under "Providence," *Literary Subaltern,* March 25, 1831, 4, refers to Jeffers having

once been known in Providence society, but if correct this may refer to his reputed 1819 visit to the United States. By the early 1820s, Jeffers's family in Newport thought him dead; a public visit under his real name to nearby Providence would have betrayed that story.

29. Chidsey, *The Wars in Barbary,* 1–31 and passim; Semple, "Pirate Coasts of the Mediterranean Sea," 149–51; Muscat and Cuschieri, *Naval Activities of the Knights of St. John,* passim; King, *The Coast Guard Under Sail,* 64. For a history of seventeenth-century Mediterranean activity, see Lloyd, *English Corsairs on the Barbary Coast.* For nineteenth-century examples, see Panzac, *Barbary Corsairs.*

30. Spencer, *Algiers in the Age of the Corsairs,* 163–66; Cave, *The French in Africa,* 35–44; Wolf, *The Barbary Coast,* 333–38; "Sentence of the Pirates," *NYJOC,* March 12, 1831, 2, which includes a statement attributed to Jeffers: "During the last Spring [i.e., 1830] he took passage for Gibraltar. . . ." "Confessions of Gibbs the Pirate," *NYJOC,* April 7, 1831, 2. Schooners named *Sally Ann* were built in Maine shipyards in 1817 and 1827. Another candidate, based at Bath, was a 175-ton brig constructed in 1824 in Topsham. Humphrey Purington was the initial owner and master; his family name was prominent among Bath mariners of the period. When this *Sally Ann* sank in a gale in 1840—the crew rescued by a passing ship—it was traveling between Matanzas and Wilmington, North Carolina. Baker, *Maritime History of Bath, Maine and the Kennebec River Region,* 1:250–51, 2:893, 951, 966.

Chapter 9: The *Vineyard*'s Last Voyage

1. Candidates for the *Lexington* include a 197-ton brig built at Scituate, Massachusetts, in 1825. It was 87 feet long and 22 feet broad and is described as having "two decks, two masts, square stern, no galleries, a billet figurehead." At the time of its 1825 registration in Boston-Charlestown, its co-owners were William Lovering of Boston and John Sever of Kingston; its master was George Brewster. In January 1828 its registration was temporarily surrendered at Plymouth. *SRE Boston and Charlestown 1821–1830,* 301.

2. Drake, *Trials of Wansley and Gibbs,* 6, 9, 10, 13; "Piracy and Murder on board the brig *Vineyard,*" *Eastern Argus,* December 7, 1830, 2 (citing the *New York Mercantile Advertiser*); "Mutiny and Murder," *Baltimore Patriot,* December 4, 1830, 2 (citing the *New York Commercial Advertiser*); "Examination, before Judges Terhune, and Hubbard," *Newport Mercury,* December 4, 1830, 2; *SRE Boston and Charlestown 1831–1840,* 398; "Confessions of Gibbs the Pirate," *NYJOC,* April 17, 1831, 2.

3. "Piracy and Murder on board the brig *Vineyard,*" *Eastern Argus,* December 7, 1830, 2 (citing the *New York Mercantile Advertiser*); "Confession of Thomas J. Wansley" and "A visit to the condemned criminals Gibbs and Wansley," in *The Confession of the Terrible Pirate Charles Gibbs,* 14, 15; untitled item, *Baltimore Patriot,* December 9, 1830, 2 (citing the *New York Mercantile Advertiser*). Wansley appears as number 439 and Butler as number 15 on the USS *Delaware* muster and pay documents in NA-RG45-T829, rolls 33 and 98.

4. Dana, *Two Years before the Mast*, 12.

5. *Mutiny and Murder*, 20, which includes Wansley's remark in court that "I knew Church in Boston . . ."; Drake, *Trials of Wansley and Gibbs*, 17; "Trial for Murder and Piracy," *Rhode Island Republican*, March 17, 1831, 2.

6. *SRE Boston and Charlestown 1821–1830*, 553–54.

7. Drake, *Trials of Wansley and Gibbs*, 4, 5, 7, 10, 17; "Postscript," *Baltimore Patriot*, December 6, 1830, 2; "Further particulars of the murder and piracy," *Baltimore Patriot*, December 6, 1830, 2 (citing the *New York Commercial Advertiser*); "Mutiny and Murder," *Baltimore Patriot*, December 4, 1830, 2 (citing the *New York Commercial Advertiser*); "Examination, before Judges Terhune, and Hubbard," *Newport Mercury*, December 4, 1830, 2. For more on French-born businessman and philanthropist Girard, who started his career as a cabin boy, see Wildes, *Lonely Midas*. Data on the Mexican dollar come from Bernhofen and Brown, "An Empirical Assessment of the Comparative Advantage Gains from Trade: Evidence from Japan."

8. Drake, *Trials of Wansley and Gibbs*, 5, 6, 10; "Definitions of Old Sea Craft," in Schonhorn, ed., *General History of the Pyrates*, xlvii, xlviii; Harland, *Seamanship in the Age of Sail*, 282; "Mutiny and Murder," *Baltimore Patriot*, December 4, 1830, 2 (citing the *New York Commercial Advertiser*); "Examination, before Judges Terhune, and Hubbard," *Newport Mercury*, December 4, 1830, 2. The description of the jolly boat appears in "Postscript," *Baltimore Patriot*, December 6, 1830, 2. Jeffers was probably asked for the details because a similar craft with three occupants landed on the Jersey shore. Eventually "a comparison of dates" showed that they could not have been the missing *Vineyard* sailors. "Further particulars of the murder and piracy," *Baltimore Patriot*, December 6, 1830, 2 (citing the *New York Commercial Advertiser*). The date of the *Vineyard*'s sailing is unclear. The November 13, 1830, *New Orleans Price Current* reported the brig "as having cleared on the 5th of that month for Philadelphia," but the aforementioned bill of lading for the specie is dated November 6 (quoted in "Further particulars of the murder and piracy," *Baltimore Patriot*, December 6, 1830, 2, citing the *New York Commercial Advertiser*). The same *Baltimore Patriot* article paraphrases Wansley as telling his examiners "On the 7th November they left New Orleans, and on the 9th they came through the South West Passage."

9. Drake, *Trials of Wansley and Gibbs*, 5, 10, 11; Jeffers is cited as referring to "Harry Atwood" under "Trial for Murder and Piracy," in a section quoting "the Commercial Advertiser of Friday," *Rhode Island Republican*, March 17, 1831, 2. Dawes also related (Drake, *Trials of Wansley and Gibbs*, 11) that "the men and I had a little quarrel about the wages I received," which might indicate a preconspiracy effort to bully him.

10. Drake, *Trials of Wansley and Gibbs*, 4, 12–13; "Mutiny and Murder," *Baltimore Patriot*, December 4, 1830, 2 (citing the *New York Commercial Advertiser*); "Examination, before Judges Terhune, and Hubbard," *Newport Mercury*, December 4, 1830, 2; "Further particulars of the murder and piracy," *Baltimore Patriot*,

December 6, 1830, 2 (citing the *New York Commercial Advertiser*); "Piracy and Murder on board the brig *Vineyard*," *Eastern Argus*, December 7, 1830, 2 (citing the *New York Mercantile Advertiser*).

11. Dana, *Two Years before the Mast*, 12.

12. Drake, *Trials of Wansley and Gibbs*, 5, 11, 13; "Mutiny and Murder," *Baltimore Patriot*, December 4, 1830, 2 (citing the *New York Commercial Advertiser*). Brownrigg may have either been slow on the uptake or else feigned ignorance, for Dawes recalled Jeffers telling him that "he had mentioned it [the conspiracy] to Brownrigg." Drake, *Trials of Wansley and Gibbs*, 11.

13. Drake, *Trials of Wansley and Gibbs*, 4–5, 8, 11, 12; "Trial for murder and piracy," *NYJOC*, March 10, 1831, 2; "Mutiny and Murder," *Baltimore Patriot*, December 4, 1830, 2 (citing the *New York Commercial Advertiser*); "Examination, before Judges Terhune, and Hubbard," *Newport Mercury*, December 4, 1830, 2; Bills of indictment filed March 2 and 3, 1831, NA-RG21.

14. Drake, *Trials of Wansley and Gibbs*, 5, 9–10, 17; "Mutiny and Murder," *Baltimore Patriot*, December 4, 1830, 2 (citing the *New York Commercial Advertiser*); "Examination, before Judges Terhune, and Hubbard," *Newport Mercury*, December 4, 1830, 2; "Trial for murder and piracy," *NYJOC*, March 10, 1831, 2; Bills of indictment filed March 2 and 3, 1831, NA-RG21.

15. Drake, *Trials of Wansley and Gibbs*, 4, 11, 12; *Mutiny and Murder*, 15; "Mutiny and Murder," *Baltimore Patriot*, December 4, 1830, 2 (citing the *New York Commercial Advertiser*); "Examination, before Judges Terhune, and Hubbard," *Newport Mercury*, December 4, 1830, 2; "Further particulars of the murder and piracy," *Baltimore Patriot*, December 6, 1830, 2 (citing the *New York Commercial Advertiser*).

16. Drake, *Trials of Wansley and Gibbs*, 4–8, 10, 11; "Mutiny and Murder," *Baltimore Patriot*, December 4, 1830, 2 (citing the *New York Commercial Advertiser*); "Examination, before Judges Terhune, and Hubbard," *Newport Mercury*, December 4, 1830, 2; "Further particulars of the murder and piracy," *Baltimore Patriot*, December 6, 1830, 2 (citing the *New York Commercial Advertiser*).

17. "Mutiny and Murder," *Baltimore Patriot*, December 4, 1830, 2 (citing the *New York Commercial Advertiser*); Drake, *Trials of Wansley and Gibbs*, 4; "Examination, before Judges Terhune, and Hubbard," *Newport Mercury*, December 4, 1830, 2; "Postscript," *Baltimore Patriot*, December 6, 1830, 2.

18. Drake, *Trials of Wansley and Gibbs*, 4–6, 11–12; "Mutiny and Murder," *Baltimore Patriot*, December 4, 1830, 2 (citing the *New York Commercial Advertiser*); "Examination, before Judges Terhune, and Hubbard," *Newport Mercury*, December 4, 1830, 2; "Trial for murder and piracy," *NYJOC*, March 10, 1831, 2; "From the N.Y. Daily Advertiser, December 4," *Connecticut Courant*, December 7, 1830, 2; correspondence from Jeff Remling, South Street Seaport Museum, New York, New York, December 17, 2004. Dawes thought the jolly boat party would head for Block Island, off Long Island's east end and very far from where the longboat would end up. Drake, *Trials of Wansley and Gibbs*, 11. This was probably because, according to

Brownrigg's statement to judges Hubbard and Terhune, Church "said he belonged to Block Island." See "Mutiny and Murder," *Baltimore Patriot,* December 4, 1830, 2.

19. Drake, *Trials of Wansley and Gibbs,* 4–8, 12; "Mutiny and Murder," *Baltimore Patriot,* December 4, 1830, 2 (citing the *New York Commercial Advertiser*); "Examination, before Judges Terhune, and Hubbard," *Newport Mercury,* December 4, 1830, 2; Smith, *Map of Long Island;* correspondence from Jeff Remling, South Street Seaport Museum, New York, New York, December 17, 2004.

20. Drake, *Trials of Wansley and Gibbs,* 4–8, 12–13; "Mutiny and Murder," *Baltimore Patriot,* December 4, 1830, 2 (citing the *New York Commercial Advertiser*); "Piracy and Murder on board the brig *Vineyard,*" *Eastern Argus,* December 7, 1830, 2 (citing the *New York Mercantile Advertiser*).

21. Drake, *Trials of Wansley and Gibbs,* 5–8, 12; "Mutiny and Murder," *Baltimore Patriot,* December 4, 1830, 2 (citing the *New York Commercial Advertiser*); "Examination, before Judges Terhune, and Hubbard," *Newport Mercury,* December 4, 1830, 2; "Further particulars of the murder and piracy," *Baltimore Patriot,* December 6, 1830, 2 (citing the *New York Commercial Advertiser*); "Piracy and Murder on board the brig *Vineyard,*" *Eastern Argus,* December 7, 1830, 2 (citing the *New York Mercantile Advertiser*).

22. "Further particulars of the murder and piracy," *Baltimore Patriot,* December 6, 1830, 2 (citing the *New York Commercial Advertiser*); Drake, *Trials of Wansley and Gibbs,* 8, 13; "Piracy and Murder on board the brig *Vineyard,*" *Eastern Argus,* December 7, 1830, 2 (citing the *New York Mercantile Advertiser*). Of the *Vineyard*'s money, a December 3 article stated that "Between $1100 and 1500 have been found," but this may have referred to or included the money taken off the men when arrested ("Further particulars of the murder and piracy," *Baltimore Patriot,* December 6, 1830, 2, citing the *New York Commercial Advertiser*). The next day, it was reported that the jolly boat had been found with a small amount of cash aboard. "The whole amount thus far recovered is about 2400 dollars." See "From the N.Y. Daily Advertiser, December 4," *Connecticut Courant,* December 7, 1830, 2. An 1891 article claimed that on Barren Island, Jeffers "had buried $30,000 of the $54,000 he and his confederates had stolen from the brig *Vineyard.* The discovery was made by the waves unearthing the silver from the sand" (see "Looking backward into antiquity," *New York Herald,* January 11, 1891, 24). But the $30,000 figure is too high, given testimony about the "lightening" of the long boat. Finally, Seitz, *Under the Black Flag,* 324–25, without specifying sources identifies "John" Johnson of Barren Island as having a younger brother, William. Of the money buried on the island, Seitz wrote: "Two inspectors from the Ocean Insurance Company went at once to the spot on Barren Island, but found the cache rifled. The Johnsons were suspected and had some quarrel over the money, according to the younger brother, who left his relative as the result. Johnson, however, gave up a few dollars, the captain's watch, a spy-glass, and a sword cane as all that had been given him for his hospitality. None of the money was ever recovered" (325).

Chapter 10: "Adjudged a pirate and a felon"

1. "Postscript," *Baltimore Patriot,* December 6, 1830, 2; "From the N.Y. Daily Advertiser, December 4," *Connecticut Courant,* December 7, 1830, 2; Johnson, ed., *Dictionary of American Biography,* 2:231; Wells, *Life and Career of Samuel Rossiter Betts,* 11–15; Wilson and Fiske, eds., *Appleton's Cyclopædia of American Biography,* 1:253; "Died," *New York Times,* November 4, 1868, 5.

2. Richmond, *New York and its Institutions,* 69, 514–15; Jackson, ed., *Encyclopedia of New York City,* 137, 608; McCarthy, "Penitentiary Origins in the City of New York."

3. "Confessions of Gibbs the Pirate," *NYJOC,* April 7, 1831, 2; Correspondence from Kenneth Cobb, director of the New York City Municipal Archives, November 3, 2004.

4. Malone, ed., *Dictionary of American Biography,* 8:188–89; "Obituary. James A. Hamilton," *New York Times,* September 26, 1878, 5.

5. Bills of indictment and court minutes, NA-RG21; Drake, *Trials of Wansley and Gibbs,* 2, 9; "Brief Notices," *NWR,* April 9, 1831, 94.

6. "Died," *New York Times,* April 11, 1854, 8; Longworth, *Longworth's American Almanac* (1831), 79; Chipman, *Report of an Examination of Poor-Houses, Jails, &c.,* 39–40; Hayward, *New England and New York Law Register for the Year 1835,* 225.

7. Jackson, ed., *Encyclopedia of New York City,* 291; Richmond, *New York and Its Institutions,* 516–17.

8. Drake, *Trials of Wansley and Gibbs,* 7, 13; "Piracy and Murder: United States' Circuit Court, Monday," *Rhode Island Republican,* March 10, 1831, 3 (citing the *New York Courier and Enquirer*).

9. "Piracy and Murder: United States' Circuit Court, Monday," *Rhode Island Republican,* March 10, 1831, 3 (citing the New York *Courier and Enquirer*); Untitled article, *NYJC,* March 9, 1831, 2; "Trial for Piracy," *Newport Mercury,* March 12, 1831, 2; Court minutes, NA-RG21.

10. Court minutes, NA-RG21; Drake, *Trials of Wansley and Gibbs,* 3–5; "Trial for Piracy," *Newport Mercury,* March 12, 1831, 2; "Piracy and Murder: United States' Circuit Court, Monday," *Rhode Island Republican,* March 10, 1831, 3 (citing the *New York Courier and Enquirer*); "Trial for Murder and Piracy," *NYJOC,* March 10, 1831, 2. For congressional acts on piracy and their interpretation at federal level, see Lenoir, "Piracy Cases in the Supreme Court," passim.

11. Hamilton, *Reminiscences,* 249.

12. Drake, *Trials of Wansley and Gibbs,* 5; "Mutiny and Murder," *Baltimore Patriot,* December 4, 1830, 2 (citing the *New York Commercial Advertiser*).

13. "Piracy and Murder: United States' Circuit Court, Monday," *Rhode Island Republican,* March 10, 1831, 3 (citing the *New York Courier and Enquirer*).

14. Drake, *Trials of Wansley and Gibbs,* 6–8; Court minutes, NA-RG21.

15. "Trial for Murder and Piracy," *NYJOC,* March 10, 1831, 2; Court minutes, NA-RG21; "Piracy and Murder: United States' Circuit Court, Monday," *Rhode*

Island Republican, March 10, 1831, 3 (citing the *New York Courier and Enquirer*); Drake, *Trials of Wansley and Gibbs,* 6–9; "Trial for Piracy," *Newport Mercury,* March 12, 1831, 2; "A visit to the condemned criminals Gibbs and Wansley," in *The Confession of the Terrible Pirate Charles Gibbs* (New York, 1831), 15. Biographical details about Davies are from the entry on him in the *National Cyclopædia of American Biography,* 3:26, *Report of Proceedings at a Meeting of the Bar of the City of New York,* 5–14, and in his obituary in the *New York Times,* December 18, 1881, 2.

16. Court minutes, NA-RG21; "Trial for Piracy," *Newport Mercury,* March 12, 1831, 2; "Trial for Murder and Piracy," *NYJOC,* March 10, 1831, 2.

17. Court minutes, NA-RG21; Drake, *Trials of Wansley and Gibbs,* 9–10.

18. Drake, *Trials of Wansley and Gibbs,* 10–11.

19. Court minutes, NA-RG21; Drake, *Trials of Wansley and Gibbs,* 12–13.

20. Longworth, *Longworth's American Almanac,* 505; Drake, *Trials of Wansley and Gibbs,* 13–14.

21. "Mr. Seth P. Staples," *New York Times,* November 8, 1861, 4; Drake, *Trials of Wansley and Gibbs,* 14–16; "Trial for Piracy," *Newport Mercury,* March 12, 1831, 2.

22. Court minutes, NA-RG21; "Trial for Murder and Piracy," *NYJOC,* March 10, 1831, 2.

23. Court minutes, NA-RG21.

24. *Mutiny and Murder,* 19–20; Drake, *Trials of Wansley and Gibbs,* 16–17; "Sentence of the Pirates," *NYJOC,* March 12, 1831, 2. Quotations from Wansley's and Jeffers's speeches are as given in *Mutiny and Murder.*

25. *Mutiny and Murder,* 20–21; Drake, *Trials of Wansley and Gibbs,* 17; "Sentence of the Pirates," *NYJOC,* March 12, 1831, 2. Despite the last-ditch attempt to incriminate Brownrigg and assign a more active role to Dawes, a newspaper reported that following Jeffers's conviction he and Wansley "both freely admitted that Brownrigg and Dawes had given a faithful relation of the circumstances, except in some trifling particulars." The writer's source was among the "persons who reconveyed them to the Penitentiary." See "Trial for Murder and Piracy," *NYJOC,* March 10, 1831, 2.

26. *Mutiny and Murder,* 21–25; Drake, *Trials of Wansley and Gibbs,* 17–20; "Sentence of the Pirates," *NYJOC,* March 12, 1831, 2; court minutes, NA-RG21; "Trial for Murder and Piracy," *NYJOC,* March 10, 1831, 2.

Chapter 11: The Arch-Pirate Emerges

1. Drake, *Trials of Wansley and Gibbs,* 19–20; Lardner and Love, "Mandatory Sentences and Presidential Mercy," 5. The cases against Jeffers and Wansley ended with the sentencing hearing. Betts only "discharged" Brownrigg and Dawes on Monday, March 28, giving them "a solemn and impressive admonition." See "Gibbs the Pirate," *NYJOC,* March 30, 1831, 2.

2. "Sentence of the Pirates," *NYJOC,* March 12, 1831, 2.

3. Longworth, *Longworth's American Almanac,* 168. Butler suffered a paralyzing stroke in 1854 and died, aged seventy-eight, on April 13, 1857, at the Natchez, Mississippi, home of his son John T. Butler, Esq. "More paralysis among Literary Men," *New York Daily Times,* January 25, 1854, 8 (citing the *National Democrat*); "A veteran printer and editor," *New York Daily Times,* April 25, 1857, 2; and "Died," *New York Evening Post,* April 15, 1857, 3. Hopson refers to Butler in "Confessions of Gibbs the Pirate," *NYJOC,* April 7, 1831, 2.

4. "Confessions of Gibbs the Pirate," *NYJOC,* April 7, 1831, 2.

5. Ibid.

6. Steuart, ed., *Passenger Ships Arriving in New York Harbor,* 1:349; "Confessions of Gibbs the Pirate," *NYJOC,* April 7, 1831, 2. Salem's published ship registers contain several entries under the name *William* from Jeffers's era. None is identified as having disappeared or fallen victim to pirates, although Jeffers's alleged modus operandi was to eliminate evidence or witnesses that could form the basis of such a report. Hitchings and Phillips, "Ship Registers of the District of Salem and Beverly, 1789–1900," 102–3.

7. "The Pirates," *Rhode Island Republican,* March 24, 1831, 2 (citing the *New York Courier*).

8. "Confessions of Gibbs the Pirate," *NYJOC,* April 7, 1831, 2. The source of the final lines in verse has not been established.

9. *Mutiny and Murder,* 28.

10. "Gibbs the Pirate," *NYJOC,* March 30, 1831, 2.

11. Ibid., and under "Providence," *Literary Subaltern,* March 25, 1831, 3, 4; "Gibbs the Pirate," *Literary Subaltern,* April 1, 1831, 3.

12. Under "Providence," *Literary Subaltern,* March 25, 1831, 4.

13. "Gibbs the Pirate," *NYJOC,* March 30, 1831, 2.

14. "Confessions of Gibbs the Pirate," *NYJOC,* April 7, 1831, 2; Untitled article, *Charleston Mercury,* April 27, 1831, 2 (citing the *Winyaw Intelligencer*); "A visit to the condemned criminals Gibbs and Wansley," in *The Confession of the Terrible Pirate Charles Gibbs,* 17. Of Jeffers's references to money, Seitz wrote the following: "He alleged that he had $150,000 in specie hidden in Cuba and $50,000 in trustworthy hands in Buenos Aires—statements undoubtedly made as feelers for aid in securing salvation from the gallows" (*Under the Black Flag,* 325). Seitz offered no source for the details.

15. "Trial for Murder and Piracy," *NYJOC,* March 10, 1831, 2; "Gibbs," *Rhode Island Republican,* April 21, 1831, 3 (citing the *New York Sentinel*). Jeffers's published letter from prison to his former lover is headed "Bellevue Prison, March 20, 1831," indicating that he was transferred from Bridewell by that date. "Confessions of Gibbs the Pirate," *NYJOC,* April 7, 1831, 2.

16. Richmond, *New York and its Institutions,* 386; Jackson, ed., *The Encyclopedia of New York City,* 608; Cooper, *The Bellevue Story,* 30–31; McCarthy, "Penitentiary Origins in the City of New York"; "A visit to the condemned criminals," in *The Confession of the Terrible Pirate Charles Gibbs,* 16

17. "Confessions of Gibbs the Pirate," *NYJOC*, April 7, 1831, 2.

18. "Gibbs," *Rhode Island Republican*, April 21, 1831, 3 (citing the *New York Sentinel*); "The Pirates," *Rhode Island Republican*, April 28, 1831, 2; "A visit to the condemned criminals," in *The Confession of the Terrible Pirate Charles Gibbs*, 15–18.

19. "Execution of the Pirates," *NYJOC*, April 23, 1831, 2; untitled article under "Charleston," *Charleston Mercury*, May 2, 1831, 2.

20. Coggeshall and Coggeshall, *The Coggeshalls in America*, 167–68; Greeley, *Recollections of a Busy Life*, 139, 317.

21. Andrew Jackson to James A. Hamilton, May 4, 1831, in Hamilton, *Reminiscences*, 218.

22. Edward Livingston to James A. Hamilton, June 7, 1831, in Hamilton, *Reminiscences*, 249.

23. NA-RG45-P, entry 72, Statements of Service from Officers ("Returns of Services of Officers"), August 1842–August 1843, vol. 2; "J. B." to Kearny, December 8[?], 1829, NA-RG45-T829, No. 14, roll 391. For the cruises of the *Warren* during this period, see Alden, *Lawrence Kearny*, 61–108.

24. L. Boyle [?] to Kearny, July 16, 1830, NA-RG45-M149, roll 19; Kearny to secretary of the navy, February 5 and February 14, 1831, NA-RG45-M147, roll 16.

25. "Execution of the Pirates," *NYJOC*, April 23, 1831, 2. Kearny's February 19, 1831, leave of absence is affirmed in documents in both NA-RG24 and NA-RG45-T829 (1/1828–1/1832, Appointments, Orders and Resignations No. 14, roll 391). Kearny's posting at the New York recruitment rendezvous ended late in 1832. Following a subsequent leave, Kearny spent three years "awaiting orders." In mid-1836 he was promoted to captain and ordered to serve on a cannon-testing board. He was later assigned to one concerned with "light houses, beacons and buoys," a far cry from the days of chasing pirates, but in August 1837 he was given temporary command of the 74-gun USS *Ohio*. At the start of 1838 he spent a few weeks on an exploring expedition, and then began stints in command of different frigates. As commodore he commanded the East India Squadron from 1840 to 1842, taking on an active diplomatic role with China. Later posts included heading naval shipyards at Norfolk and New York. He retired a few months into the Civil War and died in his native Perth Amboy in 1868. *Dictionary of American Naval Fighting Ships*, 3:605; Alden, *Lawrence Kearny*, passim; and references to Kearny contained in NA-RG24, vol. G, roll 4; NA-RG45-P, entry 72, Statements of Service from Officers ("Returns of Service of Officers") Aug. 1842–Aug. 1843, vol. 2; and NA-RG45-P, entry 73, Tabular Summary of Officers Statements of Service ("Services of Officers, 1798–1842"), August 1842–August 1843, vol. 1.

26. Alden, *Lawrence Kearny*, 44. Seitz presented without attribution another exchange that allegedly took place—"In the course of his conversation with Captain Kearney [*sic*], Gibbs remarked: 'I suppose, Captain, you think it quite a difficult matter to make a pirate, but I can assure you it is not so; on the contrary, I can make an excellent pirate in a few weeks, even of a pious young man.' Being questioned as to the method of transformation, he continued: 'In one of our cruises we

took a vessel with some eight or ten men. Among them were two stout young fellows, who we thought would be useful to use and therefore agreed among ourselves to make them join us. Accordingly all the crew were killed in their presence. After this we put a rope around each of their necks, with a block to the main yard to hang them. They were then blindfolded. When everything was thus prepared, we asked them whether to save their lives they would join us and become pirates? They gladly assented to the terms, which were not only to unite with us, but also to do all the killing required of them. Accordingly, the next vessel we captured they performed all the butchery, and, in a few weeks became first-rate pirates'" (*Under the Black Flag*, 326–27).

27. "Gibbs, the Pirate," *Newport Mercury*, April 16, 1831, 3.

28. "Execution of the Pirates," *NYJOC*, April 23, 1831, 2.

29. "An Interesting and Correct Account of the Execution of the Pirates," in *The Confession of the Terrible Pirate Charles Gibbs*, 3; Wilson and Fiske, eds., *Appleton's Cyclopedia of American Biography*, 251; Chaplin, *Duncan Dunbar*, 100–101.

30. "The Pirate Gibbs," *Charleston Courier*, April 19, 1831, 2, and under "Charleston," *Charleston Mercury*, April 20, 1831, 2.

31. "Wanton Insult," *Literary Subaltern*, April 29, 1831, 3 (citing the *Providence Daily Advertiser*).

32. Chappell, *Folk-Songs of Roanoke and the Albemarle*, 54. For more on ballads about pirates, see Turley, *Rum, Sodomy & the Lash*, 44–61.

33. "Lines, composed and written by Thomas J. Wansley," and "Confession of Thomas J. Wansley," in *The Confession of the Terrible Pirate Charles Gibbs*, 13, 14.

Chapter 12: "A dreadful thing to die"

1. Hearn, *Legal Executions in New York State*, 40–42.

2. Ibid., 39; "Execution," *NWR*, October 30, 1819, 143.

3. "Suicide," *Newport Mercury*, August 12, 1820, 3 (citing the *Baltimore Gazette*).

4. Hearn, *Legal Executions in New York State*, 41–42.

5. Ibid., 299–300.

6. "Execution of the Pirates," and untitled article, *NYJOC*, April 23, 1831, 2; "The Pirates," *Rhode Island Republican*, April 28, 1831, 2; Hearn, *Legal Executions in New York State*, 300 (citing the *New York Evening Post*).

7. Marius, *Thomas More*, 131; "The Pirates," *Rhode Island Republican*, April 28, 1831, 2.

8. "The Pirates," *Rhode Island Republican*, April 28, 1831, 2; "Execution of the Pirates," *NYJOC*, April 23, 1831, 2; "An Interesting and Correct Account of the Execution of the Pirates," in *The Confession of the Terrible Pirate Charles Gibbs*, 2–3.

9. "The Pirates," *Rhode Island Republican*, April 28, 1831, 2; "Execution of the Pirates," *NYJOC*, April 23, 1831, 2.

10. "The Pirates," *Rhode Island Republican*, April 28, 1831, 2; *Mutiny and Murder*, 36. According to one newspaper account, Jeffers "did not join in any religious

exercises, but addressed the multitude in a speech of full half an hour." If so, then all versions of his remarks are heavily abridged. "Execution of the Pirates," *New York Daily Advertiser,* April 23, 1831, 2.

11. "Execution of the Pirates," *NYJOC,* April 23, 1831, 2; "An Interesting and Correct Account of the Execution of the Pirates," in *The Confession of the Terrible Pirate Charles Gibbs,* 2–3; "The Pirates," *Rhode Island Republican,* April 28, 1831, 2.

12. "An Interesting and Correct Account of the Execution of the Pirates," in *The Confession of the Terrible Pirate Charles Gibbs,* 3; "Execution of the Pirates," *New York Daily Advertiser,* April 23, 1831, 2; "The Pirates," *Rhode Island Republican,* April 28, 1831, 2. According to an 1891 article about the holdings of the Apprentices' Library of the New York Society of Mechanics and Tradesmen, besides part of Jeffers's skull, the collection included a Mexican silver dollar "taken out of his pocket just before he was hanged" (see "Looking Backward into Antiquity," *New York Herald,* January 11, 1891, 24). But according to Dr. Janet Wells Greene of the society's library the coin is dated 1835, four years after Jeffers's execution (correspondence, April 19, 2005).

13. Marius, *Thomas More,* 131.

14. "The Pirates," *Rhode Island Republican,* April 28, 1831, 2.

15. Court minutes, NA-RG21.

16. "The Violated Sepulchres of the Dead," *NYJOC,* March 12, 1831, 2 (citing the *Greenfield* [Mass.] *Gazette*). For social opposition to autopsies in New York at this time, see Cooper, *The Bellevue Story,* 31–32. See also Humphrey, "Dissection and Discrimination: The Social Origins of Cadavers in America, 1760–1915," 819–27.

17. *Who Was Who in America: Historical Volume, 1607–1896,* 562; Jackson, ed., *The Encyclopedia of New York City,* 747.

18. "The Pirates," *Rhode Island Republican,* April 28, 1831, 2; Meschutt, "Browere, John Henri Isaac"; Adeline Adams, "John Henri Isaac Browere"; For more on Browere, see Meschutt, "A Bold Experiment: John Henri Isaac Browere's Life Masks of Prominent Americans," and Hart, *Browere's Life Masks of Great Americans.* A review of the latter appears in "Life Masks: Those Browere made of great Americans—Charles Henry Hart's comments on them," *New York Times— Saturday Review,* April 8, 1899, 226.

19. Correspondence from Robert Vietrogoski, archivist, Columbia University Medical Center, November 10, 2004; Jackson, ed., *Encyclopedia of New York City,* 747; Longworth, ed., *Longworth's American Almanac,* 715. According to one 1920s account, which cites no sources for attribution: "Both bodies were then [after execution] turned over to the surgeons for dissection. They were taken for this purpose to the medical college in Barclay Street, and exhibited for a short time. That of Wansley was found to be a perfect specimen of anatomy. Gibbs was abnormally constructed. A peculiarly confidential portion of his person, preserved by petrification, was long used in class demonstrations by no less a personage than Dr. Oliver Wendell Holmes" (Seitz, *Under the Black Flag,* 327).

20. "Looking Backward into Antiquity," *New York Herald,* January 11, 1891, 24; and correspondence with Dr. Janet Wells Greene, historian and library director, General Society of Mechanics and Tradesmen, New York, New York, March 17, 2005. For John Augustine Smith's views, see Boardman, *Defense of Phrenology* (1847). For a recent historical critique of phrenology, see Van Wyhe, "The authority of human nature: the *Schädellehre* of Franz Joseph Gall."

Epilogue

1. Correspondence from Jeff Remling, South Street Seaport Museum, New York, New York, November 4 and December 17, 2004.

2. The song is included on Foster's independent-label 2004 CD release *Cayo Hueso;* the lyrics are available on several Web sites.

3. As of November 5, 2004, the card was advertised online at www.whydah .com/store/product_info.php?cPath=13&products_id=204 and as of this writing in May 2006, a page featuring it (though apparently inactive) was at www.dead-mentellnotales.com/page/DM/PROD/C8/CardCB.

BIBLIOGRAPHY

Adams, Adeline. "John Henri Isaac Browere." *Dictionary of American Biography* Base Set, American Council of Learned Societies, 1928–1936. Republished, *Biography Resource Center*. Farmington Hills, Mich.: Thomson Gale, 2004. Available online at galenet.galegroup.com/servlet/BioRC

Alden, Carroll Storrs. *Lawrence Kearny, Sailor Diplomat*. Princeton, N.J.: Princeton University Press, 1936.

Alexander, Caroline. *The Bounty*. New York: Penguin, 2004.

Allen, Gardner W. *Our Navy and the West Indian Pirates*. Salem, Mass.: Essex Institute, 1929.

Appleby, John C. "Women and Piracy in Ireland: From Gráinne O'Malley to Anne Bonny." In Pennell, *Bandits at Sea*, 283–98.

Arnold, James N., ed. *Vital Records of Rhode Island, 1636–1850*, 21 vols. Providence, R.I.: Narragansett Publishing, 1891–1912.

The Arrogante Barcelones, 20 U.S. 496 (1822) case text. Available online at http://supreme.justia.com/us/20/496/case.html

Bailey, Thomas A. *A Diplomatic History of the American People*. 7th ed. New York: Appleton-Century Crofts, 1964.

Baker, William Avery. *A Maritime History of Bath, Maine and the Kennebec River Region*. 2 vols. Portland, Maine: Marine Research Society of Bath / Anthoensen Press, 1973.

Barbour, Violet. "Privateers and Pirates of the West Indies," *American Historical Review* 16 (April 1911): 529–56.

Bartlett, John. *Bartlett's Familiar Quotations*. Edited by Emily Morison Beck. 15th ed. Boston: Little, Brown, 1980, 355.

Beaglehole, J. C. *The Life of Captain James Cook*. Stanford, Calif.: Stanford University Press, 1974.

Beater, Jack. *Pirates and Buried Treasure on Florida Islands*. St. Petersburg, Fla.: Great Outdoors Publishing, 1959.

Berckman, Evelyn. *Victims of Piracy: The Admiralty Court 1575–1678*. London: Hamilton, 1979.

Bernhofen, Daniel M., and John C. Brown, "An Empirical Assessment of the Comparative Advantage Gains from Trade: Evidence from Japan." *American Economic Review* 95 (March 2005): 208–25.

Boardman, Andrew. *Defense of Phrenology: Containing, I. An Essay on the Nature and Value of Phrenological Evidence; II. A Vindication of Phrenology Against the Attack of Dr. John Augustine Smith; III. A View of Facts Relied on By Phrenologists as Proof that the Cerebellum is the Seat of the Reproductive Instinct.* New York: Edward Kearny, 1847.

Bonello, Giovanni. *Histories of Malta.* Vol. 4. Valetta, Malta: Fondazzjoni Patrimonju Malti, 2003.

Boston Board of Street Commissioners. *A Record of the Streets, Alleys, Places, Etc. in the City of Boston.* Boston: Municipal Printing Office, 1902.

The Boston Directory: Containing the Names of the Inhabitants, Their Occupations, Places of Business and Dwelling Houses: with Lists of the Streets, Lanes and Wharves, the Town Officers, Public Offices and Banks. . . . Boston: Edward Cotton, editions for 1810, 1813, 1816, 1818, 1820, 1821, 1822.

Botting, Douglas. *The Pirates.* Alexandria, Va.: Time-Life Books, 1978.

Bradlee, Francis B. C. *Piracy in the West Indies and Its Suppression.* Salem, Mass.: Essex Institute, 1923.

Brown, Vera Lee. "The South Sea Company and Contraband Trade." *American Historical Review* 31 (July 1926): 662–78.

Burkholder, Mark A., and Lyman L. Johnson. *Colonial Latin America.* 3rd ed. Oxford: Oxford University Press, 1998.

Carranza, Angel Justiniano. *Campañas navales de la República Argentina.* 2nd ed. 4 vols. Buenos Aires: Secretaría de Estado de Marina, 1962.

Cave, Laurence Trent. *The French in Africa.* London: Charles J. Skeet, 1859.

Chaplin, Jeremiah. *Duncan Dunbar: The Record of an Earnest Ministry.* 4th ed. New York: U. D. Ward, 1878.

Chappell, Louis W. *Folk-Songs of Roanoke and the Albemarle.* Morgantown, W. Va.: Ballad Press, 1939.

Chidsey, Donald Barr. *The Wars in Barbary: Arab Piracy and the Birth of the United States Navy.* New York: Crown, 1971.

Chipman, Samuel. *Report of an Examination of Poor-Houses, Jails, &c., in the State of New-York, and in the Counties of Berkshire, Massachusetts; Litchfield, Connecticut; and Bennington, Vermont, &c., Addressed to Aristarchus Champion, Esq., of Rochester, N.Y.* 3rd ed. Albany: Hoffman & White, 1835.

Clifford, Barry. *The Lost Fleet.* New York: Morrow, 2002.

Coggeshall, Charles P., and Thellwell R. Coggeshall. *The Coggeshalls in America: Genealogy of the Descendants of John Coggeshall of Newport with a Brief Notice of Their English Antecedents.* Spartanburg, S.C.: Reprint Company, 1982.

Coker, P. C., III. *Charleston's Maritime Heritage, 1670–1865: An Illustrated History.* Charleston, S.C.: CokerCraft Press, 1987.

The Confession of the Terrible Pirate Charles Gibbs, as Made to Justice Hopson and Others, at Different Times . . . New York, 1831.

Confessions and Execution of the Pirates, Gibbs & Wansley. New York: Christian Brown, n.d.

Cooper, Page. *The Bellevue Story.* New York: Crowell, 1948.

Cordingly, David. *Under the Black Flag: The Romance and the Reality of Life among the Pirates.* New York: Harcourt Brace, 1995.

Corrales, Manuel Ezequiel, ed. *Documentos para la Historia de la Provincia de Cartagena.* Vol. 2. Bogota, 1883.

"The Counting House Rediscovers Local Maritime History." *Counting House Times,* Fall 2003, 2. Available online at www.obhs.net/Images/OldBerwick12 .pdf.

Dana, Richard Henry. *Two Years before the Mast.* 1840. Reprint, New York: Buccaneer Books, 1984.

Dash, Mike. *Batavia's Graveyard.* New York: Crown, 2002.

Davis, Charles G. *Rigs of the Nine Principal Types of American Sailing Vessels, Illustrated in Silhouette.* Salem, Mass.: Peabody Museum, 1981.

De Grummond, Jane Lucas. *Renato Beluche: Smuggler, Privateer, and Patriot, 1780–1860.* Baton Rouge: Louisiana State University Press, 1983.

Destefani, Laurio H. "Apogeo y decadencia del corso en la guerra eontra El Brasil (1827–1828)." In *Historia Marítima Argentina.* 6:417–67. Buenos Aires: El Departamento de Estudios Históricos Navales, 1988.

———. "Cruceros de guerra y corso de Brown en 1826 con *la Sarandi* y *la Chacabuco.*" In *Historia Marítima Argentina.* 6:303–21.

———. "Guerra de corso contra el Brasil." In *Historia Marítima Argentina.* 6:257–99.

Dictionary of American Naval Fighting Ships. 9 vols. Washington, D.C.: U.S. Navy Department, Office of Chief of Naval Operations, 1959–1991. Available online at www.hazegray.org/danfs/

Douglas, John, and Mark Olshaker. *The Cases That Haunt Us.* London: Pocket Books, 2002.

Dow, George Francis, and John Henry Edmonds. *The Pirates of the New England Coast, 1630–1730.* Mineola, N.Y.: Dover, 1996.

Doyle, Arthur Conan. "The Adventure of the Sussex Vampire," in *The Original Illustrated Sherlock Holmes.* Ware, U.K.: Wordsworth, 1989.

Drake, W. E. *A Full and Accurate Report of the Trials of Wansley and Gibbs, for Murder and Piracy, on Board the Vineyard in November Last, Whilst on Her Voyage From New-Orleans to Philadelphia: with the Speeches of Counsel, Judge's Address, &c &c. From the Notes of W. E. Drake, Short-Hand Writer.* New York: Ludwig & Tolefree, 1831.

Dudley, William S., and Michael J. Crawford, eds. *The Early Republic and the Sea: Essays on the Naval and Maritime History of the Early United States.* Washington, D.C.: Brassey's, 2001.

Dugard, Martin. *Farther than any Man: The Rise and Fall of Captain James Cook.* New York: Pocket Books, 2001.

Dunham, Jacob. *Journal of Voyages: Containing an Account of the Author's Being Twice Captured by the English and Once by Gibbs the Pirate.* New York, 1850.

Ellms, Charles. *The Pirates Own Book.* New York: Dover, 1993.

Emmons, G. F. *The Navy of the United States, 1775–1853.* Washington, D.C.: Gideon, 1853.

Exquemelin, Alexandre Olivier. *The Buccaneers of America.* 1678. Reprint, Santo Domingo: Editora Corripio, 1981.

Falconer, William. *An Universal Dictionary of the Marine: Or, a Copious Explanation of the Technical Terms and Phrases Employed in the Construction, Equipment, Furniture, Machinery, Movements, and Military Operations of a Ship.* London: T. Cadell, 1780. Available online at http://southseas.nla.gov.au/refs/falc/contents.html

Farragut, Loyall. *The Life of David Glasgow Farragut, First Admiral of the United States Navy.* New York, Appleton, 1879.

Faye, Stanley. "Privateersmen of the Gulf and Their Prizes." *Louisiana Historical Quarterly* 22 (October 1939): 1012–94.

Fenwick, C. G. "'Piracy' in the Caribbean." *American Journal of International Law* 55 (April 1961): 426–28.

Finch, George A. "Piracy in the Mediterranean." *American Journal of International Law* 31 (October 1937): 659–65.

Flaccus, Elmer W. "Commodore David Porter and the Mexican Navy." *Hispanic American Historical Review* 34 (August 1954): 365–73.

Forester, C. S. *The Age of Fighting Sail.* Garden City, N.Y.: Doubleday, 1956.

Foster, Lynn V. *A Brief History of Central America.* New York: Facts on File, 2000.

Frayler, John. "Armed to the Teeth" [informational staff memo]. Salem, Mass.: Salem National Maritime Historic Site, March 16, 2001.

———. *The Arms Chest.* Pickled Fish and Salted Provisions. 7, no. 1. Salem, Mass.: Salem Maritime National Historic Site, March 2005.

———. *Everybody Wants to Get in on the Act.* Pickled Fish and Salted Provisions. 3, no. 1. Salem, Mass.: Salem Maritime National Historic Site, February 2002.

———. *Fire and Lights.* Pickled Fish and Salted Provisions. 3, no. 6. Salem, Mass.: Salem Maritime National Historic Site, October 2002.

———. *It's Only Money.* Pickled Fish and Salted Provisions. 5, no. 1. Salem, Mass.: Salem Maritime National Historic Site, September 2003.

———. *A Large-Scale Enterprise.* Pickled Fish and Salted Provisions. 4, no.1. Salem, Mass.: Salem Maritime National Historic Site, May 2003.

———. *The Medicine Chest.* Pickled Fish and Salted Provisions. 6, no. 3. Salem, Mass.: Salem Maritime National Historic Site, April 2004.

———. *Mericani.* Pickled Fish and Salted Provisions. 6, no. 6. Salem, Mass.: Salem Maritime National Historic Site, October, 2004.

———. *Officers of the Revenue.* Pickled Fish and Salted Provisions. 2, no. 2. Salem, Mass.: Salem Maritime National Historic Site, March 2000.

———. *Pickled Fish and Salted Provisions.* Pickled Fish and Salted Provisions. 6, no. 1. Salem, Mass.: Salem Maritime National Historic Site, February 2004.

———. *Rats.* Pickled Fish and Salted Provisions. 3, no. 5. Salem, Mass.: Salem Maritime National Historic Site, August 2002.

———. *Repeat Performance.* Pickled Fish and Salted Provisions. 3, no. 4. Salem, Mass.: Salem Maritime National Historic Site, July 2002.

———. *Seaman's Clothing in* Friendship's *Era.* Pickled Fish and Salted Provisions. 3, no. 2. Salem, Mass.: Salem Maritime National Historic Site, March 2002.

———. *Shoes, Ships, and Survival.* Pickled Fish and Salted Provisions. 3, no. 3. Salem, Mass.: Salem Maritime National Historic Site, May 2002.

———. *Tangled Web.* Pickled Fish and Salted Provisions. 6, no. 5. Salem, Mass.: Salem Maritime National Historic Site, August 2004.

———. *Walk Away with the Cat, Walk Away with the Fish.* Pickled Fish and Salted Provisions. 4, no. 4. Salem, Mass.: Salem Maritime National Historic Site, July 2003.

Gibbs, George. *The Gibbs Family of Rhode Island and Some Related Families.* New York: Privately printed, 1933.

Gibson, Gregory. *Demon of the Waters: The True Story of the Mutiny on the Whale-ship* Glob. Boston: Little, Brown, 2002.

Gosse, Philip. *The Pirates Who's Who.* Glorieta, N.M.: Rio Grande Press, 1988.

Gonzalez, Thomas A. *The Caloosahatchee: Miscellaneous Writings Concerning the History of the Caloosahatchee River and the City of Fort Myers, Florida.* Fort Myers: Privately printed, 1932.

Graham-Yooll, Andrew. *Imperial Skirmishes: War and Gunboat Diplomacy in Latin America.* New York: Interlink, 2002.

Greeley, Horace. *Recollections of a Busy Life: Reminiscences of American Politics and Politicians from the Opening of the Missouri Contest to the Downfall of Slavery.* New York: J. B. Ford, 1869.

Guttridge, Leonard F. *Mutiny: A History of Naval Insurrection.* Shepperton, U.K.: Ian Allen, 1992.

Guttridge, Leonard F., and Jay D. Smith. *The Commodores.* Annapolis, Md.: Naval Institute Press, 1986.

Hakluyt, Richard. *The Principal Navigations, Voyages, Traffiques and Discoveries of the English Nation.* Edited by Edmund Goldsmid. Vol. 16. Edinburgh: E. & G. Goldsmid, 1890.

Hamilton, James A. *Reminiscences of James A. Hamilton; or, Men and Events, at Home and Abroad, During Three Quarters of a Century.* New York: Scribner, 1869.

Harland, John. *Seamanship in the Age of Sail.* Annapolis, Md.: Naval Institute Press, 2003.

Hart, Charles Henry. *Browere's Life Masks of Great Americans.* New York: Doubleday & McClure, 1899.

Harlow, Frederick Pease. *The Making of a Sailor, or Sea Life Aboard a Yankee Square-Rigger.* New York: Dover, 1988.

Harvey, Robert. *Liberators: Latin America's Struggle for Independence, 1810–1830.* Woodstock, N.Y.: Overlook Press, 2000.

Hawes, Alexander Boyd. *Off Soundings: Aspects of the Maritime History of Rhode Island.* Chevy Chase, Md.: Posterity Press, 1999.

Hayward, John. *The New England and New York Law Register for the Year 1835.* Boston: John Hayward, 1834.

Hearn, Daniel Allen. *Legal Executions in New York State, 1639–1963.* London: McFarland, 1997.

Held, Robert. *The Age of Firearms.* New York: Harper, 1957.

The History of the Lives and Bloody Exploits of the Most Noted Pirates; Their Trials and Executions. Including a Correct Account of the Late Piracies Committed in the West Indies, and the Expedition of Commodore Porter; Also, Those Committed on the Brig Mexican, Who Were Tried and Executed at Boston, in 1835. 1836. Reprint, New York: Empire State Book Co., 1926.

Hitchings, A. Frank, and Stephen Willard Phillips. "Ship Registers of the District of Salem and Beverly, 1789–1900." *Essex Institute Historical Collections* 42 (January 1906).

Hohnen, David. *Hamlet's Castle and Shakespeare's Elsinore.* Copenhagen: Christian Ejlers, 2001.

Humphrey, David C. "Dissection and Discrimination: The Social Origins of Cadavers in America, 1760–1915." *New York Academy of Medicine Bulletin* 69 (September 1973): 819–27.

Huntress, Keith. "Another Source of Poe's *Narrative of Arthur Gordon Pym.*" *American Literature* 16 (March 1944): 19–25.

Ingersoll, Henry. "Diary and Letters of Henry Ingersoll, Prisoner at Carthagena, 1806–1809." *American Historical Review* 3 (July 1898): 674–702.

Innes, Brian. *The History of Torture.* Leicester: Blitz Editions, 1999.

Ireland, John De Courcy. *The Admiral from Mayo: A Life of Almirante William Brown of Foxford, Father of the Argentine Navy.* Dublin: Edmund Burke, 1995.

Jackson, Kenneth T., ed. *The Encyclopedia of New York City.* New Haven: Yale University Press / New York: New-York Historical Society, 1995.

Johnson, Allen, ed. *Dictionary of American Biography.* Vol. 2. New York: Scribners, 1929.

Johnson, D. H. N. "Piracy in Modern International Law." *Problems of Public and Private International Law, Transactions of the Grotius Society* 43 (1957): 63–85.

Keeling, David J. *Buenos Aires: Global Dreams, Local Crises.* New York: Wiley, 1996.

Kemp, Peter. *The History of Ships.* New York: Barnes & Noble, 2002.

Kendall, John Smith. "The Successors of Laffite." *Louisiana Historical Quarterly* 24 (April 1941): 360–77.

King, Irving H. *The Coast Guard Under Sail: The U.S. Revenue Cutter Service, 1789–1865.* Annapolis, Md.: Naval Institute Press, 1989.

Konstam, Angus. *The History of Pirates.* New York: Lyons Press, 1999.

Krieger, Alex, David Cobb, Amy Turner, eds. *Mapping Boston*. Cambridge, Mass.: MIT Press, 1999.

Lambert, Andrew. *War at Sea in the Age of Sail 1650–1850*. London: Cassell, 2000.

Lamson, Zachary G. *The Autobiography of Capt. Zachary G. Lamson, 1797 to 1814*. With introduction and historical notes by O. T. Howe. Boston: W. B. Clarke, 1908.

Lane, Kris E. *Pillaging the Empire: Piracy in the Americas, 1500–1750*. Armonk, N.Y.: Sharpe, 1998.

Langley, Harold D. *A History of Medicine in the Early U.S. Navy*. Baltimore: Johns Hopkins University Press, 1995.

———. *Social Reform in the United States Navy, 1798–1862*. Urbana: University of Illinois Press, 1967.

Lardner, George, Jr., and Margaret Colgate Love. "Mandatory Sentences and Presidential Mercy: The Role of Judges in Pardon Cases, 1790–1850." *Federal Sentencing Reporter* 16 (February 2004): 1–10.

Lavery, Brian, ed. *Shipboard Life and Organization, 1731–1815*. Aldershot, U.K.: Ashgate, 1998.

Lemaitre, Eduardo. *Historia General de Cartagena*, 4 vols. Bogota, Colombia: Banco de la República, 1983.

Lenoir, James J. "Piracy Cases in the Supreme Court." *Journal of Criminal Law and Criminology* 25 (November–December 1934): 532–53.

Levene, Ricardo, ed. *Historia de America: Independencia y organización constitucional*. Tomo 5. Buenos Aires: W. M. Jackson, 1940.

Lever, Darcy. *The Young Sea Officer's Sheet Anchor, or a Key to the Leading of Rigging and to Practical Seamanship*. Mineola, N.Y.: Dover, 1998.

Levine, Robert M., and John J. Crocitti, eds. *The Brazil Reader: History, Culture, Politics*. Durham, N.C.: Duke University Press, 1999.

Lewis, Daniel K. *The History of Argentina*. Westport, Conn.: Greenwood, 2001.

Lewis, Jon E., ed. *Life Before the Mast: Sailors' Eyewitness Accounts from the Age of Fighting Ships*. London: Robinson, 2000.

Little, George. *Life on the Ocean: or, Twenty Years at Sea: Being the Personal Adventures of the Author*. Boston: Waite, Pierce, 1845.

Lloyd, Christopher. *English Corsairs on the Barbary Coast*. London: Collins, 1981.

Longworth, Thomas, ed. *Longworth's American Almanac, New-York Register and City Directory for the Fifty-Sixth Year of American Independence*. New York: Longworth, 1831.

López Nadal, Gonçal. "Corsairing as a Commercial System: The Edges of Legitimate Trade." In Pennell, *Bandits at Sea*. 125–36.

Lubbock, Basil. *The Blackwall Frigates*. Glasgow: Brown & Son, 1922.

———. *Cruisers, Corsairs and Slavers*. Glasgow: Brown, Son & Ferguson, 1993.

Lynch, W. F. *Naval Life; or Observations Afloat and On Shore*. New York: Scribner, 1851.

Lucie-Smith, Edward. *Outcasts of the Sea: Pirates and Piracy.* New York: Paddington Press, 1978.

MacLay, Edgar Stanton. *A History of American Privateers.* London: Sampson Low, Marston, 1900.

MacLeish, Archibald. "Portrait of a Yankee Skipper." *American Heritage Magazine* 8 (December 1956): 1, 38–43, 97. Available online at www.americanheritage.com/articles/magazine/ah/1956/1/1956_1_38.shtml

Malone, Dumas, ed. *Dictionary of American Biography,* Vol. 8. New York: Scribners, 1932.

Manley, James R. *Exposition of the Conduct and Character of Dr. John Augustine Smith, President of the College of Physicians and Surgeons in the City of New York, and Professor of Physiology; as Exhibited in the Session of 1839–40.* New York, 1841.

Marius, Richard. *Thomas More.* New York: Knopf, 1985.

Martin, Tyrone G. *A Most Fortunate Ship: A Narrative History of Old Ironsides.* Annapolis, Md.: Naval Institute Press, 1997.

McCarthy, Thomas C. "Penitentiary Origins in the City of New York." Available online at www.correctionhistory.org/html/chronicl/nycdoc/html/penitentiary2.html

McKee, Christopher. *A Gentlemanly and Honorable Profession: The Creation of the U.S. Naval Officer Corps, 1794–1815.* Annapolis, Md.: Naval Institute Press, 1991.

Merlis, Brian, Lee A. Rosenzweig, and I. Stephen Miller. *Brooklyn's Gold Coast, The Sheepshead Bay Communities.* Edited by Robert Weisser. Brooklyn, N.Y.: Sheepshead Bay Historical Society, 1997.

Meschutt, David. *A Bold Experiment: John Henri Isaac Browere's Life Masks of Prominent Americans.* Cooperstown, N.Y.: New York State Historical Association, 1988.

———. "Browere, John Henri Isaac," *American National Biography Online,* www.anb.org/articles/17/17–0106.html

Miller, David. *The World of Jack Aubrey.* Philadelphia: Courage Books, 2003.

Miller, Nathan. *Broadsides: The Age of Fighting Sail, 1775–1815.* New York: Wiley, 2000.

Mohr, Ralph S. *Governors for Three Hundred Years, 1638–1954, Rhode Island and Providence Plantations.* Providence: State of Rhode Island, Graves Registration Committee, August 1954.

Moorhouse, E. H., ed. *Letters of the English Seaman.* London: Chapman & Hall, 1910.

More, Thomas. *Utopia.* Translated by Ralph Robinson. New York: Knopf, 1992.

Morison, Samuel Eliot. *"Old Bruin": Commodore Matthew Galbraith Perry.* Boston: Little, Brown, 1967.

Muscat, Joseph, and Andrew Cuschieri. *Naval Activities of the Knights of St. John, 1530–1798.* Malta: Midsea Books, 2002.

Mutiny and Murder. Confession of Charles Gibbs, A Native Of Rhode Island. . . . Providence, R.I.: Israel Smith, 1831.

National Cyclopædia of American Biography. Vol. 3. New York: James T. White, 1893.

Naylor, Phillip C. *France and Algeria: A History of Decolonization and Transformation.* Tallahassee: University Press of Florida, 2000.

Pack, James. *Nelson's Blood: The Story of Naval Rum.* Annapolis, Md.: Naval Institute Press, 1982.

Panzac, Daniel. *Barbary Corsairs: The End of a Legend, 1800–1820.* Translated by Victoria Hobson. Completed by John E. Hawkes. Boston: Brill, 2005.

Pennell, C. R., ed. *Bandits at Sea: A Pirates Reader.* New York: New York University Press, 2001.

Pérotin-Dumon, Anne. "The Pirate and the Emperor: Power and Law on the Seas, 1450–1850." In Pennell, *Bandits at Sea,* 25–54.

Petrie, Donald A. *The Prize Game: Lawful Looting on the High Seas in the Days of Fighting Sail.* Annapolis, Md.: Naval Institute Press, 1999.

Phillipson, David. *Band of Brothers: Boy Seamen in the Royal Navy, 1800–1956.* Annapolis, Md.: Naval Institute Press, 1996.

Poolman, Kenneth. *The Speedwell Voyage: A Tale of Piracy and Mutiny in the Eighteenth Century.* Annapolis, Md.: Naval Institute Press, 1999.

Pope, Dudley. *Life in Nelson's Navy.* London: Allen & Unwin, 1981.

Rediker, Marcus. *Between the Devil and the Deep Blue Sea: Merchant Seamen, Pirates and the Anglo-American Maritime World, 1700–1750.* Cambridge: Cambridge University Press, 1989.

———. "Liberty beneath the Jolly Roger: The Lives of Anne Bonny and Mary Read, Pirates." In Pennell, *Bandits at Sea,* 299–320.

———. "The Seaman as Pirate: Plunder and Social Banditry at Sea." In Pennell, *Bandits at Sea,* 139–68.

Register of Shipping. London: Society for the Registry of Shipping, 1816, 1820, 1821.

Report of Proceedings at a Meeting of the Bar of the City of New York Held January 18th, 1882, Called for the Purpose of Taking Appropriate Action in Reference to the Deaths of Ex-Judges Henry E. Davies, Daniel P. Ingraham and John M. Barbour, and Judge Charles F. Sanford. New York: A. Livingston, ca. 1882.

Richmond, J. F. *New York and Its Institutions, 1609–1872.* New York: E. B. Treat, 1872.

Robertson, William Spence. "South America and the Monroe Doctrine, 1824–1828." *Political Science Quarterly* 30 (March 1915): 82–105.

Robinson, William. *Jack Nastyface: Memoirs of a Seaman.* Annapolis, Md.: Naval Institute Press, 1973.

Robson, Tom. *Boy Seaman R.N.: The True Story.* Darlington, U.K.: Newton Press, 1996.

Rodriguez, Antonio Gómez. "Louis Aury: Héroe Naval de la Gran Colombia. O la diferencia entre corsarios y piratas." Available online at www.encolombia.com/medicina/enfermeria/enfermeria7104–louis.htm

Rodríguez O., Jaime E. *The Independence of Spanish America*. Cambridge: Cambridge University Press, 1998.

Safford, Frank, and Marco Palacios. *Colombia: Fragmented Land, Divided Society*. New York: Oxford University Press, 2002.

Sahni, Varun. "Not Quite British: A Study of External Influences on the Argentine Navy." *Journal of Latin American Studies* 25 (October 1993): 489–513.

Schonhorn, Manuel, ed. *A General History of the Pyrates*. New York: Dover, 1999.

Seitz, Don C. *Under the Black Flag*. London: Stanley Paul, 1927.

Semple, Ellen Churchill. "Pirate Coasts of the Mediterranean Sea." *Geographical Review* 2 (August 1916): 134–51.

Sheffield, William P. *Privateersmen of Newport: An Address Delivered by William P. Sheffield before the Rhode Island Historical Society, in Providence, February 7 A.D., 1882*. Newport, R.I.: John P. Sanborn, 1883.

Sluiter, Engel. "Dutch-Spanish Rivalry in the Caribbean Area, 1594–1609." *Hispanic American Historical Review* 28 (May 1948): 165–96.

Smith, Aaron. *The Atrocities of the Pirates*. With introduction and commentary by Robert S. Redmond. New York: Lyons Press, 1999.

Smith, Horatio Davis. *Early History of the United States Revenue Marine Service (or United States Revenue Cutter Service) 1789–1849*. Washington, D.C.: U.S. Coast Guard, 1989.

Smith, J. Calvin. *Map of Long Island with the Environs of New-York and the Southern Part of Connecticut: Compiled from Various Surveys & Documents*. New York: J. H. Colton, 1844.

Snow, Edward Rowe. *Pirates and Buccaneers of the Atlantic Coast*. Boston: Yankee Publishing, 1944.

Spain, Charles A., Jr. "Flags of the Texas Revolution." *Handbook of Texas Online*. Online at www.tsha.utexas.edu/handbook/online/articles/view/FF/msf2.html.

Spencer, William. *Algiers in the Age of the Corsairs*. Norman: University of Oklahoma, 1976.

Starkey, David J. "The Origins and Regulation of Eighteenth-Century British Privateering." In Pennell, *Bandits at Sea*, 69–81.

———. "Pirates and Markets." In Pennell, *Bandits at Sea*, 107–24.

Starkey, David J., E. S. van Eyck van Heslinga, and J. A. De Moor, eds. *Pirates and Privateers: New Perspectives on the War on Trade in the Eighteenth and Nineteenth Centuries*. Exeter: University of Exeter Press, 1997.

Staten, Clifford L. *The History of Cuba*. Westport, Conn. & London: Greenwood Press, 2003.

Steuart, Bradley W. ed. *Passenger Ships Arriving in New York Harbor, Vol. 1 (1820–1850)*. Bountiful, Utah: Precision Indexing, 1991.

Stevens, Harm. *Dutch Enterprise and the VOC, 1602–1799*. Amsterdam: Stichting Rijksmuseum, 1998.

Sugden, Philip. *The Complete History of Jack the Ripper*. New York: Carroll & Graf, 2003.

Swanson, Carl E. "American Privateering and Imperial Warfare, 1739–1748." *William and Mary Quarterly*, 3rd series, 42 (July 1985): 357–82.

Tenenbaum, Barbara A. chief ed. *Encyclopedia of Latin American History and Culture*. Vol. 1. New York: Scribners / London: Simon & Schuster, 1996.

Thomas, R. *An Authentic Account of the Most Remarkable Events: Containing the Lives of the most noted Pirates and Piracies. Also the most Remarkable Shipwrecks, Fires, Famines, Calamities, Providential Deliverances, and Lamentable Disasters on the Seas, in Most Parts of the World.* 2 vols. New York, 1836.

Tucker, Spencer C. *Handbook of 19th Century Naval Warfare*. Stroud, U.K.: Sutton Publishing, 2000.

Tucker, Spencer C., and Frank T. Reuter. *Injured Honor: The Chesapeake-Leopard Affair, June 22, 1807*. Annapolis, Md.: Naval Institute Press, 1996.

Turley, Hans. *Rum, Sodomy and the Lash: Piracy, Sexuality, and Masculine Identity*. New York: New York University Press, 1999.

Uden, Grant, and Richard Cooper. *A Dictionary of British Ships and Seamen*. Harmondsworth, U.K.: Allen Lane, 1980.

U.S. House of Representatives. 18th Congress, 1st Session. *Report of the Committee on Foreign Affairs to Which Was Referred So Much of the President's Message, as Relates to Piracies Committed on the Commerce of the United States, in the Neighborhood of the Islands of Cuba and Porto Rico, May 19, 1824*. House Report 124. Serial Vol. 106. Washington, D.C.: Gales & Seaton, 1824.

U.S. Senate. 18th Congress. 2nd Session, *In Senate of the United States, December 30, 1824*. Senate Document 6. Serial Vol. 108. Washington, D.C.: Gales & Seaton, 1825.

Vale, Brian. *War betwixt Englishmen: Brazil against Argentina on the River Plate, 1825–1830*. London: I. B. Tauris, 2000.

Valle, James E. *Rocks & Shoals: Order and Discipline in the Old Navy, 1800–1861*. Annapolis, Md.: Naval Institute Press, 1980.

Van Wyhe, John. "The Authority of Human Nature: The *Schädellehre* of Franz Joseph Gall." *British Journal for the History of Science* 35 (March 2002): 17–42.

Vargas, Carlos Cortes. "Military Operations of Bolivar in New Granada: A Commentary on Lecuna: *Cronica Razonada de las Guerras de Bolivar*." *Hispanic American Historical Review* 32 (November 1952): 615–33.

Wells, Georgina Betts. *Life and Career of Samuel Rossiter Betts*. New York: Maurice Sloog, 1934.

Who Was Who in America: Historical Volume, 1607–1896. Rev. ed. Chicago: Marquis, 1967.

Wildes, Harry E. *Lonely Midas: The Story Of Stephen Girard*. New York: Farrar & Rinehart, 1943.

Wilson, James Grant, and John Fiske, eds. *Appleton's Cyclopædia of American Biography*. Vols. 1 and 2. New York: D. Appleton, 1888.

Wolf, John B. *The Barbary Coast: Algiers under the Turks, 1500–1830*. London: Norton, 1979.

Woodbury, George. *The Great Days of Piracy in the West Indies.* New York: Norton, 1951.

Works Progress / Work Projects Administration. *Ship Registers and Enrollments of Boston and Charlestown.* The only published Boston-Charlestown serial appears to have been *Vol. 1, 1789–1795.* Boston: The National Archives Project, 1942. However, materials for subsequent volumes (including data divided into 1821–1830 and 1831–1840 periods) was compiled in 1939 by the Survey of Federal Archives Division of Women's and Professional Projects (WPA) and the National Archives. These are held at the Phillips Library of the Peabody Essex Museum in Salem, Mass., and are cited herein as *SRE Boston-Charlestown 1821–30* and *SRE Boston-Charlestown 1831–40.*

Works Progress / Work Projects Administration. *Ship Registers and Enrollments of Bristol–Warren, Rhode Island, 1773–1939.* Providence, R.I.: National Archives Project, 1941.

Works Progress / Work Projects Administration. *Ship Registers and Enrollments of New Orleans, Louisiana.* Vol. 1, 1804–1820. Baton Rouge: Louisiana State University, August 1941.

Works Progress / Work Projects Administration. *Ship Registers and Enrollments of Newport, Rhode Island. 1790–1939.* 2 vols. Providence, R.I.: National Archives Project,1938–1941.

Works Progress/Work Projects Administration. *Ship Registers and Enrollments of Providence, Rhode Island, 1773–1939.* Providence, R.I.: National Archives Project, 1941.

Zandvliet, Keez. *Mapping for Money.* Amsterdam: Batavian Lion International, 2002.

Zwanenberg, Anna van. "Interference with Ships on the High Seas." *International and Comparative Law Quarterly* 10 (October 1961): 785–817.

INDEX

About the Author

Formerly a reporter and editor on several Massachusetts newspapers, JOSEPH GIBBS holds a doctorate in policy and communication studies from Boston University. The author of *Gorbachev's Glasnost and Three Years in the Bloody Eleventh,* he is a professor of mass communication at the American University of Sharjah, United Arab Emirates.